THE MOURNER'S DANCE

THE MOURNER'S DANCE

What We Do When People Die

⌘

KATHERINE ASHENBURG

Macfarlane Walter & Ross
Toronto

Macfarlane Walter & Ross
An Affiliate of McClelland & Stewart Ltd.
37A Hazelton Avenue
Toronto, Canada M5R 2E3
www.mwandr.com

National Library of Canada Cataloguing in Publication Data

Ashenburg, Katherine
The mourner's dance : what we do when people die /
Katherine Ashenburg.

Includes bibliographical references and index.
ISBN 1-55199-074-1

1. Mourning customs. I. Title.

GT3390.A84 2002   393'.9   C2002-902217-7

Macfarlane Walter & Ross gratefully acknowledges support for its
publishing program from the Canada Council for the Arts, the Ontario
Arts Council, and the Government of Canada through the Book
Publishing Industry Development Program.

Printed and bound in Canada

This book is printed on acid-free paper that is 100% ancient-
forest-friendly (100% post-consumer recycled).

for

Sybil and Hannah

and in memory of

Scott Roche
1973–1998

Contents

PROLOGUE

During the Christmas holidays of 1997, my two daughters and I went on a long-planned trip to Vietnam. Hannah, my younger daughter, had just become engaged, and she wore a bright sapphire and diamond ring. Talk of the wedding and Hannah's future threaded in and around our travels. Fingering Vietnamese silk in tiny shops, we imagined her dress. We planned menus and counted guests. I remember joking in Hue, as we walked through the splendid tomb garden of a Vietnamese king, that this would be a fine spot for a wedding reception.

In early January, Hannah returned to medical school in Vancouver, and her sister, Sybil, went back to her job in Hong Kong. I stayed in Asia for an additional week. Returning to my hotel one furiously wet night in Shanghai, I found an urgent message from Hannah. Scott, her fiancé, had been in a car accident outside Seattle on his way to a skiing excursion. He had spinal cord damage; if he ever regained consciousness, he would be a quadriplegic. When I arrived at the Hong Kong airport the next morning, on my way to Seattle, Sybil met me with the news that Scott was going to die.

Like many Westerners at the turn of the 21st century, my family and I had not had much to do with death. In their twenties, my daughters had four living grandparents. Hannah had been to only two funerals in her life. My grandparents, aunts, and uncles had been buried after long lives, with minimal formality. This was our first experience with sudden death at a young age.

Scott died on January 10, about an hour after I reached the hospital. He had never regained consciousness. His funeral was held three days later, in the beautiful modern embrace of the Chapel of St. Ignatius at Seattle University, the place where Scott and Hannah had wanted to be married. In many ways, the funeral was a harrowing parody of what would have been their wedding. Hannah was almost always surrounded by Sybil and her three college roommates, who would have been her bridesmaids. More than two hundred friends and family crowded the chapel. Hannah's ring glinted on the lectern as she reminisced about Scott and their six years together. Scott's mother spoke too, and his brother Stephan, who was to have been his best man. Afterward, there was a luncheon for everyone at a restaurant, with an open microphone. Dozens of young people walked up to tell funny stories about Scott. It was dreadful, and ineffably comforting.

Once the funeral was over and family and friends dispersed, I assumed that custom and ceremony had had their day. Now we would be left to mourn in the modern way – utterly privately and spontaneously, in an unscheduled and mostly unmarked grief, unconstrained by repetition or expectation. This was so obvious that it never occurred to me to think of it as a deprivation. But I reckoned without Hannah.

I used to tease Hannah by telling her that when it came to much of Western civilization, she was an intelligent stranger. What I meant was that she preferred playing the piano or talking with friends to reading. A student of music and science, she had little interest in history. She had finished very few Victorian novels. And yet, in the weeks after Scott's death, something began to impress itself on me. All by herself, as if instinctively, she was designing practices that more traditional cultures had institutionalized as part of their mourning process. Some of her handmade customs involved Scott's belongings or mementoes of him. Others involved carving out times and places in which to remember Scott in a particular, recurring way. Just as older societies paid close attention to the mourner's retreat from society, Hannah wrote the rules for her own balance of seclusion and company.

In the midst of sadness and worry for her, I wondered about the source of her observances. Other than a few time-honored holiday customs, we are not especially rich in ritual as a family. True, Hannah's childhood had included the sacraments and ceremonies of the Catholic Church. Although she seemed to have left that part of her life without much lingering connection, perhaps those modernized and rather diluted rituals had left some trace.

Traditional mourning customs almost always involve a timeline, a date when the widow moves from black to grey clothes, when Kaddish no longer needs to be said daily, when a party may be attended. Hannah too had at least one date in her mind. A month or so after Scott's death, I had a dream that she moved her engagement ring from her left hand to her right. Telling her about the dream, I finished almost apologetically, "I guess that was a bit premature." She said immediately, "I'm thinking about September 6." Their wedding had been scheduled for September 5. She had already decided to wear her ring on her left hand for the full period of her engagement, then move it. I remember thinking that the Victorians, those expert mourners about whom Hannah knew almost nothing, would approve of this girl.

About the same time, I had dinner and spent the night with three friends in the country not far from my home in Toronto. We had already talked long and well about the events of the last month, and I was feeling no particular wish to discuss them again. We were relaxed and companionable. After dinner, our hosts put plaintive Irish music on the CD player, and the other guest, warm-hearted and slightly tipsy, began to cry. I was suddenly, uncharacteristically, furious. How dare she give herself to self-indulgent tears over the plight of unknown Irishmen who had died 150 years ago, when Scott had died four weeks ago that day? When the host prepared to put on another melancholy CD, I announced that I was going for a walk in the village. I knew that I was being unfair, that the weeper had proved her deeply sympathetic friendship time and time again, that my friends were simply *not in mourning*, and there was no reason they should be. But that evening showed me that, for the time being, I was on a different track.

A hundred years ago in a similar situation, I would have been at home, wearing black crape and dull jet jewelry, receiving only a few close friends who would have asked about my daughter in hushed tones. I didn't really want to repeat a Victorian mourner's seclusion, but now I understood the point of a temporary separation from a world that could not possibly care about our loss as we did.

Just as I saw the point of Hannah's practices. Not everyone did. A few male friends looked dubious, and the word "morbid" was probably murmured. But I saw a young woman surrounded by friends and coping with the most difficult year of medical school, who looked surprisingly sure-footed when it came to mourning. Once, when I uttered the usual platitude about time healing, she corrected me crisply: "Time doesn't heal. Grieving heals." I had no idea if that was true, or if Hannah would ever be happy again, but I clung to that formula.

At first, I was interested in how naturally Hannah's home-grown practices had welled up in her, and how similar they were to age-old ways. More and more, as I thought about mourning customs, many of them made psychological sense to me. Others that made no immediate sense, or that repelled me, were nonetheless intriguing.

It seemed right that individual grief should be contained and supported by traditional practices and rituals, and by a community with shared attitudes about loss and recovery. But I also had questions. How did the customs comfort people? *Did* they comfort people? Why did women bear so much of the responsibility for mourning? What has happened now that so many customs are things of the past? Are contemporary support groups, Internet mourning sites, and shelves of self-help books about grieving filling in for old practices?

A mixture of motives – curiosity, the desire to grasp what Hannah was going through, a hope of lightening or perhaps distancing my own sorrow, to name only the ones I could guess at – led me on a rich, improvised journey. It was a pilgrimage among the mourners, talking with them, reading about those in the past and in faraway places, traveling to Japan, Mexico, and around North America to see the tangible traces of grief: the days of the dead, the keepsakes, the ceremonies, the mourning clothes, the graveyards. Because it was Hannah's practices that had piqued my interest, I started not with the inner feelings of the bereaved but with their actions – the mourner's dance, as I came to think of it.

There is a powerful expression of grief in Margaret Alexiou's book *The Ritual Lament in Greek Tradition*. A mother whose child has died cries: "I will not tear my hair, nor will I rend my cloak, nor will I scratch my flesh with my nails, nor will I start up the dirge, nor will I call up the mourning women, nor will I shut myself in darkness that the air might lament with me, nor will I await the comforters, nor will I prepare the funeral bread. For such things belong to vulgar mothers, who are mothers only in the flesh."

What lingers in my mind about that long-ago mother's lament is how economically she sums up the components of "mourning" while insisting that she will have no part of it. The withdrawal, the dirge, the visitors, the making and sharing of funeral food, even the rending of cloth and the tearing of hair – those same elements recur uncannily in so many cultures over so many years that they must have spoken to something in the human condition.

And yet most of the practices in the Greek mother's list are now things of the past. The 20th century, in the West, saw the dismantling of most of our mourning customs, and for some decades it really seemed that mourning, in the sense of outward observances, had died. People still grieved, of course, but as privately and invisibly as possible. An ancient, ceremonious dance, with its own rhythm and momentum, looked to be extinct.

Now that judgment seems premature. Many old customs have vanished, but new ones spring up, and traditional ones return in new guises. The outpouring of flowers, poems, teddy bears, and homemade signs after the death of Diana, Princess of Wales, the Oklahoma City bombing, and the destruction of the World Trade Center, to mention only a few recent examples, suggests that many people do want to mark loss publicly and emotionally. Ironically, it seems easier to do that when the dead are strangers, because we still have so many inhibitions about marking personal losses. But that too may be shifting.

In place of the one traditional way our forebears followed, the mourner now faces an array of choices – bewildering for many, no doubt, and promising for others. When, in the absence of cultural cues, Hannah mourned Scott's death, she choreographed her own steps. Mourning, it seems, will out – not for everyone, but for many more than people recently supposed. The mourner's dance is changing, but it persists.

ONE

THE BUSTLE IN A HOUSE

The Bustle in a House
The Morning after Death
Is solemnest of industries
Enacted upon Earth –
　　– Emily Dickinson

Aperson dies, let us say a man. Those watching at his deathbed try to control their grief until they are sure that he is
dead. They know it is wrong to distract him while he is at the
serious business of "giving up the ghost." Then the watchers
begin to weep and lament. A close relative shuts his eyes and
mouth and arranges his limbs.

Those entrusted with the task of preparing the body, usually
the same sex as the dead, wash it carefully with warm water,
sometimes with herbs and ointments, and dress it in his last
outfit. Then, laid out on a table or bed or in a coffin, the dead
man is displayed in bedroom, kitchen, or parlor, with lighted
candles nearby, often with a bowl of water and a sprig from a
particular plant. His feet point to the door of the room.

Friends and family gather to condole with the bereaved
and to keep watch over the body, which must never be left
alone. They may touch him, kiss him, or sprinkle holy water
on him. They may cry or pray and remember the dead man

quietly; they may drink and carouse; they may do all of the above. Finally, when the prescribed time has elapsed and all is in order, he is carried to a leave-taking ceremony, and the disposal of his body takes place.

This man, allowing for minor local modifications, might have lived in Greece in the 3rd century B.C., in czarist Russia, in 18th-century France, in ancient Rome, Renaissance Florence, or 19th-century Sicily. He might have lived in the 20th century in the Bara Islands in Madagascar, in the Central Caroline Islands in the Pacific, in Palestine, Newfoundland, Portugal, or Japan. Until very recently, there was a remarkable similarity about the things people in far-flung times and places did in the first hours and days after death.

Not only were the practices similar, they were so deeply ingrained that even the weakest members of a society knew what to do. John Galt's novel *Annals of the Parish* is a closely observed account of rural Scotland in the 18th century. In it, the Reverend Mr. Balwhidder records the behavior of a feeble-minded woman, Meg Gaffaw, when her mother dies. Begging a shroud from her neighbors and straightening the body "in a wonderful decent manner," Meg places a dish holding earth and salt on the corpse, symbols of mortality and immortality that were already considered old-fashioned in her time. When the minister calls, she solemnly presents him with the customary water and bread, and he reflects, "It was a consternation to everybody how the daft creature had learnt all the ceremonies."

When the same traditions crop up again and again, and when even a "daft creature had learnt all the ceremonies," it suggests there is something critical about this short period. It is a time of shock, even when the death has been long expected; a time of disorientation, even in familiar surroundings. It is an awful time, both in the modern sense of miserable and in the word's original sense of awe-full. Modern usage has flattened words like *awful* and *dreadful* so that they mean simply very bad, but originally they referred to something that aroused awe and fear. That is how our ancestors saw the time between death and burial, as a particularly dangerous, particularly dreadful interval. More than anything, they dreaded the spirit of the dead person, because no matter how beloved the person had been, his or her spirit was now presumed to be angry, envious, and spiteful.

When someone close to us dies, it is usual to cry. We probably assume that this is a sorrowful reaction. We may observe certain customs – wearing dark clothes to the funeral, speaking only about the dead person's good qualities, holding a wake, erecting a tombstone – believing we do so out of respect if not affection. Certainly, I did. So it was disconcerting to discover that anthropologists see most of the traditions and rituals around death as born out of fear and self-protectiveness. We have rationalized and sentimentalized them since, but as the anthropologists tell it, they began as something more craven. The dark clothes hide the living from the malevolent spirit. Crying and speaking well of the dead persuade him that he is regretted. Holding a wake reassures him that he is not forgotten, perhaps even deludes him into thinking he is still living. The tombstone is an attempt to keep the spirit under the ground, where he can do less harm. So, symbolically, are the small stones Jews leave on tombstones when they visit a cemetery.

Because the spirit was thought to be especially irritable and dangerous until burial, the time immediately after death is most rich in these placating customs. Many cultures, from ancient and modern Greeks to 20th-century Italians and Irish, stress the necessity of quiet before and immediately after death. They do not want to disturb the dying or, worse still, anger the ghost.

Once death was certain, a great noise, called the *conclamatio mortis*, or death shout, used to be made. Some peoples wailed and lamented, others tolled a bell, beat a gong, clapped a sistrum (ancient Egyptians), struck copper dishes (the Romans), fired a gun (the Maoris, the Bara, Westerners at military funerals), or banged on a church door (Cluniac monks in medieval England).

Depending on whom you asked, the *conclamatio mortis* was designed to ensure that death had truly taken place, or to salute the dead person, or to scare away evil spirits.

Many European and Middle Eastern peoples opened a window in the room where the person had died, not to air it out, as is sometimes said, but to allow the ghost to escape. Mirrors were and still are covered – not, as modern people say, because vanity is inappropriate at such a time, but because it was dangerous for the spirit to see its own reflection, or that of the living. Clocks were stopped at the minute of death and not restarted until after the burial, probably to pretend that the person was not dead until he was safely buried.

Until the midpoint of the 20th century, ancient Irish superstitions lived on in many Newfoundland fishing villages, where the dead person's bed was often turned down on the first night of the wake, with pipe and slippers placed nearby, "in case they might return." In Witless Bay, among other outports, it was the custom to overturn the chairs and candlesticks when cleaning the wake-room after the funeral, probably to confuse any returning spirits so that they would leave the premises.

Did people really weep and mark a death with various solemn gestures only in the hope of sparing themselves? That troubled me and seemed to discredit the sincerity of our most long-lived observances. But when I spoke with Anne Brener, an American therapist who writes and teaches about Jewish mourning rituals, she saw it from another perspective. She pointed out that fear and awe have several faces, not all of them self-regarding. The immensity of the fact of death calls, in her words, "for some way of marking a moment on the edge of the mystery." The more energetic the marking the better, whether opening a window, overturning furniture, or preparing a body according to a prescribed ritual. "The words for 'fear' and 'awe' and 'terrible' are the same in Hebrew," she told me. "To see a custom as superstitious and self-protective is one thing; to see it as an acknowledgment of the awe and the mystery of death is another possibility." The mourner feels impelled to *do* something, as a way of saying, "There are things happening here that I don't understand."

Although Ecclesiastes distinguishes between a time to mourn and a time to dance, Brener helped me see that mourning itself can be a kind of dance, a series of actions – sometimes graceful, sometimes clumsy, sometimes closely patterned, sometimes improvised – in response to something that is almost beyond articulation. Does the dance have anything to do with sorrow? Assuming that the anthropologists are right and our ancestor donned black to hide from her husband's ghost, this doesn't necessarily mean she didn't also miss her husband. Perhaps she even felt a connection between the bleakness of her garments and the bleakness of her life without him. Presumably you could mourn a person and fear his disgruntled spirit at the same time.

Let us grant that the Jew in the ancient world begged pardon of the body before washing it (one of many apologies addressed to the dead body in cultures all over the world) and buried some of his favorite possessions with him (another widespread custom) at least partly to prevent the spirit being angry. But these are also ways of saying, "I'm sorry if I failed you," "I hope you're happy wherever you are," "I love you." Perhaps leaving a small stone on a tomb originally represented a hope that the spirit would stay buried; but today it works as a poignant sign that someone remembers the person buried there, that someone still visits his last resting place.

The fact is that we still practice some of these "primitive" customs and until recently practiced many more of them. Partly that is because death makes conservatives of us all, and it is hard – but not impossible, as the 20th century demonstrated – to break from traditional death-ways. But beyond that, some customs have staying power and others do not. We no longer deck our dead in burial crowns, as the ancient Greeks did, because that tradition ceased to speak to us. But, even though most of us no longer believe in the power of evil spirits, we still prepare dead bodies with care and make a solemn space and time between death and burial.

Apparently, these things still make some kind of sense. They are a way to dance around the unknowable profundity of death and to express – however haltingly – regret, sadness, respect, and confusion. In the case of a wake and funeral, they are also ways to find solace in company and to realign the community. The rituals that endure have what John Keats called negative capability, in that they are big enough and elastic enough to keep on being meaningful, even when the meaning changes.

⌘

When the water had come to a boil in the
shining bronze, then they washed the body and
anointed it softly with olive oil and stopped the
gashes in his body with stored-up unguents and
laid him on a bed, and shrouded him in a thin
sheet from head to foot, and covered that over
with a white mantle.

– Homer, *The Iliad*

There was reason to wash the body of Patroclus, who died in a bloody battle with Hector. But even when a clean person died gently in bed, Greek tradition demanded that the body be washed and anointed. So do the customs of many societies.

My friend Bernice Eisenstein remembers the silence that descended when her father, Ben, died in a Toronto hospital in 1991. In the quiet, behind the closed door, her mother and her aunt began to wash his body. Slowly and deliberately, they cleaned him with a washcloth, soap, and water. They clipped and cleaned his fingernails and toenails. It seemed to Bernice, watching, that they had not yet completely grasped that he was dead, and at the same time they knew this was the last thing they would ever do for him. Ben Eisenstein was a dapper man, and perhaps part of their thinking was that he should look his best before being handed over, finally, to the care of strangers. Perhaps they were re-enacting something of the washing of the dead they had known as girls in Jewish Poland. Without fully understanding it, Bernice felt proud that she was related to these women.

The washing in the hospital was followed by a much more serious ritual washing. Ben Eisenstein's body was taken to a funeral home where members of the Jewish burial fellowship, the Chevra Kadisha, follow an elaborate, ancient protocol. It begins with a thorough cleansing of the body in a prescribed order, followed by a purification rite called *taharah*. The corpse is held upright while twenty-four quarts of water are poured over the head and body in a continuous stream; then it is dried and wrapped in a pure white linen shroud that has been sewn by women past menopause.

The connection between washing and endings was a familiar one for Arnold van Gennep. In 1909, in *The Rites of Passage*, the French folklorist and anthropologist pointed out how often separation rituals involved cleansing, anointing, and purification. It was van Gennep's disarming but far-reaching idea that all of life's important changes are marked with a similar structure. No matter whether the occasion is birth, puberty, marriage, ordination, or death, the passage begins with ceremonies of separation from the old condition, continues with a transitional state in which the person is suspended between two worlds, and concludes with rituals of incorporation into the new state.

Often these stages follow closely on one another or even overlap. When an adult died early in the 20th century in Artas, a Muslim village south of Bethlehem, his body was washed on the door of his house, which had been removed and placed outside on four stones. The body, dead but not yet buried, resting on the divider between one's own place and the outside world – it is a memorable image. Strictly speaking, the washing belongs to the rites of separation, while the door points to the next, transitional stage. Doors, thresholds, courtyards, vestibules, and passageways are all natural symbols for the movement from one state to another, and these intermediate spaces appear often in the ceremonies van Gennep called transitional or liminal (from *limen*, the Latin for threshold).

In most of Western society, the awkward passage between life and death is fairly brief, ending with the burial. The best-known transitional custom is the wake of some two or three days, where the community comes to say farewell to the unburied body. Because the spirit was once thought to float somewhere between life and death until burial, wakes frequently make use of betwixt-and-between spaces. In the Roman republic, the body was often laid out in the atrium, the main room of the Roman house but one that was also open to the sky. The Etruscans and the Dayak of Borneo held their wakes in the vestibule of their houses. In 16th-, 17th-, and 18th-century Europe, after a period inside, the body was briefly exposed in the open doorway of the house, usually close to the time of the funeral.

Even when the physical space used is not particularly transitional, the feeling immediately after death is. When a friend's niece was killed in a car accident in Idaho at the age of sixteen, her parents had her embalmed at the local funeral parlor, then brought her home to her own bedroom. Many people thought it was bizarre, and it was certainly unusual in North America in the 1990s. But it seemed that the girl's parents needed her to spend one more night in her own bed, until they began to comprehend what had happened. Friends and family gathered in her bedroom, where her favorite music played. Her father stayed up all night with her, as he had stayed up all night during her birth.

In the case of difficult relationships, death apparently ends the possibility of resolution. But just as people often ask a corpse for forgiveness, they sometimes make one last, postmortem attempt at reconciliation. That too is a kind of transition. The dead body is no longer the other person in the relationship, but it still looks like that person. And it may "listen" better than the person could in life.

Helen Ryane describes her mother's feelings toward her as "mostly indifferent." They had never been close, and Helen was convinced that her mother found her the least lovable of her five children. When Grace Eggie died in Saskatchewan in the early 1990s, Helen was in her mid-forties. She went to the funeral parlor early in the morning and asked for the coffin to be opened. Holding her mother's hand, she spent some time alone with her, reminiscing, saying goodbye. Then, with the coffin still open, she wrote her a letter about their relationship, the hopes she had had for it, the disappointments, the good and bad parts. She tucked the letter in at the side of the coffin, and it was buried with her mother.

Judaism, which shares so many mourning customs with Middle Eastern and European cultures, negotiates the interval between death and burial differently. The period is short, ideally no more than twenty-four hours. The brevity made sense in a hot climate, and their Mediterranean neighbors joined them in that. Where they, and many other cultures, parted company with the Jews was in the attitude to the body. The Jews liken the corpse to a broken Torah scroll. No longer useful, it is something to be treated respectfully but quickly entrusted to people outside the family – to the burial society for washing and to an official called a *shomer* who stays with it until burial. It is not dwelled upon by the family and is certainly not the object of a wake.

Jewish scholars and rabbis muster studies about the psychological harm caused by viewing the dead, embalming, and holding a wake. Cultures that do all these things could point to studies from equivalent sources indicating that such practices are consoling and healing. There is very little research that conclusively demonstrates that one particular mourning practice produces a better outcome than another. The truth seems to be that as long as a culture supports the individual mourner in its particular traditions, whatever they are, the result is more likely to be good than bad.

But saying farewell to your dead is a healthy impulse. It confirms the death and concludes the relationship with a living person. Jews do spend some time with the body before the burial society takes over, and Lisa Newman expected to have that opportunity when her mother died. Ironically, because her mother, who was Orthodox, died on the Sabbath, she ended up spending much more time with the body than is usual in a Jewish bereavement. Not only did Lisa find these hours unexpectedly precious, they mollified a hurt that was more than thirty years old.

When Lisa was twenty-one, her father was taken to Toronto Western Hospital one Friday evening with chest pains. His wife did not accompany him because the Sabbath had begun and car travel was forbidden; she planned to walk to the hospital the next day. In the middle of the night, a doctor called to say that Lisa's father had died.

What greeted Lisa and her mother in the hospital was unsatisfactory on every level. The doctor who talked with them didn't know the dead man or them. No one seemed able to tell them whether he had died alone or in pain. They weren't able to see the body. All they knew then and all Lisa knows now is that her father entered the hospital alive and died there of a massive heart attack. As with many cases when a family is unable to see the body after a sudden death, a residue of pain lingered around the circumstances of the death, in addition to the loss itself. For years it was hard for Lisa to look at a photograph of her father. She tried to see the hospital records without success. Coincidentally or not, she later worked as a social worker in Toronto Western for eleven years in the 1970s and 1980s, almost as if she were haunting the corridors, looking for the father who had gone there and never come back.

On a Saturday afternoon in the spring of 1999, Lisa Newman arrived back at Toronto Western "with all my baggage." Her ninety-four-year-old mother was brought there by ambulance, after she had choked and lost consciousness at home with Lisa. She was immediately pronounced dead in the emergency department. This time, things unfolded differently. The doctor explained thoroughly what had happened and assured Lisa there was nothing she could have done. The outcome was inevitable. When she asked if her daughters could see their grandmother, she was told, "Take as long as you like."

Because it was the Sabbath, the burial society and the Jewish funeral home could not take possession of the body until after sundown. Lisa did not want her mother to go to the hospital morgue, and since in Jewish tradition the body must never be left alone, she decided to stay with her until the Sabbath was over. The emergency department gave the family its trauma room, which could be closed off from the rest of the ward. Lisa and her two daughters watched over the body for about nine hours, in privacy and comfort.

Very quickly, Lisa realized that "there was no place else in the world I wanted to be." It was peaceful, and even the interruptions were thoughtful. A nurse kept bobbing her head in. Would they like some coffee? No, thank you. Perhaps a cup of tea? Some ice water? No, thank you. The nurse looked at the thin old woman extended on the bare stretcher. Would they like a pillow for her head? Yes, they would. When the nurse had made her look more relaxed, she told Lisa, "She's with the angels now."

Lisa remembers, "I had a strong sense of my mother's presence in the room. At first she was warm and I would reach out and touch her, the way you touch a pet that you're fond of, when it's there and sleeping beside you. I felt her comforting me, as if she were saying, 'You'll be okay. You'll be okay.'"

Lisa had not eaten, and her daughters brought her some food. She wonders why she didn't feel strange about eating there (something strictly forbidden to the *shomer* who watches with the dead), but "I was hungry and it just made sense." Her daughters were grateful to have this time with their grandmother, and they sat and talked: "I can't even remember what we talked about, but it felt like a really holy time."

As the day wore on, they phoned family from the room and made funeral arrangements, ordered cakes and percolators for the after-funeral reception. Lisa's oldest friend visited. Gradually, as they watched, her mother changed. She grew colder, lost her characteristic expression. "Initially I felt her spirit there," Lisa says, "and then, slowly, without my even noticing it, it left. By the end of the time, this was not my mother. This was the physical remains that had to be properly cared for. She was gone. And it felt so right, so peaceful. I was exhausted and it was sad, but it didn't feel wrenching or painful."

The hospital, which had complicated her loss when her father died, redeemed itself with the simple gift of time and space. All the family needed, as Lisa says, was that the hospital "let us be," while a natural process happened. That night she told one of her daughters, "Toronto Western Hospital doesn't owe me anything now." When the burial society representative showed up late in the evening, Lisa was ready to let her father go, as well as her mother.

⌘

> When I was young, goin' to a wake was the
> most enjoyable thing of all.
> – schoolteacher on the Southern Shore
> of Newfoundland, 1973

Angela Burke is eighty-three, a big-boned, vigorous woman who likes to sit on her porch in Brigus overlooking the Atlantic Ocean. Her house is tall and plain, its clapboard a dark green popular in the outports of Newfoundland. The Burke family bought the house in the 1840s, and Angela Burke moved here in 1942, when she married her husband, Jim. Jim's father, grandfather, great-grandfather, and great-great-grandfather were all named James. Until Angela, they had all married women named Ann and brought them to this house.

Now Angela Burke lives alone. The deaths and burials she knew in her first thirty years were almost medieval in their calculated simplicity. And even in her old age, although she scorns the "heathenish" modern ways she sees developing, death in her outport remains remarkably unpretentious and communal.

The first death she remembers well was that of her grandfather Patrick Lamb, who died at home in his sleep in 1930. One of the first things done when he was discovered was to open a window in his bedroom, "to let the soul go out," as Angela says. Because it lingered in the vicinity until the burial, people knew not to stand in doorways during the wake, in case the soul wanted to leave.

Patrick Lamb was washed, shaved, and laid out by male neighbors. If necessary, his eyes would have been closed with big Newfoundland pennies and his mouth would have been secured shut, either with a piece of cloth around his head or by propping a prayer book under his chin. He was dressed, as Catholics in Newfoundland were until the 1950s or '60s, in a brown, Franciscan-style monastic habit. It was embroidered on the breast with a large, padded Sacred Heart, a drop of blood, a sword, and the letters I.H.S. They stood for *In hoc signo*, the Latin beginning of Constantine's motto, "In this sign you will conquer," but were believed all over Newfoundland to mean "I have suffered." Men and women, rich and poor, were buried in this costume, and people kept their habits in readiness for years before they died.

(The habit was strictly reserved for the dead. But the story is told of Joany Power, an old woman who lived in Placentia Bay, who wore hers when her son was away, to save her neighbors the trouble of dressing her body in case she died. One day, wearing her habit, she was gathering firewood at the beach and so terrified some fishermen in a nearby boat that they never fished in that particular bay again.)

One of the first calls in an outport after a death was to the local shipbuilder or furniture maker, who would set to work making a plain pine box, covered with grey cloth for adults, white for children. In Brigus in 1930, the call went out to Mr. Farley, the furniture maker. But the coffin was not ready until the second day, and the body spent the first night on the sofa in the parlor, or wake-room, as it was called in this part of Newfoundland. Throughout North America, the seldom-used, best room in the house was reserved so consistently for waking the dead that when funeral parlors began to offer that function, at the beginning of the 20th century, a new name was devised for the room. To distinguish it from its associations with the dead, it became the "living room."

The typical Newfoundland wake lasted two nights and three days. The wake-room was prepared by covering the pictures and mirrors with white cloths; the sofa on which the body was laid was also shrouded. Virtually all the adults in the outport, dressed in good clothes, entered by the front door, which was used only for ceremonial occasions. After greeting the family with the traditional Irish condolence, "Sorry for your trouble," the visitor went to the dead person. It was widely believed that if you kissed him or touched his forehead, he would not return in your dreams. The custom of saying something nice about the person was also believed to prevent his return.

On a special table close to the body, two candles in brass candlesticks were kept perpetually burning. "That was a job in itself," according to Angela Burke, and a bereaved family would usually buy two pounds of candles for the wake. In Brigus, the brass candlesticks belonged to a Mrs. Hearn, who always lent them out. On the same table, if the dead was a man, lay a pile of snuff and an array of cheap clay pipes, called "God be merciful" pipes because with each intake of breath, you were supposed to say, "God be merciful to Patrick Lamb."

Visitors moved back and forth from the hushed, candlelit wake-room to the kitchen, the social heart of the Newfoundland house. There the neighbors had brought food – "That was the first thing you did when you heard someone died, you made a boiler of soup or some fresh rolls," Angela says – and the talk was more relaxed, recalling the good qualities of the dead as well as other topics.

Angela Burke's son Tom, now a lawyer in St. John's, remembers the wake of his great-aunt Phine (short for Josephine), a pious woman known for sewing dozens of brown habits for other people's wakes. Phine's women friends were perhaps not quite as devout as she was, and the boy Tom Burke watched them toss back bathtub gin in the kitchen before repairing to the wake-room for one of the three rosaries prayed around the body through the night, at 10 P.M., at 2 A.M., and just before breakfast. The rosary said, they returned to the kitchen for more gin.

It was the all-night wake that distinguished Newfoundland Catholic deaths from those of their Anglican and United Church neighbors. The neighbors' food – ham, rolls, shorebirds, baked beans, fish cakes, sweets – would be served at at least three "lunches" or "scoffs" during the night. Angela recalls the surprise of going to a Protestant wake in nearby Burnt Head at what she considered a normal evening hour, "and they'd gone to bed!" Various reasons are given for the Catholics' all-night wake: the body could never be left alone; the candles needed attending; the rosaries needed saying. But mainly, Angela admits, "I think they probably stayed up for a party."

Once the immediate family retired, around midnight, the party or the "time," as Newfoundlanders call any social gathering, could begin. It might be as decorous as ghost stories and affectionate rhymes made up about the dead person or as outrageous as tying fishing line to various parts of the corpse to make it nod, wave, or rise in its coffin. The more extreme shenanigans, almost always carried out by intoxicated men and closely patterned on Irish precedents, had a long history in Newfoundland. In the 1850s, a supervisor for an English firm went to an outport wake. He reported:

> Poor Paddy [the corpse] was often appealed to, to say if any of the present party had wronged him, and what for. Sometimes the corpse would be taken up, and, in drunken madness, embraced by one of his friends; then another would come up and dispute the right; then a scuffle would ensue, and the dead body would be thrust first in this corner, and then in that, but oftener would be laid flat in the middle of the floor. A little of this wake went a long way, and I speedily left the party, and walked home in the moonlight.

Twentieth-century corpses had their faces blackened with soot and their feet pressed to make the head rise. They had ice cream cones fixed in their hands or hot potatoes lobbed at them, and they were propped up to fall into a newcomer's arms when he opened the wake-room door. Games were played in which the penalty was kissing the corpse or biting the corpse's toes. Not all practical jokes involved the corpse; it was also common to smear soot on the faces of visitors who fell asleep, to put pepper in callers' tea, and to seat mourners in pans of water.

Pranks of this kind generally took place only at the wake of an old person. A young person's or child's wake was a much sadder, more solemn affair. In addition to the other diversions, the death of an elderly person promised a few not-terribly-well-chaperoned late nights and an opportunity for courting. It was said that the gain in population nine months after a wake more than made up for one death, an exaggeration but a telling one. An outport resident rationalized the goings-on: "The nights were long, the family was in bed, so I guess everything was done; there was tricks and riddles and begar there was even some lovin' done."

"Merry wakes," as they were called, are receding into the mists of legend. Ken Broughton followed his father as the funeral director in Brigus. The elder Broughton, who died in 1971, was sometimes summoned to a Catholic home wake to repair the damage done to the corpse by an exuberant party the night before, but this has never happened in his son's tenure. While maintaining the ecumenical balance necessary in his business, Ken Broughton, who is a Protestant, believes that Catholics accept the loss of a loved one more easily than do Protestants. Hence their wakes and post-funeral feasts, which Protestants find baffling if not disrespectful. When I asked Newfoundland Catholics if they thought they accommodated death more readily, I always got a jocular variation of "Of course we do! It's because we know *we're* going to heaven!"

A wake full of practical jokes is, to modern sensibilities, disturbing. How could you use a corpse as a prop in a drunken party? How could you go to bed, leaving the body of your father or your aunt to be possibly played with and manipulated? The standard answer given by the folklorists who study the merry wake is that it is a vestige of the old belief in the malign spirit. Faced with a ghost who envied the living, your best strategy was to act as if he were still alive – give him a hand of cards, a glass of rum, an ice cream cone; enlist him in tricking the timid newcomer. Above all, make him part of the party.

Rollicking, boisterous wakes had been scandalizing the respectable throughout Europe at least since the 4th century, and the clergy had been railing against them from the start. Scandinavians were notorious for their unruly vigils until the Protestant Reformation, when they were effectively sobered by Lutheran pastors. The European merry wake lived longest in Ireland, where it remained in vigorous health until the end of the 19th century. It lasted even longer in Newfoundland, until the clergy and conventional opinion finally triumphed around the midpoint of the 20th century. It was a battle between ancient folk practice and the authorities, and the fun of defiance no doubt aided the merry wake's persistence. But, as the Newfoundland folklorist Peter Narvaez argues eloquently, anti-authoritarianism and the fear of the spirit probably counted for less in 19th- and 20th-century Newfoundland than the sheer, body-centered pleasure afforded by the traditional wake.

Licence – in the form of smoking, drinking, eating, ridicule, practical jokes, bawdy behavior – trumped mourning at these vigils. The living kept riotous company with the dead in a way that can look, depending on your vantage point, callous or heartbroken. Evasive in that it avoids the reality of the loss, subversive in that it flaunts bad behavior, such a wake may try, hopelessly, to assert the vitality of the dead. But even more than that, it asserts the vitality of the wakers.

It is a thought that makes people uncomfortable, but death can make those left behind feel piercingly, singularly alive in a way that nothing else can. Caterers will tell you that people eat much more at a funeral than at a wedding. Jokes at a wake or after a funeral can seem disproportionately funny. And grief can mutate seamlessly into fierce energy. At a traditional 18th-century Highland wake, the widow or widower, often with tears streaming, would lead a dance around the body. It began solemnly and became more and more aggressive, more frenetic, until in one case the floor shook so that the body fell from the bed into the crowd. Once again, licence triumphed over mourning, the demands of the living took precedence over the dead.

The Irish folklorist Sean O'Suilleabhain tells the story of a peaceful wake and funeral in Leinster. Immediately after the burial, the son shouted, "This is a sad day, when my father is put into the clay, and not even one blow struck at his funeral!" In tribute to his father's memory, he proceeded to strike the man next to him. A scuffle broke out in the graveyard, more fights ensued, and the dead man's son went home well pleased. The physicality, the ferocity, the insistence that the dead are best celebrated by a demonstration of animal spirits are close kin to the "tricks and fun" that animated a Newfoundland wake.

Aside from the pranks, the communal and volunteer quality of a pre-1950 Newfoundland wake is notable. In a small outport, a death diminished everyone, and all hands came together to support the family. The goods and services a modern city dweller pays for at the time of death came from neighbors, and the only expense was the wood for the coffin. Its making was free, as was the laying out, the food for the wake and funeral reception, and the digging of the grave. (A man in Patrick's Cove in Placentia Bay remembered that once a fellow had offered to pay for the digging of a grave, and "it was a number of years before they came to understand and forgive what they termed his 'ignorance.'") The layers-out and the gravediggers would be given a bit of rum for their trouble. Angela Burke remembers the death of a man named Bill Finn, when her own squeamish husband and another neighbor were drafted to lay him out. Once they began drinking the customary rum, they forgot their qualms, and by the time they had finished, "it was just like a wedding."

The homelike aspect of the traditional wake is what Angela misses most. Since Ken Broughton opened the first funeral parlor in the three-hundred-year history of Brigus in the 1970s, home wakes have gradually become uncommon. (There was no need for a commercial funeral parlor in his father's day, since people were waked in their own front rooms.) Angela scorns the vast, "heathenish" coffins on sale at the funeral parlor ("With lights inside!") and the very idea of taking your dead to a business establishment. In fairness to Ken Broughton, it must be said that his funeral parlor is about as modest and neighborly as a business could be. All the arrangements are made at the kitchen table at the back of the building. Visiting hours can stretch from 10 A.M. to 10 P.M. without a break if the family wishes, and most people in Brigus do. Broughton's lunchroom has replaced the kitchen in a home wake. He provides tea and coffee, and the neighbors still contribute the food.

Even so, it was not good enough for Angela Burke. When her husband died in 1980, he was laid out in the parlor where his sisters and parents and all his forebears since the 1840s had been waked. The Burkes had not discussed his wake, since he died unexpectedly of a stroke at sixty-six. But, although some people thought it was foolish, his widow never considered doing otherwise. When she is asked why she chose a home wake, this articulate woman is briefly speechless. It is as if you asked her why she stood up before walking. Finally she says, "I thought, well, why take him out? There was no need . . . Why be all night at Ken Broughton's? They might as well have buried him! . . . I can't see why, if you've got to leave him at night, why you don't bury him." She adds that when death stays at home, so to speak, it's less frightening. Her grandchildren and great-grandchildren fear death and dead people because they have become rare, but in the past "you knew what death was. People knew they were going to die, and it didn't come as any surprise."

For Angela Burke, it seemed only natural that her husband should move from his own house to his parish church to the Brigus graveyard. But she departed from tradition in one important way, declaring that there would be no alcohol at the wake. Her five sons, three daughters, and extended family had gathered from around the world, but she did not want a party. Perhaps she had vivid enough memories of the old merry wakes to want to ensure that one did not take place. Yes, his mother's order was unusual, Tom Burke admits, but "she ruled."

Donna Burke, Tom's wife, has seen both her parents waked at home in the 1990s. Ken Broughton embalmed them in his funeral parlor, another innovation he introduced to Brigus in the 1970s that is now standard. Then he returned them to their apartment in their son's house. Donna remembers their wakes as informal family occasions where there were no "hours of visitation." If the spirit moved you, you could pad downstairs in the middle of the night for a visit with the dead. Initially awed grandchildren quickly accepted that Nanny and Grandfather Hayes had come home to be in their bed one last time. Told that it wouldn't feel like Nanny when they asked if they could touch her, the younger children gently tried to bend her fingers. Watching the children play outside, Donna saw them taking turns imitating the corpse, while the others would approach and make the sign of the cross. They were "playing wake."

"What it showed me was that children will incorporate whatever is around," she says. "They will make it part of their life. Of course, the older kids were sad and upset, but seeing your loved ones in their own environment, not in some cold place that is only about death, is a comfort . . . The death is really and truly part of the living that continues, and it all falls within the same house." Even the cat, a favorite of Nanny Hayes, took it in stride. Coming down one morning, the family found her sleeping on Nanny's still, cold chest.

Will Angela Burke be waked in her tall green house? Once again, it is so taken for granted that her children have not even discussed it. Although the brown habit was, in her opinion, "a good thing," none is lying in readiness for her. She has forbidden her family to deck her in gold jewelry, another innovation she considers pagan. But she did ask one of her sons to bring her a black shawl on his last visit home from Australia. She plans to wear it over a plain white blouse, in her coffin, in her own parlor.

⌘

The "Bustle in a House / The Morning after Death" that Emily Dickinson describes is indeed solemn, but it remains a bustle. It often struck me that Scott's parents, Marilyn and D'Arcy Roche, were organizing, in about two days and in grievous circumstances, ceremonies and gatherings only a little less complicated than the wedding we had been looking forward to planning over the next nine months. To compound their difficulties, they lived in California, and Seattle was not their city.

On Sunday morning, about eighteen hours after their son died, I went with the Roches to shop for a funeral. Looking at a few churches and a school chapel, balancing available times, ambience, parking, and flexibility when it came to music choice and the number of eulogies allowed in each case, Scott's parents maintained a focus that was more than impressive. I felt sure that, in their situation, I would have taken the first church, however inadequate. They did not. The music was important: Scott loved singing, and he and his mother often shared new discoveries in vocal music. So were the eulogies: the traditional Catholic funeral allows for only one, and Marilyn, Hannah, and Scott's brother Stephan all wanted to speak.

After the tour of funeral sites, we went to a friend's house, and the Roches and their four living sons sat down with lists of more than fifty incoming relatives, times of arrival, places for them to stay. A restaurant for a lunch after the funeral had to be chosen. Tasks were assigned. Sons and parents got busy on cellphones. On Monday, a church was selected, the priest consulted, readings and music chosen. Marilyn went shopping with her daughters-in-law to buy clothes for the funeral. She also bought a present for Hannah, something that Scott had been threatening for years to give her – a pair of black velvet slacks.

Monday evening the Roches gave a buffet dinner in Scott's house, with Thai food from his favorite carryout restaurant, for the family and friends who had convened in Seattle by then. After the funeral, having experienced their attentiveness and generosity in marking a tragic time, I told them I wished more than ever that we could have designed a joyous one together.

Hannah, in contrast with Scott's parents, spent the days before the funeral refusing to leave my sister's house in Everett, just outside Seattle. There she simply sat on the couch, so entwined with her three college roommates that they sometimes looked like a hydra-headed beast, two dark-haired, one red-haired, and one light brown.

She had been very different while Scott was in the hospital, going almost without sleep for forty-eight hours. There she ushered visitors in and out of his room, fielded telephone calls, talked with the medical staff about his care almost like the doctor she would be. She and her roommates, who had flown in from New York, Washington, and San Francisco, spent the last night of Scott's life with him in his hospital room. He had been reading Kipling's *Kim*, saying he was going to read all the books he had been assigned in college but left unread, and the book was found in the car after the accident. Although he was unconscious, Hannah read it to him in his hospital room. She sang his favorite songs to him, and every so often she would order her friends out of the room so she could spend some time alone with him.

The minute he died, she withdrew. Psychologists call it "recoil." I noticed it first at Scott's house, where we went after leaving the hospital, to pick up Hannah's things. On the dining table was a photograph of Scott holding a colleague's newborn baby. She picked it up, looked at it briefly, and said, "That's sad." I was shocked at the smallness and flatness of her voice. When Marilyn and D'Arcy invited us to go looking at churches, she stayed at my sister's; I was sent in her stead. Nor would she meet with the priest to arrange the funeral, although she chose the music and discussed her preferences over the telephone. Apparently numb, she was very clear about what she would and would not do. When she talked, she talked only about Scott.

There is no judgment implied in this description of Scott's parents' and Hannah's responses. Both Marilyn and Hannah describe themselves as in shock in those first days. One turned to activity; the other to stasis.

Months later, I recognized Hannah in something I had been noticing in my reading about bereavement. Again and again I would come across descriptions or pictures in which a mourner sits stunned and unmoving. A miniature from the Flemish mid-15th-century *Hours of Philip the Good* is typical. It is a bedroom scene with a corpse being swathed in a winding sheet by two women. The casement window is open to allow the spirit to leave, the plain wooden coffin is ready. A woman, probably the widow, sits apart, resting her face on her hand, averting her gaze from both the body and the prayer book she holds. I began to think of this woman and others like her as the "immobilized widow," although any close mourner could qualify.

Some cultures institutionalized the mourner's inertia. In fishing villages on the east coast of Scotland, it was the custom for the widow to retreat immediately to her bed and receive visitors there. Middle-class European widows were confined in bedrooms hung with black cloth, and aristocratic widows received callers in special mourning beds, hung heavily with black and lent out to family members as the need arose. At the Burgundian court in 15th-century France, the widow of a knight was consigned to her bed for six weeks after her husband's death.

The polar Inuit of a hundred years ago had the most strange and evocative custom I encountered along these lines. For five days after her husband's death, the widow sat by his body, never standing and never lying down, with her husband's trousers upon her head. As sometimes happens with an apparently bizarre tradition, this one had an eerie rightness I found hard to articulate. In a culture where clothes were few and treasured, a man's widow sat by his side, not moving, crowned with his trousers. Except for the trousers, it reminded me of Hannah on my sister's couch.

Sometimes expectations coupled with necessity meant that the widow had to do all the arranging and *then* look helpless. Elizabeth Grant's *Memoirs of a Highland Lady* describes one such woman, an elderly relative whose husband died in 1814. The vignette has all the elements of the good death, Scottish Highlands style: the body laid out on the bed in the best room, wearing a ruffled shirt and nightcap, with hands crossed over the breast. White sheets and napkins were everywhere, on the chests and tables, pinned over the pictures and cushions. Refreshments (wine and seedcake for visitors of the first rank, whiskey and cheese for the others) were dispensed by a relative who watched by the corpse. The widow sat in a spare bedroom, playing what Elizabeth Grant calls the "serious part" of the Highland widow: silent and motionless, she nodded or whispered, but only if an answer was absolutely necessary. The scene, as Grant observes tartly, was letter-perfect, for it was truly a scene. The widow had in fact been up since early morning, "streaking the corpse" (arranging the limbs), organizing the wake-room and her own room, seeing to all the food and drink. Her culture dictated that she look the part of the stunned mourner, while at the same time it demanded that all the customary arrangements be in place.

We'll never know if the backstage bustle or the public pose of numbness suited that Highland widow better – or if both served some purpose. But that nameless woman has been a reminder to me, when I'm tempted to wax nostalgic about cultures with firm protocols for the distracted or confused mourner. Sometimes those rules must have been a welcome support and sometimes, when they clashed with the mourner's temperament, an uncongenial burden.

Modern permissiveness when it comes to the mourner's behavior can look like a deprivation one minute, a blessing the next. In the case of Hannah and Marilyn, in those first days, it was a blessing. It helped, too, that the cast of characters was large enough to allow those who wanted to bustle to bustle, and those for whom activity was impossible to sit apart. Marilyn's nervous energy found a purpose in organizing Scott's funeral. Hannah, on the other hand, needed time to retreat, to absorb the shock, to absent herself for a while before she could contemplate life without Scott.

TWO

WAILING TIME

How good are tears, how sweet are dirges,
I would rather sing dirges
Than eat or drink.
    – lament by a contemporary Greek woman

When I called Hannah from Shanghai and learned about the accident, she said that if Scott turned out to have brain injuries as well as quadriplegia, perhaps it would be better if he died. Then she began weeping, saying she could not bear the thought of never talking with him again. Her sister called her that night from Hong Kong, and at the sound of Sybil's voice, she cried again. When I arrived at the hospital and put my arms around her, she sobbed briefly. That was the last time I saw her cry.

The Jews call the day or so between death and burial the "wailing time." The official name for this period is *aninut*, from the Hebrew verb meaning to wail, to complain, to lament. I saw no wailing at Harborview Medical Center, where Scott died, or in the places where we congregated before the funeral. Of course people did cry, and had cried during the two days in the hospital when Scott's fate was at first unknown, and then horribly known. My ex-husband, who had rushed down to Seattle from his home in Vancouver, made Hannah and her roommates smile because he spent considerable time in the waiting room with shreds of Kleenex adhering to his moist face. Hannah had almost never seen her father cry before.

Probably the most dramatic burst of tears I witnessed occurred in the intensive care unit, within minutes of my arrival. A young man walking down the corridor stopped suddenly, banged his fists hard on the wall, and wept fiercely for a few minutes, facing the wall. It was a surreal moment for me, partly because this stranger looked disturbingly like Scott and partly because such an outburst is rare in contemporary North America. He turned out to be Scott's brother Matthew.

We do not wail much, as a society, and there is plenty of evidence that shows how effectively such expressions of emotion are culturally reinforced or discouraged. When Jessie Janowitz, one of Hannah's college roommates and a Jew, heard that Scott's funeral was going to be held in a Catholic church, she joked about the Jewish aversion to crucifixes, saying she intended to look at the cross above the altar whenever she felt tempted to cry, and that would stop her. But the very idea of not wanting to cry at a dear friend's funeral or of calling the impulse a temptation would strike many people in other parts of the world as bizarre.

In the past, it would have been an even more outlandish notion. The clamor that greeted death and went on intermittently until burial, the *conclamatio mortis*, took many forms, but wailing was probably the most widespread. In India, the Kol women were expected to cry in the funeral cortege, while the men were expected not to. Nineteenth-century explorers reported that Maoris of both sexes wailed, and the formation of a long stream of mucus from the nose (a *huupee*) was cultivated as a praiseworthy sign of grief.

Vase paintings from ancient Greece show women surrounding the body on its couch, clasping the dead person's head or pulling at their own hair while they sing a mournful chant. Relatives might stand on one side of the body, with professional

lamenters on the other. Together they traded the lament back
and forth, weaving improvised, personal parts in with traditional complaints. The professionals tended to more ordered,
polished segments (called *threnos*), which the kinswomen sometimes responded to simply with doleful wails (*goos*). The laments
for Hector sung by his wife, Andromache, his mother, Hecuba,
and his sister-in-law, Helen of Troy, in *The Iliad* are typical in
that they praise the dead man while bitterly bewailing their
own fate now that he is gone. The Greek model – the combination of familial and professional mourners; the dirge, both
celebratory and self-pitying, sometimes accompanied with
reed pipe and movement so that it looked like a funereal dance;
the prominence of female mourners – spread throughout the
Hellenic empire and beyond.

Not everyone approved of wailing and lamentation, on the
grounds that they were excessive and disruptive. In *The Laws*,
Plato sensibly allowed that "either to ordain or to prohibit
weeping for the dead is unseemly," but he drew the line at hired
mourners and loud lamentations outside the house. Solon
prohibited howling women and hired singers, the Spartan
Lycurgus limited mourning to eleven days, and Cicero would
permit no more than ten flute players in the funeral procession.
None of it had much effect. Mourning, at least in the ancient
Mediterranean world, was determined to have its say. It would
take more than a patrician distaste for noise and vulgar display
to temper the outpourings of grief.

The early Christians had a more serious objection to florid
mourning. For them death was not an unmixed evil but a birth
into a new and better life. Howling and lamentation were worse
than unruly; they disparaged the doctrine of the afterlife. It is
impossible to know how much the belief in heaven really comforted mourners in the 1st century A.D. or in our own time, but
Christians in all eras have at least attempted to find solace in that
doctrine. (A 1992 study does indicate that faith in an afterlife is

associated with less evasion of grief and greater recovery.) And it represented a major shift in attitude, as the tombstone epitaphs for young children in the Roman empire before and after Christ suggest. The pagan inscriptions are fatalistic; the death is sad but foreordained. A little girl identified only as Ampliata, not yet five years old, urges her mother not to mourn because fate has decided her death:

> *Noli Dolere Mamma*
> *Faciendum Fuit*
> *Properavit aetas fatus*
> *Quod volvit meus*

> Don't grieve, Mama,
> It had to be done.
> What my fate had in mind for me,
> My lifespan speeded up.

Beyond the acceptance of stark necessity, Ampliata has no comfort for her mother. The Christian inscriptions, by contrast, are joyful. A three-year-old assures the parents that weeping is futile when their child lives forever in heaven. Another child reminds his parents not to mourn, because he is in paradise:

> *Ne tristes lacrimas, ne pectora tundite vestra,*
> *O Pater et Mater nam regna caelestia tango.*

> No tears of sadness, no beating of your breast,
> O Father and Mother, I have reached the
> kingdom of heaven.

Even so, the Church Fathers had an uphill struggle when they tried to legislate mourning. It was one thing to believe your little daughter was in heaven; it was quite another not to long for the sight, the sound, the feel of your three-year-old. Not only are death customs deeply entrenched, but the Christian injunction to see death as a joyful release pitted theological conviction against natural human affection.

That tension was much in Saint Gregory of Nyssa's mind when his sister Macrina died in 379. An abbess and a saint in the Orthodox Church, Macrina was by Gregory's account something even rarer: an eldest sister whose bossiness her brothers (three of them bishops, two of the bishops saints) welcomed. Gregory saw her as a woman informed by "philosophy," which the 4th century understood as a combination of Christianity and asceticism. In particular, the strength of her belief in an afterlife impressed him, and at least half of Gregory's short, very likable biography of his sister is devoted to her reactions to others' deaths and her own.

Born in Cappadocia, Asia Minor (now Turkey), Macrina was a student of the Scriptures and extremely beautiful. She was promised in marriage by her father, but the young man died before the wedding. In a pre-emptive strike against the returning swarm of suitors, she declared that she would be faithful to her father's choice and remain single. From that point, Macrina devoted herself to prayer and to helping her mother raise her family. When her brother Basil returned from university studies in rhetoric "puffed up beyond measure with the pride of oratory," his sister "took him in hand" and convinced him to renounce worldly ambition. He founded a monastic settlement on one of the family estates and is now known as Saint Basil the Great.

When another brother, the hermit and philosopher Naucratius, died suddenly, their mother was overcome with sorrow. Macrina grieved too, but she schooled her mother in bravery. According to Gregory, thanks to his sister, their mother "did not behave in any ignoble and womanish way, so as to cry out at the calamity, or tear her dress, or lament over the trouble, or strike up funeral chants with mournful melodies." Gregory's description of what his mother did *not* do is a concise summary of the pre-Christian practices the Church Fathers were trying to suppress, and calling them "womanish" points to the source of the trouble, as far as the Fathers were concerned.

On her own deathbed, Macrina, by then the abbess of a monastery and probably in her early fifties, was cheerful, looking forward to meeting her "bridegroom," as she called Christ. She died while beginning to make the sign of the cross. She had asked her brother to close her eyes and mouth and cross her hands on her breast when she died, but her body had fallen naturally into the correct position. (Things have a way of working out more neatly for saints than for lesser mortals, at least as reported in their official biographies.) In an echo of the old taboo against noise while the soul struggled to leave the body, she had expressly forbidden the attending nuns to weep as she lay dying. Once she was dead, though, "grief like some inward fire was smouldering in their hearts, [and] all at once a bitter and irrepressible cry broke out."

The nuns lamented as women in the Greek world had for centuries, using the familiar images, oppositions, and parallelisms to tell the soreness of their loss. They sang:

> The light of our eyes has gone out,
> The light that guided our souls has been taken away.
> The safety of our life is destroyed,
> . . . .
> The bond of restraint has been taken away,
> The support of the weak has been broken
> . . . .
> In thy presence the night became to us as day,
> Illumined with pure life,
> But now even our day will be turned to gloom.

Undone by the sight of his sister and "the sad wailing of the virgins," Gregory felt a "flood of emotion, like a watercourse in spate," sweep away his reason, and he abandoned himself to grief. But not for long. Macrina's face seemed to reprimand him, and he reminded the nuns that they must turn their lamenting into psalm singing. At that point, Gregory more or less took control of the mourning rites, improvising a compromise between Christian and pagan ways and reconciling Macrina's purism with his own more yielding, affectionate character.

At a few key points, Macrina seemed to get the best of both pagan and Christian traditions. She had made no provision for special burial clothes, and Gregory and one of the deaconesses dressed her in a linen robe Gregory had brought with him. As a result, she looked like a bride, which is how unmarried Greek women had been dressed for burial long before the time of Christ. The deaconess objected, saying it would not do for the other nuns to see Macrina arrayed in bridal splendor, so they covered her finery with a dark robe. The symbolism could hardly be more apt, for Macrina and the early Christian world as a whole: the old pagan costume close to the body, obscured by a somber, monastic-like robe.

During their all-night wake, the nuns mingled their lamentations with psalms, the approved, joyful music for a Christian death at least since the 2nd century. By dawn the entrance hall of the monastery was full of people from the surrounding area, who broke out in wailing. Cleverly Gregory divided the visitors, placing the women with the nuns on one side, the men with the monks on the other. Just as the paid lamenters and the bereaved family wailed in response to each other at a pre-Christian wake, Gregory arranged that the women and men should alternate singing psalms, "in rhythmical and harmonious fashion, as in chorus singing." It was the antiphonal structure these people knew well from the old laments, but sobered and Christianized.

The funeral march to church, with Macrina borne uncoffined on her bed by two bishops and two priests, escorted by deacons and servants with wax tapers, accompanied by followers singing hymns and crowds desperate to see her body, was an exquisitely slow procession that took the best part of a day. On these occasions, anguish and disorder threatened constantly to break through the skin of Christian resignation, as had happened during the recent funeral procession of Macrina's brother Basil. A Christian onlooker described that scene as "psalms giving way to lamentation, and philosophy overcome by passion. It was a struggle between our followers and the outsiders – Greeks, Jews and immigrants . . . and the body only just escaped their clutches." The dualities are significant: psalms versus lamentation, philosophy versus passion, the Christians versus the "outsiders."

In Macrina's case, the crisis came inside the church, where her parents' grave had already been opened to receive her body. (Corpses were simply placed in the earth without coffins. Mindful of the biblical prohibition against uncovering the nakedness of one's parents, Gregory hastened to cover their decomposing bodies with a cloth.) The psalm singing had stopped, so that the priests could pray, and in the lull, "a woman cried out impulsively that after this hour we should see that divine face no more." The rest of the nuns took up that doleful thought, wailing, and the priests restored order only with difficulty.

When the formalities were over, Gregory prepared to return home. He had done his best to respect his sister's serious spirit, to put philosophy before passion. But before he left, feelings for Macrina that had not been voiced in the sweetness of the antiphons demanded expression. No matter how certain he was of meeting her in another life, the sister who had scolded, inspired, taught, and loved him was no more, at least in this world. "I first threw myself on the grave and embraced the dust," he wrote, "and then I started on my way back, downcast and tearful, pondering over the greatness of my loss."

⌘

Look at her, how she lies,
Like a felled lemon tree!
— a 20th-century Greek woman,
lamenting over her daughter

My treasure and my love,
My little dark-headed boy,
Whom I thought whiter than new milk
Or than water on a summer day!
— a 20th-century Irish woman,
lamenting over her son

Gradually, the Church Fathers softened their stand against the expression of grief. Just as the Greek and Roman elite's distaste for excessive mourning had not much affected the behavior of the people, the doctrine of the Resurrection had not managed to wipe out sorrow. Very definitely it had not wiped out ritual lamenting, which seems to strike deep in the cultures where it takes root.

In the Muslim world, Muhammad's teachings also forbid wild wailing and keening, but more than thirteen hundred years after the Prophet, Muslim women continued to wail and keen. By then, the opposition between the lamenting women and the men who attempted to control them had taken on a ritualistic character of its own, as they acted out two reactions to bereavement.

In the village of Artas in the Palestine of the mid-1920s, the anthropologist Hilma Granqvist was present at the mourning for a sheikh. When women arrived from a neighboring village, she reported, "Weeping loudly they loosened their hair, jumped up and down on the earthen floor, whirled about, slapped their faces, all the while singing their mourning songs." Other women blackened their hands with soot, tore at their hair, literally skipped about in grief. As each mourner entered the house where the sheikh was laid out, she threw herself on the dead man and re-energized the group, which danced and lamented to the point of exhaustion. The newcomer added a fresh note, varying with her relationship to the dead, to the continuing improvised song of lamentation. A half-sister of the dead man, living in another village, rushed in, rent her dress, and sang:

> The tidings came to me
> I was frightened
> The tidings were about
> The light of my eyes!

A daughter of the sheikh sang to her uncle:

> O father's brother
> Canst thou not see
> We have become orphans.
> My mother and I
> Are dressed in mourning!

Meanwhile, there were protections and checks built into the scene. Granqvist noted that it was a point of pride with the women to lose themselves in grief, but there was no fear of real harm. Each close mourner had a "comforter" whose job was to make sure she did not hurt herself seriously as she whirled into hysteria. The men, praying outside the house, entered periodically, trying to quell the wailing, telling the women their behavior was sinful, that it hurt the dead man. The women paid no attention.

Granqvist believed that the dualism in their mourning satisfied both ancient, pre-Muslim practice and Muslim teachings then current: "Bewailing is required, bewailing is prohibited, the women must lament the dead and yet the men prevent them from doing so. When the men raise difficulties, they feel justified in that they are protecting their religion, defending the Muslim faith. Their raging against the women's behaviour is a holy anger."

The lamenting of women inside the house of death (and the more subdued congregating of men outside the house) was such a constant that Boccaccio noted its absence in the Florentine plague of the 1340s as one of the clearest signs of disaster: there were too many sick, too much fear of contagion for the usual observances. Whether they chanted, ululated, sang, or droned, Maori, Coptic, Fijian, Portuguese, Ghanaian, Highland Scots, Irish, Italian, Greek, French, and Russian women continued to lament vocally and publicly, many of them into the 20th century. And many employed similar devices, from the hesitant beginning ("How can I tell your story?") through the reproaches ("How could you leave me to bring up our child alone?"), the praise, the genealogy, the biography, above all the bitter contrast between the past and the present, between the fortunate then and the miserable now.

In addition to the family, professional mourners would lament for money, for barter ("Sing me a fine lament for him, and you shall have a pile of beans," as a modern Greek lamenter was promised), or simply because they were good at it. They too performed all over the world, from China to Spain, but in the West their position was ambiguous. By the Middle Ages, the Church roundly disapproved, although it had not been above hiring them for funeral processions in the early days of Christianity. At least since the 17th century, synod after synod of the Irish Church had forbidden paid keeners, obviously without success. In 1800 the Archbishop of Cashel prohibited "all unnatural screams and shrieks, and fictitious, rueful cries and elegies, at wakes, together with the savage custom of howling and bawling at funerals."

Most of the disapproval focused on the professional mourners' mercenary motives, which is like complaining that a professional string quartet will not perform except for money. In a poetic tug-of-war between an Irish keening woman and a priest, the characters quarrel over who profits most from a death. The priest taunts her, "You would keen over a dog, you hag, / If you found him dead!" and she ripostes, "No need for you to be so bitter, Father; / What you don't get from the living, you get from the dead."

The professional keener still commands respect in countries such as Greece and Portugal. Engaging one is a way to show special respect for the dead, to procure a good send-off, to help organize the family's inchoate grief. Much like a choir director, the skilled keener knows where to take the lament, how to lift the burden of improvisation and inspire the family. Margaret Alexiou describes kinswomen and professional mourners in modern Greece sustaining each other, passing the song from one side of the bier to the other, the relief singer grasping the hand of the current singer to indicate that she will take up the lament. And their professional or semiprofessional status need not imply heartlessness. Often a woman took up lamenting because of tragedy in her own life. A Macedonian woman explained to Alexiou that she became a mourner because her husband and son died early in her life. Lamenting at the wakes and funerals of others became a way to remember them: "I weep for my own, not for theirs."

There were no professional mourners, called *ciangiulini*, in Maria-Carmela and Paolo Pietropaolo's village of Maierato in Calabria, in southern Italy. Maierato was too small and humble to support professionals, but there were some in nearby Pizzo, which had a bourgeoisie and even an aristocracy. In Calabria, the more prosperous you were, the more likely you were to hire professionals. The poor lamented for themselves, as Maria-Carmela Pietropaolo has for all the bereavements in her long life.

Her greatest losses were the deaths of two babies during World War II. Sitting at her kitchen table in Toronto, she weeps easily when she thinks about the little boy and girl who died in Italy almost sixty years ago. She leaves the kitchen briefly to return with her one dim photograph of the boy and a recent, brightly colored one of their tomb in Maierato. Remembering her chants when they died, she describes them as "a cry of pain, but not like when you hurt yourself and you cry in pain. It was as if a despair had entered my life . . . So I chanted, 'I am left empty-handed, this is the despair of my life to be without my children, to be all alone without my husband who is away at war.'"

The unapologetic self-pity of her plaint reminds me of Andromache bewailing Hector in *The Iliad*, and rightly so. Calabria is part of Magna Graecia, the Greek colonial empire, and Maria-Carmela Pietropaolo is one of the last practitioners of the ancient Mediterranean lament. As she recalls the lyrics she sang for her babies, she does not quite chant but she comes close. Later her son Damiano shows me what the chants he has witnessed in Calabria and in Toronto's Italian community sound and look like. It is as if one of the ancient Greek vase paintings of a mourning scene has come to life. He rocks back and forth, sometimes with his head in his hands, sometimes with his hands spread out. The sound he makes is more like the recitative in an opera than a melody, in that the note rarely changes. Its rhythm is trochaic, a two-syllable foot with the accent on the first syllable. In its melancholy, it is almost Asian, and Damiano prolongs the significant word in each line or thought.

The plaintive, un-histrionic sound of the chant interested me, as did Maria-Carmela's description of it as an expression of despair. Somewhere between the speaking voice and either a full-blown cry or melody, the chant signaled that this was no ordinary statement, no ordinary situation. I thought of Marilyn in the hospital, as she and D'Arcy were about to go into their son's room to say their last goodbye. She said, apparently casually and in passing, "It's so hard to let go." It sounded absent-minded (literally absent-minded) and almost worryingly understated, as did Hannah's "That's sad," on seeing the photograph of Scott holding a baby. When I imagined those sentences as part of a chant, they sounded perfectly natural.

Lamenting in Maierato when the Pietropaolos lived there took place mostly during the wake and the funeral procession. After World War I, the priests had forbidden chanting during the funeral mass itself, but they relented when "the grief was just too great," as Paolo Pietropaolo puts it – whether because of the person's youth or in the case of an accident. A mourner might also break out in a lament long after the funeral. Maria-Carmela would find herself lamenting her babies while working in the fields, "as my heart moved me."

When Paolo's father died in Calabria, his mother grieved quietly until she saw her son begin to shave the dead man to ready him for the wake. Then she started chanting, addressing her husband, "I don't know how your son Paolo can muster the courage to shave you like this." At that point, the other women in the room joined in the lamenting. Some were genuinely moved, according to Paolo, while others sang "out of respect for her grief, so that there would not be gossip about how unmoved they were by this tender scene."

During the wake, which typically lasted about twelve hours, family and friends took turns lamenting when inspired, perhaps only for a few minutes at a time or longer. In a pattern similar to the passing back and forth of the lament in Greece, as described by Margaret Alexiou, Italian women in Maierato would spell one another off. Their words when relieving the current chanter suggest something of the satisfaction, even the pleasure, afforded by the exercise: "Let me take over, you must be sated with it by now, let me have a turn ... Take a rest now ... Let me enjoy a bit, too."

Although Maierato had no professional mourners, it had a few women known for their skill at chanting. When they arrived at a wake, people would show their appreciation by making room for them at the bedside and falling silent. One of them, a Signora Nunziata, complained that even if she was not moved to chant, her reputation preceded her and she felt obliged. Paolo Pietropaolo explains that it was a mark of respect not just to appear at a wake but to be willing to share in the family's sorrow by chanting, and Signora Nunziata was much honored for this. His wife adds that Signora Nunziata was no stranger to loss, as her own brother had died tragically in a fire. Signora Nunziata and her mother grieved and lamented for years "and so they became very good at it."

Most chanting was done by women, but there were memorable exceptions. Maria-Carmela Pietropaolo remembers a male cousin running from the next village to be with his dead father and chanting his grief "as loudly as any woman." Another family connection, a doctor, had been widowed early with three little daughters, whom his sister raised. When the sister died, the doctor was inconsolable. Maria-Carmela tried to stop his crying, reminding him that we are born to die, that other people have sisters, but this only spurred him on. He chanted, over and over, "I have lost not only a sister, but also a mother to my daughters . . . and my wife died before her, and our mother before her." With the doctor, as with many mourners, past as well as present sorrows found their way into his song.

Chanting has become more and more rare since the Pietropaolos moved to Toronto in 1959. When Maria-Carmela's mother died in Canada in the 1970s, she chanted in the funeral home. (This confused her eight-year-old nephew, Rocco, who associated singing with joy. He asked his mother, "Why is Aunt Carmela happy when Nanna has died?") But the rise of the funeral parlor has proved a major deterrent to lamenting, because it strikes Italian Canadians as an alien place to voice their grief. Paolo Pietropaolo's cousin died about seven years ago and one of his daughters, while at home, began to chant. People tried to stop her, including Paolo, until he decided that she would feel better if she were allowed to grieve "in the old way."

Grieving in the old way has become difficult even in an out-of-the-way village like Maierato. As the children of the Pietropaolos' peers become bourgeois, they become ashamed of their parents' peasant ways, which, as they see it, include lamenting. Paolo's sister lives in Italy and wants to chant when the occasion arises, but her daughter, a high school teacher married to an architect, stops her every time she tries.

Paolo Pietropaolo says he does not miss the old customs: they were restrictive, and it's better that people get on with their lives sooner than they were able to. His wife is more ambivalent. She agrees it was "ugly" when men in mourning were not allowed to shave for a year, and it was difficult when fires could not be lit even for cooking during the mourning year. But lamenting has served her well. After she chanted for her father, she says, "I felt better, a sense of relief, also a sense of having done my duty, a sense that I was showing my great love for him. And the chanting and the tears were a release for me."

I asked Damiano about the continuation of the custom. "Let me put it this way," he answered. "If I died now, my mother would chant for me. When she dies, there will be no one who knows how to do it." I did not have the courage to ask Maria-Carmela, who has three living sons and a daughter, whether she minds that no one will chant for her. But when I asked her son, he nodded: "It's one of the first grievances she mentions when she regrets coming to North America, or when she sometimes complains about her heartless modern children."

⌘

Bewail the dead, hide not your grief.
 – Ben Shira, a 4th-century sage

Like their Middle Eastern neighbors, the Jews made use of paid lamenters and wailing women. In the first centuries after Christ, one of the duties of the burial society was to engage "chanting women," along with musicians and funeral orators. Fourteenth-century Jewish mourners in Saragossa, Spain, walked home from the synagogue with a wailing woman who accompanied her dirge on a tambourine. The other women, presumably unprofessional mourners, joined her chant with clapped hands and vocalizations.

Most lamenting of this public variety happened during *aninut*, the tense, tightly circumscribed period between death and burial. The "wailing time" is ostensibly dedicated to the dead, but it's also a time of great indulgence for the mourner. Called an *onen*, which literally means trouble or sorrow, the mourner is considered too raw to be comforted, and his needs take precedence only after burial. With help from family and friends, the *onen* must make the relatively simple arrangements for the Jewish funeral and burial. But his grief is so apparent, and some normal obligations so obviously impossible, that he is granted special licence. For example, Jews must celebrate the Sabbath with joy, but the Rama, one of the great 20th-century Talmudic teachers, ordained that if an *onen* "takes pleasure in crying, because it relieves the anguish from his heart, then, he is permitted to cry on the Sabbath."

Beyond that, he is forbidden to work, to wash or shave, to have sexual intercourse, to eat meat or drink wine, even to study the Torah. Most striking of all, he is prohibited during *aninut* from uttering benedictions or responding "Amen" to a benediction, and cannot be part of a minyan, the quorum of ten males necessary for a Jewish service. Contemporary Jewish teachers explain these last prohibitions by noting that the mourner at this stage is likely to be enraged at the God who has taken away his loved one, and no one angry at God can fulfill his religious obligations. Coming from a Catholic background, where anger at God was never acceptable, I admired what seemed a psychological sophistication and compassion for the mourner's angry desolation.

As I learned more about the origins of *aninut*, it sounded less straightforward and understanding. Many ancient cultures, including the Jews, relegated close mourners to a temporary death-in-life. Unwillingly, the mourner had stepped too close to the thing we most wish to avoid, and he carried something of its impurity or threat. In his exemption from normal activities and obligations – washing, praying, having sex – the *onen* mimics the state of death. Jewish scholars have noted a rationale even more specific to Judaism and its central commitment to life. As those closest to death, *onenim* are temporarily exiled from full humanity, and hence from full Judaism. Like other traditional mourning customs, the laws of *aninut* are ambiguous. They can look superstitious and punitive, which seems to be how they began. They can also look wise and permissive, an externalization of the new mourner's inertia or lack of interest in everything but his loss.

Our wailing time for Scott, although not rich in wailing, had rightly included this element of indulgence for the close mourners – up to a point. Torn between my concern for Hannah and for Scott's parents, especially his mother, I insisted that my exhausted, numb daughter go with me to the relatives' house where the Roches gathered after Scott died. That was for the Roches' sake, and was probably a mistake. Similarly, the dinner the family gave the night before the funeral in Scott's house was an ordeal for Hannah, who retreated to a bedroom with some close friends and closed the door.

Whatever its origins, *aninut* now is a brief shelter that indulges mourners at the peak of their misery and disorientation, expects almost nothing from them, and even tolerates the possibility of rage at God. Believing that there can be no comfort "at a time when the deceased lies before him," Jewish law discourages the community from visiting until after burial. The *onenim* are left to howl in despair, to rail against the injustice of their fate, to curse God, to stare dumbly at the wall. As Rabbi Margaret Holub says, "It is as though the angel of death were still in the house, stalking with sword raised. Until the burial, the death is still happening, body and soul are shaking apart throughout the household. The community stays away, as rebuilding cannot begin until the earthquake is over."

The earthquake may be over by the time of burial. But the aftershocks, the survey of the destruction, and the woeful task of rebuilding have not yet begun.

THREE

THE CELEBRATION

Celebrate *v.* 1. To perform publicly and in due form (any religious ceremony, a marriage, a funeral, etc.) . . . 4. To make publicly known, proclaim, publish abroad. 5. To speak the praises of, extol, publish the fame of.
     – *The Oxford English Dictionary*

Separation is a bilateral process requiring vigorous and determined efforts on both sides: as the body must leave the group, so the group must leave the body.
     – Robert Garland, *The Greek Way of Death*

From a practical point of view, a funeral is unnecessary. The body must be disposed of in some way, but why should people gather, usually shortly before or after the burial or cremation, to remember, to mourn, to celebrate, to condole one another? Because, as Robert Garland says, "the group must leave the body." The important word is "group." The other important words in Garland's sentence are "vigorous and determined efforts."

By Sunday morning, when I went with Scott's parents to look at venues for the funeral, they had already made some decisions. The choice of Seattle itself was not obvious. The Roches and three of their sons lived in San Francisco, which is where Scott had gone to high school. He had lived a bachelor's life in Seattle for less than two years. But the Roches reasoned that Seattle was Scott's home, that the family would already be gathered there, that it would be closer for his friends in Vancouver, where Hannah lived, as well as for his friends on the east coast. "The group must leave the body," and this would be easier for the group.

D'Arcy Roche was concerned that the funeral should not be a "dirge." Marilyn still found the events of the last three days so unbelievable that she had to remind herself every five minutes or so, "He's dead. He's dead." She was determined that, since they had only one chance to honor Scott publicly, they would get it right. They wanted to choose the music and the readings as broadly as possible, and to have at least three eulogies. Scott was to be cremated, and his parents felt his life would be easier to celebrate without the presence of his body or his cremated remains.

The Roches are nominal Catholics, although their connection had become tenuous over the years. The Church still seemed more like home than anything else, but devising the funeral they wanted took precedence over any lingering affiliation. Together we visited the chapel of an Episcopal school, a Catholic parish church, and Seattle's Catholic cathedral. (We also talked about an Episcopal church recommended by some Seattle friends. D'Arcy, whose links with Catholicism were stronger than Marilyn's, joked darkly, "But will God be there?") The school presented timing and parking problems, and a minister would have to be found. The parish church struck us as dim and gloomy. The cathedral was beautiful and had a fine choir, but the music would have to be chosen from its liturgically approved repertoire and only one eulogy was allowed. We separated at noon without having made a choice.

That evening, I spoke with D'Arcy on the phone and, unthinkingly, I asked him how he was. "Much better than I should be," he said ruefully, "because we're getting things done." It was an honest answer that pointed to one of the functions of a funeral: it gives the bereaved some control in the midst of turmoil. To be bereaved originally meant to be robbed or dispossessed; the mourner has been robbed not only of the beloved but also of the sense that life can be ordered. Creating and planning a funeral does not restore the balance, but it can help, a little.

The key thing the Roches had accomplished since the morning was finding an ideal place for the funeral: the Chapel of St. Ignatius at Seattle University. When I visited Seattle in the summer of 1997, Scott took Hannah and me to see Steven Holl's brand-new chapel at the city's Jesuit university. Acclaimed as one of Seattle's finest buildings, the ocher-colored chapel is rather secretive on the outside. Inside is a curved white space mysteriously lit from above by a combination of stained glass and painted baffles. Scott loved it, pointing out the bronze door handles that furl like a priest's stole, the beeswax-encrusted walls of a side chapel, the bell tower at the end of a reflecting pool.

Hannah and Scott had wanted to have their wedding there, but they were told that only members of the university community could be married in the chapel. Ironically, what had been denied in life was granted in death when the friend of a friend secured the use of St. Ignatius for the Roches. Their son's funeral, on Tuesday, January 13, 1998, would be one of the first to be celebrated in the Chapel of St. Ignatius. Scott Anthony Courtenay Roche, who had been welcomed into the world with a Catholic baptism almost twenty-five years before, would leave it with a Catholic funeral.

⌘

The Hopi in Arizona bury the body without ceremony and have no public gathering, but they are unusual. Almost every culture has a leave-taking ritual for the dead. Even so, the funeral we are familiar with arrived relatively late in the Western world.

The modern ceremony, held most often in church, synagogue, funeral parlor, or hall, typically from one to five days after death, had no real counterpart in the ancient Greek or Roman world. The Greeks concentrated on what Robert Garland calls the "three-act drama" of laying out the body, proceeding to the place of interment, and finally cremating or burying the remains. The first act, the *prothesis*, or laying out, took place at home and contained the ritual laments by family and professional mourners around the body. It was the most ceremonious of the stages and corresponds to a traditional wake. No prayers or words to be said at the burial or cremation have survived, although it seems likely they existed. Offerings – food, water, animals, ointments, pottery – were made to the dead, placed either in the grave or near it, depending on the period. Mourners witnessed the libations, and the ceremonies ended with the funeral banquet.

The Western funeral is a gathering that in earlier times happened between two solemn processions – from home to church, and from church to the burial place. The aristocratic families of the Roman republic devised such a collective moment, on their way to burying their dead outside the city walls. Accompanied by horns, flutes, and actors masked to impersonate important family members in the past, the cortege stopped at the forum. There, at the speakers' platform, the dead man would be propped up, near the masks representing his ancestors, and an adult son or other family member would deliver a memorial oration while everyone listened. It was a public farewell for a public man, designed to awaken family pride in the relatives and civic pride in the populace. But it was reserved for elite males, and women and ordinary people were dispatched with a minimum of ceremony.

Christianity changed that, as it changed much else. A novel mourning form grew out of two of the new religion's central convictions: every human being was equal in the eyes of God, and death was a happy release into a better life with Christ. Seeking to dispel the pagan disbelief in an afterlife, the Christians crafted a ritual for everyone that unfolded from prayers at the deathbed to masses celebrated years later.

The anthropologist Victor Turner sees ritual as the action that reintegrates a disturbed social group after a crisis. The medieval rites for the dead were designed to knit an unraveled community, whether a parish or a country, back together after the crisis of death. Progressing deliberately from the smallest affected group to the largest, they began by attending to the dying person, moved after death to the immediate family ranged around the deathbed, then to the larger group at the wake, then to the full community gathered for the funeral. At least from the 7th century, the funeral or requiem mass (whose name comes from the first words of the opening prayer, *Requiem aeternam dona eis, Domine*, or "Grant them eternal rest, O Lord") was the center of the extended ritual.

In the medieval mind, the rites for the departed served both living and dead. They comforted the living through communal gatherings, which sometimes included feasting and gift giving. Mourners were not abandoned to their own devices soon after the burial but were enmeshed in a protective schedule of prayers and masses that were celebrated at lengthening intervals. The rituals kept pace with the progress of mourning, and vice versa.

The rituals helped the dead, in the medieval understanding, through the doctrine of purgatory. The idea of a transitional realm where the souls of those who had died in a state of grace waited until they were worthy of heaven became an official Church doctrine in 1254, but it had been widely believed during the previous century. The connection between purgatory and the funeral was a direct one: the funeral prayers specifically called upon God to take the dead to heaven, and the more people who said those prayers, the more the soul's way to heaven was quickened.

As a result, it behooved everyone to ensure as large a turnout as possible for his own funeral. It was not uncommon that one-third of a person's fortune would be spent on his "soul." This included inducements to attend the funeral – food, drink, commemorative objects such as rings – as well as bequests for memorial masses and special prayers. (The very rich founded whole buildings, called chantries, designed for the continuous chanting of prayers and masses for their souls.) Because the poor were believed to have powerful intercessionary powers, their presence at a funeral was sought through promises of food, clothing, and money.

The doctrine of purgatory was by no means an unmixed blessing. The rich had a grossly unfair advantage, and the Church profited mightily from the faithful's attempts to shorten their journey to heaven. (Nor was the thought of the place, interpreted literally by the nuns who taught me in the 1950s as a fiery bog, consoling. I spent too much of my childhood worrying about the flames.) But the positive side of purgatory was the connection it forged between the living and the dead. Mourners could do more than mourn; their prayers could actually help the dead. In addition to the communal support that a secular funeral offers, the medieval ceremony carried with it a conviction that the dead were not beyond our reach and care.

That belief ended for the people who embraced the Protestant Reformation. Scandalized by the abuses committed in the name of purgatory, the Protestants disavowed it. In England, Parliament condemned the doctrine in 1547; it found no place in the theologies of Luther, Zwingli, or Calvin. Protestantism held that the individual's fate was in his hands alone and was thus sealed at the instant of death. No amount of prayers or masses or good deeds done by the living could affect it. The dead were on their own, the mourners were left with no purposeful work, and the blurry line between living and dead encouraged by Catholicism was sharpened and thickened.

When belief changes, the ritual changes. The doctrine of purgatory had tainted the whole funeral rite as far as the Protestants were concerned, and the most rigorous reformers tried to throw the baby out with the bathwater. Since there was no longer any theological point to a funeral, the least ceremony was the best ceremony. In England in 1553, all psalms, prayers for the dead, and the service of Communion were ordered omitted from the funeral service. In 1644, during Cromwell's rule, the authorities went further. The dead were to be carried from their house to the place of burial without an intervening ceremony of any kind. Kneeling and praying by the corpse was considered superstitious, and reading, praying, and singing en route to or at the grave "have been grossly abused, are in no way beneficial to the dead, and have proved many ways hurtful to the living."

Even the sensory accessories of funerals – candles, incense, and the ringing of bells – incurred the wrath of reformers, as too redolent of papistry and its errors. In Geneva, funereal minimalism reached such extremes in 1643 that even a Lutheran visitor, Elie Brackenhoffer of Strasbourg, was shocked. He reported, "No funeral prayer, no song, no commemoration, much less any ringing of bells for the occasion. When a man dies, he dies. He is not given so much as a Paternoster for alms. The bereaved and others thus return home without consolation and without exhortation." The further removed a denomination was from Catholicism, the more unadorned the rite for the dead, as Queen Victoria saw when the father of her gillie, John Brown, died in the Scottish Highlands in 1875. The queen noted in her diary the plainest of Presbyterian farewells, simply the saying of prayers over (but not for) the dead man in the hallway of his house, after which the body was carried to the place of burial.

Protestants only slightly less austere than those in the Highlands did contribute something important to the funeral, and that was the sermon. A Calvinist funeral that took place in 1819 in Dutch New York, described by the Reverend Peter Van Pelt, was almost as pared down as that of John Brown's father, with one significant difference. A group of men sat around a table, solemnly passing wine and pipes. On the table was the coffin. The *dominie*, or minister, gave a sermon in Dutch and said a prayer, and all assembled took the coffin out to the churchyard. The center of this understated service was the minister's address.

Just as the Scripture readings and the sermon inspired by them replaced the Catholic consecration as the dominant feature in the Protestant service, so the funeral sermon, in several denominations, replaced the prayers for the dead in the requiem mass. At its peak, from the 17th to the 19th centuries, it evolved into a hybrid of devotional and biographical art, which began with a meditation on the Scripture reading of the day and proceeded in the second half to an oration on the dead person's life – a eulogy, in other words.

As Protestantism became more secure, some of the old practices crept back. Singing of hymns and psalms and some discreet candles and bell ringing gradually lost the taint of Catholicism in many Protestant denominations. The practice of praying for the dead never became acceptable, but it too proved a difficult habit to stamp out entirely. John Evelyn, John Aubrey, and Samuel Johnson, all good Protestants, all admitted to praying for dead family and friends.

Meanwhile, the Catholic funeral remained unaffected. With minor tinkering and local permutations, it persisted in a form that would have been recognizable to a medieval man or woman until the Second Vatican Council of the 1960s. Out of the liturgical reforms inspired by the council came a revamped funeral mass – unchanged in its essentials, but now celebrated in the vernacular rather than Latin, by a priest wearing white vestments to signify hope. At first it was called the Mass of the Resurrection. Later, when it was felt that the pendulum had swung unrealistically far in the direction of joy, it was renamed the Mass of Christian Burial.

⌘

> There's a push for "do it yourself" funerals
> – as if grief were ever anything but.
> — Thomas Lynch, "Socko Finish"

On Monday, the day before the funeral, Marilyn and D'Arcy went to Seattle University to discuss the Mass of Christian Burial with John Whitney. A Jesuit in his thirties, Father Whitney spent about an hour and a half with them, listening hard as they described Scott and the funeral they wanted. The Roches were fortunate that they had arrived at a university chapel, and a Jesuit university at that. Where a parish church might well insist that the readings all come from the Bible and the music from the Catholic hymnbook, Father Whitney took a more permissive stance. The funeral mass, he believes, is "meant to be a reflection of the family's grief. It gives you a shell, but allows for a lot of individual development."

Not that the Roches wanted to talk about grief, nor did they want the funeral to be about grief. It was tragic, Marilyn told Father Whitney, "but it is. Now what we want to do is celebrate Scott's life . . . to let people know that his life was meaningful and that his presence was significant. We don't want to hear about God's plan. We want people to feel joyful to have known him."

"We don't want to hear about God's plan" – it was an audacious wish to bring to a Catholic priest. Luckily, John Whitney knew that the Catholic service was flexible enough to accommodate them, and he sympathized with the desire to give thanks for a life. "We're not celebrating because a person died," he says, "but because a person lived."

D'Arcy wanted to avoid scriptural passages that stressed loss and sorrow, as well as theological consolations. "Any rationalizations would have been offensive and cloying," he explains, "and that's the part I didn't want to get into – neither the bitter wailing and 'it's not fair,' nor these pat explanations about God's will. Give me a break. It was avoidance, I admit it, but I thought maybe if we pick another path, we don't have to get into that." (In the months after Scott's death, D'Arcy read books about grieving that urged mourners to walk through the very bitterness and resentment he was intent on bypassing. "Maybe so," he concedes. "But not that week.")

Marilyn told Father Whitney that it should not be "an old person's funeral," that it should express something of Scott's spontaneity and optimism. A simple request, which would have been impossible to achieve a generation or two ago. The Catholic funerals I remember from my childhood balanced sadness, hope, and impersonality in roughly equal measures. The sadness came from the priest's black vestments, the hope from the stress on the Resurrection, and the impersonality from the fact that no eulogies were permitted. The funeral always seemed to be, as our missals put it, for "N., our brother or sister in Christ," and not for Mary Sweeney, whose milestones, not to mention her quirks and sweetness and failings, went unmentioned.

Now, reluctantly in some parishes, more willingly in others, the Mass of Christian Burial allows for some individuality and human feeling, mostly through eulogies given by friends and family after the Communion service. Something else that was going to make eulogies valuable at this service, in Father Whitney's opinion, was the absence of the body. When there's no body, he feels, there's a particular need to say a personal farewell. He accepted the Roches' decision not to have the coffin or the cremated remains present, something else that would not have been allowed a few decades before.

(Technically, the lack of a body or cremated remains made this a memorial mass rather than a funeral, but everyone, including Father Whitney, referred to it as "Scott's funeral.") Personally, he disagrees that a body would make it "too sad," which was the Roches' rationale: "This is the chance to say goodbye to this body, and then to internalize his memory."

One way of tracking the history of Western attitudes to death would be through our changing reactions to the corpse, from the matter-of-fact acceptance of bodily decay in the Middle Ages to the embalmed and cosmeticized face of death in 20th-century North America to the complete absence of the body at the memorial service that is now preferred by many people. The lack of Scott's body was probably the only point on which I too differed from the Roches. There is something so real about the presence of the coffin, and something very tender and protective about the way it is treated during the ceremony. Harrowing as it is, it seems it should be there.

Thomas Attig, the author of *How We Grieve*, tells of a funeral director who put a rocking chair in his office so that parents could rock their dead child while planning the funeral. There was no rocking chair in the Jesuit residence and Scott's body was not there, but he was powerfully present in that room. The young man Father Whitney heard about – outgoing, hopeful, apparently carefree yet a meticulous planner – surfaced in the prayers the priest wrote and the liturgy he shaped.

One of the notes he heard sounded frequently was that Scott was a great gatherer of all kinds of people. Because the majority at the funeral would be non-Catholics, the Roches wanted the service to be as inclusive as possible. They wanted their Jewish daughter-in-law to read from the Old Testament and Scott's Jewish co-worker to ring the chapel bell at the end. Father Whitney offered to invite even those not taking Communion to come forward, if they wished, and receive a blessing. He provided the Roches with some collections of readings, which they could use or not. No one knew ahead of time what every person was going to read or say. The word *liturgy*, Father Whitney tells me, means the work of the people, and he trusted these people, who were strangers to him, to do their work.

The day of the funeral was mean and grey, with melting snow and a thin wind. At first the chapel, in the uncolored light of the entrance, was a continuation of that world. But something else lay ahead in the chapel proper, a rounded space that offered the protectiveness of a cave with the inspiration of brilliantly colored light that fell and pooled on floors and walls. For Ignatius Loyola, the founder of the Jesuits and the namesake of the chapel, spiritual life was a play of light and dark, of consolations and desolations. When Steven Holl read that, he found the dynamic he wanted for his chapel. How strange that Scott's favorite building was designed around the ideas of deprivation and solace, which made it particularly apt for his funeral.

At the back, at the turning point between the cold light of the entrance and the warmth of the chapel, stood the baptismal font, a great round cedar bowl. That is where the service began. As a baby dressed in a white robe is carried to church, blessed, and welcomed into the community, so a dead person is carried to church, blessed, and welcomed into eternal life. The new liturgy stresses the family resemblance between baptism and the funeral, but the Church has always marked the link between the first and last ceremonies of a person's life. (It is a reminder of Arnold van Gennep's idea that all rites of passage are essentially similar.) At the start of a funeral, the priest meets the coffin and the family at the baptismal font. There he drapes the coffin in a white pall that echoes the baptismal robe, and sprinkles it with water from the font.

When there is no body, this step is usually omitted. But Father Whitney had heard so much about Scott as a diver, a swimmer, and a water polo player that he began at the font, with some spontaneous words about Scott's love of water. Then he prayed, "In the waters of baptism, our brother Scott was washed in the love of the Lord. As we begin this memorial, let us pray that the waters of life, which welcomed Scott, will wash away our tears, renew our hearts, and refresh us in the sure and certain hope that we shall see our brother again." He gathered up some water from the font and sprinkled the people as he walked down the aisle to the sound of the opening hymn.

It was a triply poignant beginning. The reminder of baptism hurt because Scott was too young, not far enough removed in time from his baptism. The mention of Scott's ease in water was such a true detail that my eyes filled with surprised tears as I listened. It was my first inkling that this funeral was going to be about the Scott I knew, not some generic young man who had died tragically. And finally, we, the assembled friends, stood in for Scott's body, as the priest sprinkled us with water from the baptismal font.

When there is a death, people often turn to a ritual they believe in imperfectly or not at all, because it offers the comfort of the familiar. But there are problems with a service based on a particular religion, both for those who know it well and those who don't. I have been to Catholic funerals where the emphasis on hope sounded heartless, and where the repeated emphasis on the Resurrection alienated many. Because of the Roches' insistence and Father Whitney's tact, Scott's funeral struck a fine balance between the noble spine of the age-old rite and a pluralistic, welcoming spirit.

Even the unavoidable tension involved in a religious ceremony had something of necessity in it. Why were we lauding God's fatherly care – in the opening hymn, "All Creatures of Our God and King" – at a time like this? I didn't know. But Christians, Jews, Muslims, and the followers of many religions respond to death with similar affirmations of God's justice and omniscience. The problem of trying to make sense of Scott's death was inevitable. Unsatisfactory and even grating as this particular resolution might be to many, a church was probably as good a place as any to start struggling with the question.

I suspect that a good part of the appeal of Scott's funeral lay in its use of ritual elements so profound that they transcend particular beliefs. The first element is simply motion. In 1998 I heard a lecture given by Todd Van Beck, a Presbyterian minister and funeral director. He said, "Unless there's walking, it isn't a ritual." When I see a bridal procession, a graduation, a bar mitzvah, a christening, I remember that. (It suggests that a Quaker memorial service, where people sit or stand in place and speak about the dead person when inspiration strikes them, is a memorial service but not a ritual.)

At a funeral, walking has an additional point, the one Anne Brener makes when she speculates that the immensity of death compels us to do something physical in the face of it. In the New Orleans jazz funeral, the parade to and from the church is a stylized, jiggling walk, designed in long-ago Africa to shake off malign spirits. In the past, Western funerals usually involved two processions and the hard, significant work of carrying the coffin (literally bearing one another's burdens). Sometimes, when a person died many miles from his parish, relays of bearers were arranged, and it was called a "walking funeral."

At Scott's funeral, there was no formal procession, but the assembled had their chances to walk – up and down the aisle for Communion or for a blessing, to and fro on the altar for the various readers and speakers. The main walker in a Catholic funeral is the celebrant, and in addition to the abundant choreography of the mass, Father Whitney makes a point of using the chapel's processional space as much as possible.

At Scott's funeral, water was poured, candles lit, bells rung. A ritual needs things that speak to the senses, preferably things that have as wide a symbolic meaning as possible, even contradictory meanings. Because ritual aims always at consensus, the more ambivalent an object or a prayer the better. Water is a symbol of life and death, of renewal as well as tears. Bells peal to announce joyful and sorrowful events. Candles, which suggest the light of life as well as the vulnerability of the flame that can be instantly snuffed out, have an ancient connection with funerals. At the funeral of an English Carthusian monk in 1556, an onlooker recorded only that he had been dispatched "with grett lyght" – an eloquent image that summons up a dark church and dark-clad mourners lit by numerous flickering flames. In several cultures, one of the first announcements of a death was made to the beehives, probably because plenty of beeswax candles would be needed for the wake and funeral.

The candles, water, and bells, as well as other real things – flowers, the Communion wafers, and wine – were part of Scott's funeral's non-verbal power. (Todd Van Beck also says, "When words fail, have a ritual.") But we spoke and sang about those symbols as well, used them to express our feelings as well as to distance them.

As his parents wanted, there were many references in Father Whitney's prayers to the joy that Scott's life brought to those who knew him. But grief entered too, which was only sensible, and it was more bearable in that it usually entered symbolically. Scott's brother Sean and his wife, Cindy, read from Isaiah 25.6–9, about God swallowing death in victory and wiping "tears from off all faces." We sang about sorrow and danger in two modern hymns that are favorites for funerals: about wandering in barren deserts and unknown lands in "Be Not Afraid," and about the snare of the fowler, the terror of the night, and "the arrow that flies by day" in "On Eagle's Wings." The biblical nature of these tribulations put our grief in a vast context: tragedy is a constant of life, we sang together, for untold men and women before us and after us.

For me, the joyous refrain of "On Eagle's Wings" was more painful than the verses. It runs, "And He will raise you up on eagle's wings, / Bear you on the breath of dawn, / Make you to shine like the sun, / And hold you in the palm of his hand." It brought to mind a black-and-white photograph I had seen of Scott diving, taken when he was a young teenager. His body, arcing in the sun with his arms outstretched like an eagle's wings, was at once perfect and vulnerable. I wished very much that there were someone able to hold him in the palm of his hand.

The most unexpected reading came from Scott's brother Matthew. Never having been to a funeral and with no idea what to read, he took the obvious course for a man in his late twenties. Early on the day of the funeral, he went on the Internet, to sites that offered readings about death and mourning. There he found A.E. Housman's poem "To an Athlete Dying Young." It is a poem I know well. But I had never really grasped its pathos until I heard it that morning. The poet's pretense that the athlete has chosen to depart at the peak of his prowess ("Smart lad, to slip betimes away / From fields where glory does not stay") seemed to echo a certain whistling-in-the-dark aspect of Scott's funeral. That Scott, like Housman's athlete, had arrived at a moment of youthful perfection was cause for celebration, but we dearly wished that he could have outlived that moment. The poem ends with an image of the athlete's laurel-crowned head in death: "And find unwithered on its curls / The garland briefer than a girl's." In my mind's eye I saw Scott's glossy, dark head in Harborview Hospital, not crowned but surrounded by tubes and pulsing machines.

When a Catholic church permits eulogies, they take place after the Communion service, close to the end of the mass. As Father Whitney puts it, first the liturgical ideal, then the human reality. There were three eulogies, from Scott's mother, his brother Stephan, and Hannah. Marilyn, in a pale blue dress she had bought the day before in a deliberate choice not to wear "mourning," shaped hers in the form of a telephone message to Scott. It was a wry device, suited to a young man who talked on the phone a lot, and to his mother every day. It was also a device that could have descended to bathos but did not, thanks to Marilyn's deft use of specific moments from the life of her youngest. The one that struck me most sharply, one of those details that only a mother would remember, was: "And, in spite of what the doctor predicted, you were *not* a late bloomer."

Years later, I asked Marilyn how she summoned the courage for that eulogy. She didn't remember thinking it through, only having the sense that "this is my little guy, and my only chance to do this." When her son Matthew and her sister Gerry wept during their readings, she did say to herself, "Marilyn, you can't cry." (She didn't.) I suggested that she might have thought of it as an obligation, but that wasn't quite right: "It's more a reward you get when you have such a lovely child, to be able to honor him in that way."

When it was Stephan Roche's turn, four handsome men, looking eerily like Scott but bigger (he was the smallest as well as the youngest), went up to the lectern. Stephan was flanked by his three brothers, who would have been groomsmen. His speech was a funny, warm summation of Scott's gift for friendship, from age two, when he had an imaginary friend named Urnell, to the last day of his life. As Stephan talked, a smile of great sweetness played across his face, a smile that made sense as long as we concentrated on Scott's gifts and not Scott's fate.

Hannah's eulogy began artlessly. "I'm not a public speaker," she said, "but Scott would never forgive me if I didn't speak today." She looked pathetically young but poised, as if she stood on an altar at her fiancé's funeral on a regular basis. The poise was reasonable: she had lost much of her future, so there was no point in being nervous. She told of being introduced to Scott by a roommate during her freshman year at Princeton, at a point when she was not interested in meeting anyone. She reported Scott's reaction the next time he ran into the roommate: "Hannah's cute, but what a bitch."

The audience sat silent for a fraction of a second. Was it possible to say "bitch" in church? I looked at my lap, wondering how I had failed to teach my daughter proper behavior for church. Father Whitney, sitting on the altar, laughed. Taking their cue from him (apparently, it *was* possible to say "bitch" in church), the audience laughed.

Hannah talked about their six years together, a recollection more like the teasing toast a bride gives at the rehearsal dinner than a eulogy. Full of stories of Scott's drinking at Houseparties Weekend when he should have been writing his English thesis, their falling asleep together when he should have been writing his thesis, his sneaking into the library at night to pinch books for Hannah while she was writing *her* thesis, it was wildly inappropriate in a Catholic church by the standards of most people over forty-five. And wonderfully appropriate for Scott. She finished by talking about his generosity, his accommodating spirit, how much he had looked forward to having children. The audience applauded. Was it possible to clap in church? Apparently.

⌘

During the funeral, another ceremony was never far from our minds: the wedding of Scott and Hannah. In the bright, open space of the chapel, the priest wore the white vestments he wears to celebrate a wedding. The three eulogies were not terribly different from wedding toasts. The feelings aroused by the formal ceremony flowed into the reception with its spontaneous speeches about Scott.

There is something piercingly sad about the death of a young person on the brink of marriage. Traditional cultures found it a particularly difficult death, for the obvious reasons and also because it aroused sharp anxieties. A young, unmarried person was thought to make an especially angry spirit in death, keen to exact vengeance on the living. To minimize the danger, the survivors tried to convince such spirits that they had not died unfulfilled, with their marriage unconsummated and their destiny frustrated.

The ancient Greeks laid out the unmarried (and the newly married) in wedding finery, and modern Greeks still bury an unmarried young woman in a wedding dress. A minor tractate of the Talmud directs that a *huppah*, or wedding canopy, be erected for a betrothed man or woman who died before marriage, and that unripened or inedible foods be hung from it. (The symbolism of the inedible foods is an unusually realistic note.) The hair of dead engaged women would be covered, as a married woman must cover her hair, and pen and ink would be tucked in at the side of a betrothed man's coffin, to suggest that he might still write a *ketubah*, or marriage contract.

When an unmarried girl died in Cheremis villages in western Russia as recently as the 20th century, cloth and ornaments to make her wedding dress were placed in her coffin, as well as a married woman's head covering. Other cultures went further, actually combining a wedding with the funeral. Not all such examples are in the dim, peasant past. When the daughter of a naval officer died just before her wedding in Portsmouth, England, in 1881, she and her attendants were dressed in their wedding clothes and the hearse was trimmed with orange blossoms. The distraught groom stood by the upended coffin while the minister read first the marriage service, then the funeral service. Mad? Perhaps temporarily, but no more than the occasion warranted.

Watching such a death-wedding, as they are called, in the 1960s in Romania, a peasant woman explained to the folklorist Constantin Brailoiu, "You know, it's necessary to deceive the dead a little." That was the ancient motivation, but in the Portsmouth case it sounds as if this ceremony was also for the bridegroom. Accounts of death-weddings in 20th-century Europe are surprisingly numerous. The Balkan countries are particularly attached to the custom (with

Romanian death-weddings still performed in the 1970s), but there are records of such ceremonies in France, Germany, Italy, Austria, Hungary, and the Scandinavian countries.

Much of this sounds folkloric and Old World. But I have a copy of a photograph taken in America in the 1920s. A group of people are standing in front of a brick house, perhaps a farmhouse, with a front porch – a prosaic, down-to-earth American house. The older women wear cloche hats and street-length coats. At the front of the picture, a young woman is dressed in a festive-looking white headdress. Her dress, stockings, and shoes are white, and she carries a large bouquet. Around her stand six girls in white, dropped-waist middy dresses, with pearls, and about as many young men in white ties and boutonnieres. Some twenty-five older people stand behind them and to the side.

A wedding, apparently. But no one is smiling. The bridesmaids' ties and belts are dark, perhaps black. Where the bridegroom would be, next to the solemn bride, there is a closed coffin on a stand, with a spray of flowers on top. Behind it, one of the groomsmen holds up a wreath. It is a death-wedding in the heart of America, the participants dressed in the insouciant clothes of the flapper era.

The photograph is in the collection of postmortem pictures in the Strong Museum in Rochester, New York. It was taken by the Hughes Studio, and on the back it says, "Please return to Eleanore Naffziger, 2050 Upper Chelsea Road." The name suggests a German community, but nothing more is known about it. Whether the bride was engaged to the dead man or simply playing that role is unknown. It is an unforgettable scene, at least partly because every one of these modern men and women looks perfectly at home in this sad charade.

Surely not all these people believed in the malevolent potential of the unmarried spirit. Death-weddings may have begun in self-protective worry, but they probably endured for more purely affectionate motives. Behind the grave faces, I see the impossible wish to give the dead what life denied them. They address the camera with equanimity, as if to say, "Death came too soon, cheated him of his rightful expectations. Let us give him, if only symbolically, what should have been his."

⌘

In the goodwill that prevailed on the morning of Scott's funeral, even the most dogmatic aspects of the ritual were somehow poignant. Probably few people in the Chapel of St. Ignatius trusted that their prayers would move Scott out of purgatory more quickly. The Catholic Church, too, interprets purgatory more abstractly these days, not as a place but as a waiting period while the soul chooses God, or not-God. But the Church persists in praying for the dead. "The dead are still our companions," Father Whitney says with certainty. "Our conversation is not finished."

We did pray for Scott, in terms a medieval Christian would have understood without any difficulty. After the opening song, Father Whitney entreated, "Admit him to the joyful company of your saints, and raise him on the last day to rejoice with all your people in the glorious and eternal banquet of your reign." Friends and family responded, "Amen." At the end he prayed, "Forgive Scott his sins, and grant him a place of happiness, light, and peace in the kingdom of your glory for ever and ever." Again, the assembled said, "Amen."

Something latent in those prayers retained their power – not necessarily that our intercession would hasten his way to heaven, but that our love for Scott was palpable, that it meant something and was *doing* something for Scott, not just for ourselves. It was honoring him, and he deserved honor. It was wishing him Godspeed, whatever that meant.

We left the chapel to the sound of bells. In the tall, slim tower beyond the reflecting pool, Scott's cousin Drew Macmillan and his colleague Mike Frost were hand-tolling two bronze bells. Mike, who sold computer systems with Scott, remembers standing in the tower and pulling those ropes for what seemed like a long, effortful time. "Bells are such an ancient thing to mark a death," he says. "I had the sense that the whole university community was hearing those bells, and somehow that meant that Scott was really dead."

He harked back to one of the meanings of "celebrate" – to make known, to make public. The main celebration was over, but there was one final step.

⌘

Many cultures include the giving of food and gifts as part of a funeral. What began as an attempt to placate the dead person became complicated by other motives, including the wish for as large a congregation as possible, to pray for the soul of the dead. But long after the doctrine of purgatory was condemned, the sums spent on food, drink, and mementoes for funeral guests in Protestant countries were immense. The giving of small gifts, often food, to funeral-goers acquired a deep significance in traditional societies and died hard. Dorothy Wordsworth recorded the funeral of a poor married couple in England's Lake District in 1808. Their death in an accident had left six children orphans. When each guest at the funeral was given the traditional threepenny loaf of bread, Dorothy's sister Mary tried to refuse, "thinking that the orphans were in no condition to give anything away." Then she realized that it was a custom too weighted with meaning for them to abandon.

In more citified circles, the gifts of scarves, rings, and pipes and the ruinously expensive dinners that marked European and colonial funerals finally ended in the 19th century – replaced, in one theory, by the costly coffins and other funereal accessories demanded by the new masters of ceremony, funeral directors. Today in the West, we satisfy our desire to give something on behalf of the dead with bequests, scholarships, donations to hospitals, and similar public-spirited gestures. Gift giving persists in similar places, like Japan, where the complicated bestowing and receiving of goods and money at a funeral reaffirms a delicate web of relationships.

A funeral feast was a place to flaunt your wealth, but it also did honor to the dead, "gave him a good send-off," as we say. Often a seated, solemn dinner or lunch, it could include particular, symbolic foods. Chinese people, for example, still prepare a Buddhist meal of all-white, vegetarian dishes after a funeral. With or without symbolic foods, such a meal is a consolidation of the remaining family, the first social gathering of the diminished clan. Eating is an affirmation of life, even when it is half-hearted – perhaps particularly when it is half-hearted.

There are cultures where the affirmation of life at a funeral feast, as at a wake, turns deliberately defiant and uproarious. The Basques hold a banquet after the burial that begins gravely with a prayer and a eulogy. Gradually the feast becomes gay, even ribald. No doubt it is part of mending the tear in the social fabric, but it must be hard for close mourners. Not every part of a mourning ritual is designed for every mourner.

⌘

The custom of refreshments after the funeral persists – as a hospitable gesture, a way to thank those who came to the funeral, a way to bring the fractured group together. The Roches were conscious of those motives when they invited everyone to a post-funeral lunch, and they also wanted to give people a chance to say something about Scott. They had hoped to open the way for spontaneous memories while in church, but Father Whitney urged them to stop at three eulogies and then pick it up at the restaurant. The Roches worried more about the after-lunch speeches than about any other aspect of the funeral. They hoped there might be four or five.

D'Arcy made a graceful speech about the blessings of Scott's life and invited people to come forward to the microphone. As it happened, there were between twenty and thirty speeches. Many faces crumbled into something close to a sob at the end of the first sentence, and then recovered. I remember no speech that was not fine in some way, funny or heartfelt or eloquent or revelatory of a side of Scott that was new to me. I had not known that he was Scooter for his first seven years or so. I had not known (but was not surprised to learn) how much of his conversation revolved around Hannah.

The speakers ranged in age from eighty-six to eight. The eldest was Scott's maternal grandmother, Lillian Scott Miller. A notable soccer player in her day, she recalled watching Scott play water polo at Princeton. She didn't think much of it as a game, but it was clear to her that her grandson was very good at it. The youngest and briefest was my sister's younger daughter, Madeleine. Scott had been her father's hiking companion, her older cousin's boyfriend and then fiancé, her babysitter, and – being Scott – her uncondescending playmate. She said, "My name is Madeleine and I've known Scott most of my life. I loved him and I'm really going to miss him."

At the end, Scott's oldest brother, Sean, did something that would have frightened our ancestors. He stood at the microphone and said, Enough of the beatification of Scott. Yes, he'd devised all those clever pranks we'd just heard about, but he was also a couch potato who could sit mesmerized by dumb television for hours. Yes, he was magnanimous, but he was also a bit of a mooch, the baby in the family who was used to having his way smoothed. He did make friends with most people he encountered, but sometimes he could have been more discriminating. Sean put it wittily, warmly. The rest of us laughed affectionately; these too were sides of Scott. To our ancestors, this breach of the taboo against speaking ill of the dead – especially the newly dead, who were particularly irritable – would have been courting disaster. Sean got away with it.

It was the first funeral for my sister's older daughter, Kate, who was ten at the time. Later, when I asked her what she had thought of it, she said she was surprised that people laughed. Did she think that was good or bad? Neither, she said with her usual seriousness. She just didn't know people did that at a funeral.

⌘

To paraphrase Malvolio on greatness, some are born adept at ritual, some become adept, and some have ritual thrust upon them. In other words, funerals are not everyone's cup of tea. But avoiding them or denying them to others is a dubious enterprise. People sometimes make it known that they want no funeral for themselves, no visitation hours, no memorial service of any kind. In my experience, it is WASP men who leave these instructions, but no doubt this mentality crosses ethnic and gender lines.

Their motivations are various: modesty, a horror of senti-mentality, the wish "not to make a fuss," as well as more mysterious ones. But since the dead person won't be there to be embarrassed, ashamed, or feeling fussed over, and the effect on his family is to deny them the enclosing embrace of a group farewell, the order, in effect, has an element of hostility. (And sometimes, perhaps, that is the intention.) A friend whose father imposed such a ban before he died more than two years ago describes herself, her mother, and siblings as wandering in an emotional limbo where mourning can neither begin nor end.

Equally presumptuous is the friend or adviser who decides, on behalf of a close mourner, that the deceased should not be given a funeral or that the bereaved should not attend the funeral. This attitude is much less frequent now but was once typical in the case of a stillbirth or the death of a newborn child. Todd Van Beck tells the story of a newborn's death in the American Midwest in 1979. His funeral home arranged for a perfunctory funeral and buried the child before the mother got out of the hospital. Four months later, the mother bought a cucumber that weighed two pounds. She rocked it, crooned to it; later she buried it. Van Beck learned his lesson: embalm the baby so that the funeral can wait until the mother comes home. Let parents diaper their dead babies, comb their hair, and attend their funerals, "or they'll end up babying cucumbers."

Did Scott's funeral work for everyone? Of course not. Probably no ritual that includes more than a handful of people ever does satisfy everyone. I would guess that most people outside the close family circle found the funeral moving, cathartic, and comforting in varying measures. I would guess that people in the close family circle found it good according to the degree of their involvement. The more you shape something, the more meaningful it will be for you, but that is not always possible for someone in full-blown, traumatic grief. Hannah kept herself more or less aloof from the funeral planning; that was the form her particular distress took.

Aside from the speeches, which she enjoyed, she found the reception after the funeral as overwhelming as the dinner at Scott's house the night before. Bewildered by the necessity of responding to everyone's condolences, she was angered by the snippets of normal conversation she overheard, as college friends from all over the country caught up on one another's news. The funeral at least was a quiet space where "no one was trying to hug me." Two years later, when I asked her what parts of the funeral, if any, made an impact on her, she mentioned the beauty of the chapel, Marilyn's and Stephan's eulogies, and the music. Then she added, "But of course I chose the music."

Scott's parents worked so bravely and inventively to avoid his funeral being "too sad." But how could the funeral of a young man, a week away from his twenty-fifth birthday and looking forward to a wedding, not be sad? The tributes to his joie de vivre and kindness and boyishness evoked the real

Scott. They celebrated him accurately. But, for all that we concentrated on its silver lining, the dreadful cloud never lifted for a minute. The funeral was heartbreaking, but something would have been very wrong if it had not been. Being sad together is no bad thing. It is, after all, a necessary part of how the group separates from the body.

FOUR

FINAL DESTINATION

I am not resigned to the shutting away of loving
    hearts in the hard ground.
So it is, and so it will be, for so it has been time
    out of mind:
Into the darkness they go, the wise and the
    lovely. Crowned
With lilies and with laurel they go; but I am not
    resigned.
        – Edna St. Vincent Millay,
          "Dirge Without Music"

Nor were the Roches resigned to the shutting away of
Scott's body in the hard ground. True to their pragmatism and their desire that Scott's life continue in some helpful
way, they had settled quickly on organ donation and cremation.
Unfortunately, the laws in the state of Washington prohibit
organ donation except in the case of brain death and, although
Scott died of a brain injury, he did not match the clinical crite-
ria for brain death. Much to his parents' distress, his superbly
healthy heart, lungs, and other organs were cremated with him,
and only his corneas and graftable skin could be used.

Once Scott was dead, Marilyn regarded his body as a shell,
and neither she nor D'Arcy imagined wanting to visit a place

where the body was interred. As it turned out, they did not collect Scott's ashes from the crematorium in Seattle for more than a year. They delayed partly because it was painful, partly because they were ambivalent – feeling that the remains were not to be disregarded but without a strong sense of what to do with them.

When they did take possession of the ashes, D'Arcy scattered some near the summit of Mount Rainier, on a climb he made in 2000 in memory of Scott, who had climbed the mountain the September before he died. Hannah had asked for a small amount, and she scattered them on English Bay in Vancouver, near the spot on the beach where Scott had proposed to her, and in front of a bench inscribed in his honor. When I asked her about burial versus cremation, she said that she would have liked to know that all of his ashes were buried somewhere. It was a mild, even theoretical preference, because she has never visited a grave. It didn't occur to her to bury her token amount; that would have seemed "weird" and inappropriate. Scott's bench is her stand-in for a grave, her special place dedicated to him, but she thinks there is "something more real" about a grave.

The Roches' tentativeness about Scott's ashes is not uncommon. Cremation has gained acceptance in the West only in the past 150 years, and many people are still a bit at sea about what to do with the cremated remains (or cremains, as funeral directors call them). When the subject comes up in almost any group, a story or two surfaces. Often it has an element of comedy or embarrassment. A Jewish widower in a bereaved spouses' support group I observed still widens his eyes at the memory of a Newfoundland widow who kept some of her husband's ashes in a little vial on her key chain. Thinking of her, he says of the support group, "That's when I knew I'd really stepped out of my culture!" What he doesn't seem to appreciate is that the widow isn't operating out of her traditional culture, either. Her solution is purely personal – and satisfying. As she says, patting her key chain, "I always have him here with me."

My friend Ivan told me about another friend who showed up at Ivan's office one day, bearing his father's ashes. He had cared for him long and tenderly but could not cope with his remains: the dilemma of what to do with them paralyzed him. He begged Ivan, "I don't care what you do with them, but you must never tell me." Ivan promised and disposed of them in his office's Dumpster.

No doubt these uncertain and eccentric solutions will diminish as we become more familiar with cremation. It is, after all, an ancient method, used thousands of years ago by peoples who later shunned it, such as the Greeks and the Jews, as well as by peoples who continue to cremate, most notably Hindus. The fact is that humans have contrived only a handful of ways to dispose of a corpse. It can be burned, exposed, or consigned to water. It can be placed in a protected location above ground or below. Depending on their climate and geography, long-ago societies chose what seemed the most effective way to avoid the malice of ghosts, the wrath of the gods, the threat of disease.

Practices can change, as the increasing popularity of cremation demonstrates. But for most cultures the "correct" disposal of the dead, however it is defined at that moment, is powerfully significant. Sophocles' tragedy *Antigone* is based on the king's refusal to let Polynices be buried in the ground. The dead man's sister, Antigone, dies in an attempt to give her brother what the gods decreed was proper for the dead. The king, Creon, dies, along with his wife and son, because he disobeyed the gods. But exposure, which is Creon's punishment for Polynices' treachery ("Leave his corpse disgraced, a dinner for the birds and the dogs"), is exactly what many societies see as the most respectful course of action. For the Parsis, who leave their corpses to be picked clean by vultures within a matter of days, it is burial and the resulting decay of the body that is an affront to the dead.

Like other mourning customs, those designed around the body's last destination offer the comfort of the familiar during a time of unique pain – even when the familiar has an element of horror. As death has become entrusted to institutions and technicians, whether hospitals or funeral parlors, morticians or nurses, a close connection with the corpse is harder and harder to bear. Yet customs persist that involve intimate contact with the dead body. Westerners, for example, often find the details of Japanese cremation startling. The family views the procedure through a window in the crematorium. Afterward, guided by the crematorium attendant, the close mourners transfer the important bones, ending with the Adam's apple, into the burial urn that holds the ashes and other bone fragments. The moment when the mourners, sharing a special large pair of chopsticks, move the bones is a solemn one, and the only occasion when two Japanese are permitted to use the same pair of chopsticks.

I asked my friend Reiko Ryuzoji, a Japanese woman in her sixties, if it had not been difficult for her and her sister to transfer their father's leg bone and Adam's apple into the urn, mere days since he had been alive. She shook her head. "We are so accustomed to it from our youth," she said, giving the response people often make about a daunting ritual. And even daunting rituals can be adjusted to circumstances, as Reiko points out. The spouse of the dead person can avoid the cremation, and close mourners are not expected to attend the cremation or the transferral of bones when the death has been particularly shocking. When their mother died suddenly in her early fifties, Reiko and her sister, then young women, did not watch the cremation. Even more so when a death violates the expected order: parents do not attend the cremation of their child.

For Reiko's friend Fumiko McDonald, the Japanese style of cremation is something better than customary. Its bracing realism is reassuring. More than thirty years of marriage to an Englishman have given Fumiko a forthright cross-cultural perspective on Japan and Britain. Her spacious, well-upholstered Tokyo apartment might be in London, except for the Japanese maid who offers mid-morning coffee and chocolates, Fumiko herself, and the manual of Japanese funeral etiquette she consults occasionally during our conversation.

Compared with the unblinking Japanese death customs, Fumiko found the cremations of her parents-in-law evasive and worrying. She never saw them dead and last saw their closed coffins in an English funeral chapel. She was assured that they were cremated and their ashes scattered in the chapel's rose garden, but she sounds almost suspicious as she asks, "Where are they? Cremated? So they say, but where are the ashes gone? They say they scattered them in the garden – does that mean I am walking on them in the garden?" She does not really fear foul play, but she misses the concrete experience of seeing a familiar body in death, then transmuted into clean, white bones. She says wistfully that she would have liked to watch the cremation: "I would like to know where my father-in-law has gone."

When she visits Japanese cemeteries, Fumiko takes flowers and puts them in the vase that is typically part of the gravestone. Other Japanese visitors bring cigarettes or sake. But when she visits England and takes flowers to her parents-in-law, she leaves them in the funeral chapel. There is no grave to decorate.

In 1999, when a close Japanese friend of the McDonalds died, Fumiko found his cremation and burial conclusive in the best possible way. For her, the saddest time was when the body was laid out, dressed in traditional Japanese style as a pilgrim, with the straw sandals called *zōri* and the *yukata*, or cotton robe. Her friend looked, she says, as if he were sleeping, and she was tempted to say, "Enough, Yamasa! The joke has gone far enough." Her husband, Christopher, gave the eulogy in Japanese, addressing Yamasa directly as he lay in his coffin, thanking him for his friendship. He had died two days before his birthday, and Fumiko slipped a birthday card into his coffin, a contemporary variation on the custom of providing money, food, and other commodities for the next world.

When her friend had been reduced to bones, Fumiko felt a wave of relief and clarity. "I felt, That's it . . . He's gone to another place, so you cannot be sad any more. It's real, you have to be facing it." She and her husband were given the honor of transferring the important bones into the burial container, and the sight of the tall Englishman and the tiny Japanese woman sharing the ritual chopsticks in the crematorium must have been a remarkable one. Yamasa's bones were buried in the graveyard in his ancestral village, surrounded for the ceremony by his family living and dead, something Fumiko found profoundly touching: "My dear friend Yamasa is now sleeping where he was born."

Christopher McDonald plans to sleep far from where he was born, but it is a decision Fumiko wholeheartedly approves. Not for them the scattering of ashes, a custom that is gaining interest but few adherents in Japan. The McDonalds have bought a small plot in the section of the Yokohama graveyard where Fumiko's family is buried and have designed a simple gravestone. Under "McDonald," it says "Together always." It is easy to imagine Christopher McDonald's English family's reaction to the idea of watching his cremation and depositing his barely cooled bones into an urn. And it is tempting to conclude that the customs of one's own group are meaningful and consoling only because they are the customs of one's own group. Which, when faced with the loneliness of bereavement, is by no means a trivial reason.

But everyone knows people whose own mourning customs emphatically do not work for them. Or people like the Roches, one of the first generations in their Catholic family to be intellectually committed to cremation and not yet certain what the ashes required in the way of ceremony or permanent home.

And there are others, who expect nothing from rituals they barely know or consider bizarre and then find themselves inexplicably moved. Neil Bissoondath was one such mourner. It is almost twenty years since he cremated his mother, and he still does not completely understand his response to the experience.

A novelist and non-fiction writer, he was raised in Trinidad in a nominally Hindu family. His grandparents occasionally held prayer meetings at their house, which the boy Neil enjoyed solely for the food. His parents' generation, which includes his maternal uncles, the writers Shiva and V.S. Naipaul, is mostly non-observant. A skeptic from an early age, Neil attended Christian schools and knew the Hindu cremation ceremony only through television. Impatient with ritual, he was and is quickly irritated by what he sees as its absurdity.

When his mother died in Trinidad at fifty, from a ruptured aneurysm, Neil was told for the first time that it is the duty of the eldest son to officiate at the Hindu funeral pyre. Bewildered, innocent of what that entailed, exhausted after three days of watching by his mother's comatose body, he agreed for the sake of his father, aunts, and grandparents.

Neil put himself in the hands of the local pundit, or Hindu priest, a man apparently both ignorant and careless. The pundit arrived late at the funeral home, where Sati Bissoondath lay in a Styrofoam open coffin, wearing a favorite dress, her nails painted by her sister. He explained nothing, chanted in Hindi, which Neil did not understand, ordered him to sprinkle water on the body using a mango leaf, to make such-and-such a mark on her forehead with a particular paste. When the time came to carry the body in a sheet to the pyre, Neil was one of six bearers, unable to grasp the complicated directions that involved stopping frequently for more incomprehensible prayers. He obeyed as if in a nightmare.

At the pyre itself, some six feet high and sited close to a river, about a hundred people were gathered. Sati Bissoondath had been a popular teacher in a suburb of Port-au-Spain, and her son, now living in Toronto, found himself surrounded by faces he had not seen since childhood. He was told to climb to the top, where his mother's body had been placed.

Now the pundit passed up cans of ghee, clarified butter, and Neil and his younger brother Ved, who had volunteered to help him, were ordered to spread it liberally on their mother's body, from her face and neck over her whole body to her feet. Neil remembers the intimate contact of covering her dress, her hands, "the fingers we knew so well," first with the ghee, then with layers of rice and sugar. When her sons had dutifully made her unrecognizable, Sati Bissoondath's body was studded with chunks of camphor, including one placed between her lips. It fell to Neil's brother, who was placed at her head, to find her lips under all the layers. It was, according to Neil, the "one moment of horror, but he did it stoically."

When the body was prepared, the sons climbed down. Neil was given four flaming torches to insert into the corners of the pyre, which flared up immediately. Meanwhile, there was an apparently unimportant addition to the scene. Another pundit, dressed more resplendently than the first priest, with an air of self-possession and elegance, had arrived while the brothers had been at the top of the pyre. A cousin of Neil's mother, he too took a hand in directing the ceremony. Neil did not know him, but something about the man's demeanor, his sense of being in control, contributed to a startling shift in his feelings.

Watching the flames shoot high into the sky, he realized suddenly that the "days of torpor and heaviness had lifted. It's something that I still find difficult to explain, but I think it comes from having done this ceremony. I walked away from that pyre with a sense of great satisfaction, almost happy." He later wrote, "I had set my mother free, and in sending her into a sky of infinite blue, I had, unexpectedly, set myself free, too." A corner had been turned. He remembers returning to his parents' house feeling "light," having a beer and relaxing. "The healing process really started for me at that point," he says. "I missed her and I would for the next two years, but the weight of her death, that sense of being crushed, was over."

There were other ceremonies, formal and informal, in that first week. On the evening of the cremation, Neil's uncle Shiva Naipaul arrived from London, bearing Camels and whiskey. With his nephews he visited the pyre, by now a square of glowing coals, where he spent a few minutes in thought. Then uncle and nephews went home and sat up much of the night smoking, drinking, and laughing. Fresh from adventures in Australia, Shiva was full of stories at which his nephews roared. It was a kind of wake, strangely joyful and hilarious as wakes often are. In Neil's case, the euphoria sprang from his sense of having given his mother the proper farewell, coupled with his conviction that she, who loved to laugh, was laughing with them.

The next day he went with his brother-in-law to the pyre, to shovel the ashes into the river. That night they observed another Hindu ritual. Like many peoples, the Hindus consider the newly dead person to be wandering the earth, hungry and in need of protection. Accordingly, Neil, his brother, Uncle Shiva, and the unimpressive priest took food to a dark spot on the road on the way to the pyre, along with a machete. Neil was amused by the bizarre picture the quartet made in the dark, with their food, their brass bowl of water, and their machete: "But we did it and came away lighthearted, just because I think it was a kind of distancing from the death."

There is a significant difference between a ritual that satisfies profoundly, if inexplicably, and one that cheers you up because it strikes you as goofy. At this point, aware again of the "absurdity" of ritual, Neil began pulling away from it. His uncle V.S. Naipaul arrived in Trinidad in time for a ceremony that takes place about a week after the death. He had marked the day of his sister's cremation at his home in England in the modern, rational way – setting out his pictures of her and meditating on her life. No doubt, had he been given a choice, Neil would have chosen something similarly simple and private. Instead, having been surprised into entering "the heart of the ritual," as he calls it, he was ready to move on. He drafted his brother to stand in his stead for the one-week ceremony. The magic moment when ritual had worked was over.

Nor has it returned. When his father moved to Toronto a few years later and became ill with cancer, Neil said goodbye to him there. He did not go to Trinidad, where the father returned, for his death or cremation. The man who says, "Deep down, ritual generally does not speak to me," chalks up only one exception to that rule.

What made his mother's cremation the anomaly? There are a few logical reasons. The cleanliness of cremation, the idea of purification by fire, struck an intellectual as well as emotional chord with him. His mother's body would suffer no decay, something that she, who always identified herself as a Hindu, would have wished. Her death was a complete shock, so the ritual may have substituted in some way for the goodbyes he had no chance to say, the resignation he hadn't achieved before her death. When his father became ill, Neil said goodbye and needed nothing else. As for the elegant pundit, he helped to dignify the ritual at a crucial point. When a priest who is "a bit of an idiot" is the master of ceremonies, it's hard to take the ceremony seriously. Someone who looked credible, even aesthetically pleasing, and in control made it easier for Neil to reap what benefit he could.

On a less cerebral level, there is the fact of "going through the motions," which was all Neil planned on doing. An expression we use negatively is all-important in ritual. As Neil says of the priest who provided no intellectual justification, "where he served was in leading us through the gestures. The gestures were what made the difference." He is sure that simply witnessing the cremation would have done nothing for him. It was the chance to move, to become involved, that was decisive.

"Going through the motions" became for Neil Bissoondath the mourner's dance. He did not dance when his father died. He may never dance again. But once, when he needed it, it worked.

⌘

> To know the character of a community, I need
> only visit its cemeteries.
> — Benjamin Franklin

Throughout history, Westerners have favored burial over the other methods of disposal. But the definition of a proper burial has been far from static. Fearing the impurity and the malice of the dead, the ancients buried them out of town, along the main highway in the case of the Appian Way of Rome. Graves were respected and marked with individual inscriptions, but it was against the law to be buried within the city limits.

Gradually, as the French historian Philippe Ariès writes in *The Hour of Our Death*, the Christians developed the novel idea of living near their dead. Their belief in the resurrection of the body had diminished the old fears of the corpse. While an outlawed sect, they had worshiped in catacombs, which accustomed them to the idea of religious services held in close propinquity to the dead. Once Christianity became legal, in the 4th century, and they were allowed to build churches, they often located them on the sites of martyrs' tombs. Martyrs were believed to have special protective powers, and people wanted to be buried near them. So burials began to take place in the church floor, as near to the martyr as possible, and later in the churchyard, which was considered an extension of the church.

These "burying churches" were still outside the city proper, but beginning around the 6th century, burial in city churches became legal. It represented a profound change in thinking, from the dead who were considered polluting to the dead whose nearness was attractive. As Ariès writes, "Henceforth and for a long time to come – until the eighteenth century – the dead ceased to frighten the living, and the two groups coexisted in the same places and behind the same walls."

Certainly the dead and the living seem to be cohabiting very pleasantly at Trinity Church in Newport, Rhode Island. Wanting to spend some time in a traditional churchyard, I chose this white clapboard church with its tall spire and the tidy enclave of gravestones that borders it on two sides. Trinity's particular origins are British colonial, but its close cousins flourished all over Europe from the Middle Ages to the mid-19th century.

Soon after Newport's Anglicans, Huguenots, and Quakers banded together in 1698, they built a church inspired by Christopher Wren and began burying their dead around it. The churchyard's two hundred or so inhabitants range in age from the stillborn to ninety-three, and their solemn stones date mostly from the 18th century. Many commemorate young children and women in their twenties, many presumably dead of childbirth.

Aside from its prettiness, two things are notable about Trinity Churchyard. The first is the restraint of the inscriptions. The occasional person, usually one with a full-sized stone laid flat on the ground, called a ledger, is commended for his exemplary life or her blessed soul that will reunite with her "clay" on Judgment Day. More frequently, their fate is recorded laconically: "In memory of Elizabeth the wife of David Melville, died December 1738 age 31. Also Mary their daughter, two months and Lovelace their son aged 17 days."

Compared with the steady understatement of the epitaphs, the various creatures carved on the tombstones evolved in front of my eyes as I walked from row to row. The oldest stone in the churchyard is a ledger commemorating Thomas Mallet. He died in 1704, but the incised skull and crossbones that top his vital statistics spring from an earlier sensibility. The skull is pear-shaped, with oversized teeth. Two cartoon-like bones with prominent knobs are crossed beneath it. Such a straightforwardly grisly reminder of our physical destiny looks more like the 12th century than the urbane 18th, and Mallet's skull and crossbones represent the tail end of a long tradition. Within a decade, the skull began to grow wings, even to float a small, crown-like accessory above the head. Sarah Fitch, who died on January 1, 1727, in her twenty-third year, has such a winged, crowned skull on her stone.

The winged death's-head, as it is called, is a softening and pulling back from the graphic skeleton that functioned as a memento mori, and perhaps as a salutary bit of reality therapy for mourners. The winged death's-head was followed by something even more genial, the so-called winged soul-head, a pleasant bald head that was a transition between the skeleton and the cherub. As the head became more and more recognizably human, the wings, placed sometimes directly behind the head, sometimes underneath the head like an ill-controlled ruff, became increasingly exuberant. Dependent on naive and intermittently individualistic carvers, these stages did not proceed neatly. Sometimes a particular carver would revert to a more primitive-looking form while his peers were forging something more naturalistic. But it is the general movement that is significant, a progression from a warning reminder of bodily corruption to a curly-haired, winged angel who spells goodwill, solace, and the promise of another life.

While the skeleton was mutating into a chubby-cheeked cherub, during the 18th and early 19th centuries, there was a shift in Protestantism. At the Calvinist end of the spectrum, people were moving from a frightened helplessness about damnation to a new confidence that everyone who tried could attain salvation. The shift spread across denominational lines; at the other extreme of Protestantism, even the Anglicans, who had never preached predestination, shared in this more hopeful attitude to death.

This new mood can be read in the stones of another churchyard, this one around the Anglican church of St. Matthew in Quebec City. For ninety years, beginning in 1770, this downtown graveyard was the English community's chief cemetery. Cherubs' heads were already outmoded when the first people were buried here, and the milder character of this churchyard shows itself in the inscriptions. Christian stoicism is still in evidence, but mixed with a natural regret.

Frequently the choice of Bible quotation, resigned but poignant, conveys feeling. That chosen for Richard Vivian's wife, Ann DeVerna, who died in 1836, aged twenty-six, comes from the Book of Job: "I know that My Redeemer Liveth" (19.25). Sometimes a stone suggests the almost superhuman acceptance demanded of 19th-century believers, along with a sharp sense of what has been lost. Over four years, James and Mary Whittington lost four babies. On a tomb sacred to the memory of Martha, who died at twenty months in 1815, Elizabeth, who died at six weeks in 1816, James, who died at seven months in 1817, and Jane, who died at fourteen months (how they must have hoped) in 1819, the parents inscribed:

> The Lord gave
> And the Lord hath taken away
> Blessed be the name
> of the Lord.

When James Ellis died at the age of thirty-five in 1825, his "afflicted Widow" asked, in beautifully cut letters whose balance of thick and thin strokes seems to echo her mingled heartbreak and faith, "Why should I grieve / I shall go to him." And inscriptions began to make reference not just to the dead but to the mourner. Thus John E. King, aged eighteen, who was drowned in 1846 while a midshipman on HMS *Vindictive*, has a stone erected by "his widowed mother." The plaintive calling attention to her widowed state, like the "afflicted Widow" of James Ellis, is something new.

These people are from the same stock and the same religion as those buried in Trinity Churchyard in Newport. What has changed is the times. The Newport graveyard breathes the cool, dry Christianity of the 18th century. The graves at St. Matthew's date mostly from the early 19th century, a moment when feeling and Christianity were converging. Their inscriptions are the next chapter in an evolving expressiveness about the dead, and a new focus on the grave as a place to remember them.

Added to these sentiments was a rising concern about the state of graveyards. Trying to persuade his coy mistress to make the most of her youth, the 17th-century poet Andrew Marvell reminds her, "The grave's a fine and private place, / But none I think do there embrace." In fact, many of the graves of Marvell's time were neither fine nor private. Trinity and St. Matthew's were not unhealthy, but these were church-yards in sparsely populated colonies. A 19th-century traveler, Basil Hall, described the usual English burying place as a "soppy churchyard, where the mourners sink ankle deep in a rank and offensive mould, mixed with broken bones and fragments of coffins."

In crowded European cities, where in some cases people had been buried around the same church for a thousand years, conditions were disrespectful to the dead and dangerous to the living. By the second half of the 18th century, the foul air around churchyards was believed to fade cloth, tarnish silver, and turn soup rancid. In 1744, several funeral-goers in Montpellier, France, were asphyxiated by toxic vapors from a vault. When a family grave was reopened for a funeral in Saulieu, in Burgundy, in 1773, 140 people became ill. Twenty-seven of them died.

Shortage of space and a traditional lack of concern about the exact whereabouts of a grave, as long as it was within the precincts of the church, meant that the poor were buried in common graves and then reburied as the space became needed. In Paris's notoriously overcrowded Cemetery of the Holy Innocents, mephitic gas from a recently filled mass grave invaded the cellars on the adjacent Rue de la Lingerie. People became seriously ill, and quicklime was poured into the grave as a disinfectant.

The confluence of public health crises, a more promising view of the afterlife, and the beginnings of the Romantic movement called forth a new kind of burying place. No longer a bleak, unavoidable necessity, it was to be a beauty spot, a retreat into the consoling arms of Nature, an inspiration to meditation and renewal. This pastoral, carefully composed destination, as the historian Richard Etlin writes, would have been inconceivable during the previous thousand years. And almost as soon as it opened, imitations sprang up in Europe, Britain, and North America.

Père Lachaise, the first ornamental or garden cemetery, as these innovations were called, was launched by the French government in 1804. Named for François d'Aix de La Chaise, the confessor of Louis XIV and a keen gardener, it was located on Lachaise's former estate. Mixing English landscape theories of the picturesque with the formal French style, it afforded splendid views of Paris and took the French bourgeoisie by storm. Fashionably dressed ladies and gentlemen picnicked and promenaded there on weekends, following what was probably the first guidebook to a burial place – an astounding novelty. Everyone wanted to be buried at Père Lachaise, and so many succeeded, erecting ornate and individualistic statues and monuments, that by the second half of the century most of its rural or garden aspect was effaced.

But while Père Lachaise still looked like a garden, its influence was extraordinary. The first and most celebrated American imitation was Mount Auburn, which opened in Cambridge, Massachusetts, in 1831. More wholeheartedly (and permanently) naturalistic than its French forebear, Mount Auburn became Boston's primary tourist attraction almost instantly. Visitors including Charles Dickens, Emperor Dom Pedro of Brazil, and the future King Edward VII toured this phenomenon and wrote about it in letters, poems, and essays. The English actress Fanny Kemble pronounced it "a pleasure garden instead of a place of graves," but that was a distinction that would soon be passé. Guides to Mount Auburn proliferated, as did stereoscopic cards with bucolic views. Six hundred people a day walked in it, pondering its beauties and its lessons. Legend has it that Franklin Pierce, the future fourteenth president, was discovered sitting under one of Mount Auburn's trees in 1852 when the messenger arrived with the news that he was the Democratic Party's presidential candidate.

Even the word used to describe it was new. No longer a churchyard or graveyard, much less the French *charnier*, or mass grave, it was called a cemetery, from the Greek word for a dormitory. (*Cemetery* was an English word, but before the 19th century it was relatively rare and usually described catacombs.) More specifically, the Anglo-Saxon world called it a "rural cemetery." That pointed to the fact that cemeteries were slightly outside of town, for emotional as well as hygienic reasons. Even after big cities had grown up around them, the name – suggestive of contemplative values in danger of being lost in the hurly-burly of 19th-century life – remained.

As Père Lachaise begat Mount Auburn, within the first two decades of its life Mount Auburn begat ample, landscaped cemeteries all over the Northeast and as far west as St. Louis and Detroit. Before Père Lachaise, cemeteries did not have names. They were usually known by the name of the church they adjoined, occasionally as the Old Burying Ground or the New Burying Ground. Now these new-under-the-sun descendants of Mount Auburn were given names redolent of the pastoral consolation Americans wanted from them: Laurel Hill (Philadelphia, 1836), Greenmount (Baltimore, 1838),

Harmony Grove (Salem, Massachusetts, 1840), Forest Home (Milwaukee, 1850).

Most of the rural cemeteries were private enterprises whose landscape and statuary came at a price too steep for working-class and even many lower-middle-class families. But only seven years after the opening of Mount Auburn, the city fathers of Rochester, New York, founded· America's first municipal rural cemetery – a place where rich and poor, black and white, Jew and Christian and freethinker could be buried in the same poetic landscape. When I was growing up in Rochester, Mount Hope was "my" cemetery – not in the sense of a future home, because Catholics are the only large group unrepresented here, but in the sense of a neighborhood landmark. My friends and I rode our bikes through its hill-and-dale topography, used the stout little temple mausoleums as backdrops to our make-believe, and attached ourselves to angels and other sentimental favorites among the statuary. I had no idea I was playing in a distinguished example of a particular type of cemetery. I probably assumed all cemeteries were like Mount Hope and equally diverting for children.

While Boston was the country's undisputed cultural center, Rochester in the 1830s was a brash boomtown. Thanks to abundant water power, canal and lake transportation, and a promising seed and nursery industry, the town's population had ballooned from its founding in 1812 to ten thousand in 1834. Its growth, plus cholera and typhus epidemics that emphasized the dangers of in-town graveyards, determined Rochester to have its own rural cemetery.

The city council bought fifty unfarmable acres on the east side of the Genesee River. While they dithered over a name – some wanted Mount Auburn, while others chafed at such servile imitation – a workman on the site persisted in submitting bills for "labor at Mount Hope." Exactly how he came up with the name is unknown, but it was perfectly in keeping with the optimism of the rural cemetery movement, and it stuck.

The site too was an inspired choice, for Nature herself had done the Romantic landscaping so carefully contrived at Mount Auburn. The glacier that had covered Mount Hope some twelve thousand years ago left in its wake a sharply varied place of serpentine ridges, kettle-shaped depressions, undulating valleys, and dramatic ascents. Its highest point measured 675 feet, some 175 feet beyond the elevation of the city's main intersection. The original forest, preserved as much as possible when the cemetery was laid out, included white, red, and black oaks, tulip trees, chestnuts, beeches, white ashes, red and sugar maples. When the Reverend Pharcellus Church claimed, in his dedicatory address on October 3, 1838, that Mount Hope's scenery was "even more bold and picturesque" than that of the gold standard, Mount Auburn, it was no idle piece of local patriotism.

Mount Hope had more than good looks to recommend it. With his century's blend of rhapsody and pragmatism, Church found time in his oration to praise the cemetery's "dry and light soil, peculiarly favorable alike to the opening of graves and the preservation of them from the intrusion of water." That, along with its glorious terrain and a retired location that was still only one and a half miles from the center of town, made Mount Hope "among the most inviting cemeteries in the world."

Church welcomed visitors to the new cemetery "to revive the memory of departed friends and to anticipate the exalted scenes of eternity." In addition, people thronged to Mount Hope, as they did to all the rural cemeteries, for less elevated reasons. An English traveler in America named Henry Arthur Bright wrote, "Cemeteries here are all the 'rage,' people lounge in them and use them (as their tastes are inclined) for walking, making love, weeping, sentimentalizing, and every thing in short." The first landscaped public places, these cemeteries were used as we now use city parks, which were unknown in the 1830s. Ultimately they led to the creation of our parks system. They were also seen as religious and moral schools. Mothers were encouraged to take their toddlers there, instilling in them important lessons about mortality, everlasting life, and the exploits of local heroes.

Within a few years of its birth, Mount Hope was a magnet for tourists and a place of serious, if self-conscious, contemplation. In 1841, the *Rochester Gem and Ladies Amulet* carried an account of a day trip made by about a dozen young men and ladies from the nearby country town of Clarkson. After a four-hour trip on the Erie Canal to Rochester and a brief stop for lemonade at Dawley's Saloon, the young people took a hack for Mount Hope Cemetery.

The writer, one of the young people and identified only as H.R., muses on the transition between "the city of the living and the city of the dead" represented by the entrance gate, on the necessity to think on the next world once past that gate, on the great democracy of death, "where the dust of my neighbor mingles side by side with that of the pilgrim from foreign lands – of the infant babe with the grey headed patriarch – of the goodly saint with the midnight assassin." The party alighted from their carriage to walk about the cemetery and later re-entered it for a climb to the pinnacle. Then home to Clarkson, well pleased with a "holiday ride" that would have been as unthinkable for young people in the 18th century as in the 21st.

Other visitors were moved to poetry, like the 18th-century poets known as the Graveyard School. But the graveyard poets stressed the sadness of mortality, while the 19th-century poets found hope, comfort, and morality in the cemetery. Looking forward to "a bright world, beyond the darksome grave," Marcia Webster, in the *Rochester Gem and Ladies Amulet*, urges:

Go to Mount Hope, and let thy soul be cheered
By the instruction that is given thee there.

Although the idea of being "cheered" by the instruction available at Mount Hope strikes an odd note now, its lessons were by no means all lugubrious. The landscape is indeed beautiful, made more so by judicious thinning of the original forest and the addition of fifty choice trees in 1847. Those specimens, among them European purple beeches, variegated sycamore maples, Caucasian spruce, and Nikko firs, are now more than 150 years old. Among its other faces, Mount Hope is a notable arboretum as well as a birders' delight.

The statuary, while not as impressive as at Mount Auburn, is a complete anthology of 19th-century styles, and the design of the monuments rings all the changes from neoclassical to late-20th-century kitsch. The architecture includes seventy-four mausoleums, mostly in classical styles, two Gothic Revival chapels, a doughty little Second Empire gatehouse, a gazebo, and a show-off, two-tiered Florentine fountain.

Because Mount Hope was open from the beginning to anyone, bluebloods, immigrants, ex-slaves, and the city's founder, Colonel Nathaniel Rochester, all found a home along its winding paths. There are plots reserved for the Rochester Orphan Asylum, the Home for the Friendless, nine Jewish congregations, the Rochester German Benevolent Society, the Society of Friends, the Odd Fellows, the Masons, and the city's firemen. Revolutionary War soldiers were buried here, and there are military sections for Civil War, Spanish-American War, and World War I soldiers. The history of Rochester is here for the viewing.

It is easy to trace the rural cemetery's influence on American cultural life, where it inspired the profession of landscape architecture and greatly stimulated the development of American sculpture. Its effect on the mourner is harder to judge. Most of those who wrote about the rural cemeteries were not mourners, and they tended to generalized bromides about the moral and emotional power of these new resting places. Did burying the dead in Mount Hope, as opposed to a 17th-century churchyard or a 20th-century memorial park, make any difference to their family and friends?

Impossible to know, but the rural cemetery has one undeniable advantage for the bereaved: it knit death, the dead, and the mourners into the everyday fabric of society. The paradox of the old-fashioned graveyard versus the rural cemetery is that the graveyard was close to the center of the city but often ignored, while the new cemeteries were designed to be out of the hustle and bustle of life, yet intimately part of its being. Far from the modern situation, where grief is shamefaced and kept behind closed doors, in the 19th century the mourner knew that he was engaged in one of the central human activities. Furthermore, there was evidence all around him that the cemetery was one of the most valued places in society.

Mount Hope offered other consolations. Aside from the balm of its landscape, the new expressiveness about death meant that a monument could be as personal as one's pocketbook allowed. At the expensive end, the parents of Henry Selden, who died at twelve in 1858, commissioned a realistic statue of a schoolboy, with book in one hand, leaning against a pillar entwined with morning glories, symbolic of early death. Underneath is inscribed:

> He is not dead, this child of our affection,
> But gone unto that school,
> Where he no longer needs our poor protection
> And Christ himself doth rule.

Even a simple gravestone could be powerfully poignant. A tomb believed to hold an ex-slave has a plain stone inscribed only: "We called her Anna." Charlotte Perry and Elisha Sibley, a married couple, are buried under a double headstone that resembles a matrimonial bed. It is decorated only with sculpted ivy, representing undying affection. The Bembel family also arranged for headstones and footstones that look like beds. In their case, the grave of their daughter, E. Wilhelmine, who died in 1860 at the age of eight, is tucked protectively between that of her mother and her father. The stones of the parents, who lived to ripe ages, have sheaves of wheat, symbolizing God's harvest, laced with ivy for lasting love. Wilhelmine's has a small hand holding morning glories.

The 19th-century stones in Mount Hope typically put a period after a single name – "Mary." – in a succinct expression of finality. And there is much use of the possessive – "My Baby," "Our Charlie." The heartbroken wish to keep what cannot be kept is strong on these stones, particularly when the dead is a child. A stone for "Herbert," decorated with an anchor for hope, is inscribed "Ours for a Day." The use of smaller stones for children was a 19th-century innovation, and many adult tombs are ringed round with small ones for the children of the family. In one of the plots bought by a Jewish congregation, three miniature stones stand in a row, marked "Little Julie Ehrlich," "Little Carry Ehrlich," "Little Lizzie Ehrlich."

The 19th century made much of the cemetery's civic aspect, believing that the visitor would be inspired and the mourner comforted by the nearness of great local figures. This was not a particularly convincing argument to me, when it came to mourners, but I was wrong in at least one instance. Susan B. Anthony's simple grave in Mount Hope, once the scene of suffragist demonstrations, almost always has a few stones placed on it by visitors. At the end of the 20th century, a letter was discovered at the base of her grave from a man whose mother had died that day. The letter thanked Anthony for all the advances that had made a better life possible for his mother.

Mount Hope and the other rural cemeteries retained their drawing power through the 19th century. But beginning with the devastating losses of the Civil War, cemeteries, funerals, and death in general lost some of their appeal. At the same time, the rural cemeteries were in a certain sense the victims of their own success. They had been the original people's parks and fine art museums, institutions that society in the second half of the century refined and launched on their own, without the graves. The Rochester parks system was born in the 1880s; New York City's Central Park opened to the public in 1858, and the Metropolitan Museum of Art in 1870. People now had alternatives when it came to enjoying nature and art, but the change was gradual. In the 1870s Mount Hope was still a prime spot for picnics and carriage rides. In 1909, from five to eight hundred visitors passed through the entrance gates on a weekday, with three to five thousand on Sundays.

But in 1909, a new cemetery would not have been designed with Mount Hope's picturesque clutter of hills and valleys, monuments, and eclectic gravestones. The rural cemetery had been neatened and suburbanized in the second half of the 19th century into the so-called park cemetery, which featured lawns and more standardized graves. That in turn was succeeded by a cemetery that was in some ways a logical extension of its predecessors, but that also marked a radical departure in its attitude to death and mourning. It was appropriately born, at the beginning of the 20th century, in another boomtown, Los Angeles.

⌘

MONUMENTS MAY TOPPLE
– warning sign in a cemetery

The newcomer was the memorial park, and the first and still the most famous example of the genre is Forest Lawn. Behind its rolling greens and flush-to-the-ground markers was an unspoken and very 20th-century thought: there was something not quite acceptable about death. Slightly embarrassing and perhaps even tasteless, it was definitely a downer.

As revolutionary as Père Lachaise and Mount Auburn, a phenomenon that ranked in its day with Universal Studios and Disneyland as one of the top three tourist attractions of Los Angeles, Forest Lawn had dismal beginnings. In 1912, a young

Midwesterner with a science degree, Hubert Eaton, came to work at a dusty, unsuccessful cemetery in suburban Glendale. (It was not forested, nor did it have any lawn to speak of. Water from the Sierra Nevada arrived on an aqueduct in Los Angeles in 1913 and allowed Forest Lawn to live up to its name.) Eaton was not particularly interested in the business and was depressed by the bleak look of the place. But he proved such a success at the new practice of selling graves on a "before need" plan that within a few years he had risen to general manager.

The events of New Year's Day, 1917, are the cornerstone of the Eaton legend. As the story has it, he walked alone on a hill overlooking Forest Lawn and had a vision of what a cemetery should be. Far from the "unsightly stoneyards" full of "misshapen monuments" that they had become, Eaton dreamed of a great park that would express his belief in a happy eternal life and a "Christ that smiles." It would be a place for strolling lovers, for artists in search of inspiration, where those "who are left behind" would be glad that their loved ones had gone to a better place. Commemorating the dead, but only in stained glass and marble, would be "encouraged but controlled by acknowledged artists." Forest Lawn would be as different from other cemeteries "as sunshine is unlike darkness." "The Builder's Creed," as Eaton called his mixture of upbeat Christianity and marketing, is carved in stone near the cemetery's Memorial Terrace.

Eaton wasted no time in revamping Forest Lawn. The Pan-Pacific International Exposition in San Francisco in 1915 had impressed him with its inspirational art, fountains, grandiose plantings, and curving roads. The fair furnished Eaton with a working model for his cemetery, and it was there that he bought the first piece in Forest Lawn's art collection. *Duck Baby*, a saccharine statue of a plumply naked toddler clutching a brace of ducks, stands with a like-minded group of sculptures at the pond by the cemetery's entrance. They include a gleeful child with frogs, a burro, a boy wielding a panpipe, a pubescent girl, and a copy of *The Little Mermaid* given by the actress Greer Garson in honor of her mother. Across the pond, a replica of the Venus de Milo is visible.

Sweetly pretty originals and copies of Western masterworks sum up the art at Forest Lawn, which now numbers almost a thousand statues and hundreds of square yards of stained glass. Along with Forest Lawn's layout, Eaton also borrowed its artistic mission from the San Francisco exposition: to bring Californians the great art of Western civilization, particularly that which expressed an optimistic, non-denominational Christianity. (Eaton's personal search for an artistic representation of the "Christ that smiles" was long and not terribly successful.) Forest Lawn has been derided as a theme park, but Eaton would not have considered that a criticism. Like a world's fair, a memorial park needed a theme, and what better one than his own brand of "let not your heart be troubled" religion, expressed whenever possible by artists?

Mocking Forest Lawn is like shooting fish in a barrel, a pastime neither Jessica Mitford nor Evelyn Waugh scorned. Waugh used the memorial park to delicious advantage in his 1948 novel, *The Loved One*. Mitford derided its kitsch and salesmanship in her 1963 exposé of the American funeral industry, *The American Way of Death*. The surprise in visiting Forest Lawn after reading these mordant satirists is seeing that their descriptions are restrained: the reality is even more extraordinary.

The sections of the cemetery really are named Slumberland, Inspiration Slope, Blessed Promise, Abiding Love, and so on. The "shooting-gallery statuary," as Mitford calls it, really is a dubious assortment of chalk-white, marble copies of Michelangelo's and Leonardo's most famous works mixed with original pieces celebrating bare-breasted women, babies being bathed, and heavily muscled men defending their family. There is a huge (195-by-45-foot) oil painting of the Crucifixion unveiled every hour with attendant hoopla, a version of Leonardo's *Last Supper* executed in stained glass, a Freedom Mausoleum dedicated to the American heritage, a museum with a coin collection that includes every coin mentioned in the Bible, and a gift shop selling replicas of Forest Lawn treasures. Eaton intended the Great Mausoleum to become America's Westminster Abbey, where the nation's "immortals" would be entombed in the Memorial Court of Honor. The first two so honored were Gutzon Borglum, the sculptor of the Mount Rushmore Memorial, and Carrie Jacobs-Bond, the composer of "I Love You Truly" and "Just A-Wearyin' for You."

There are finely executed copies of three British village churches, each replica heavily freighted with cultural baggage of the manly, Anglo-Saxon variety Eaton admired. The Little Church of the Flowers is based on the Buckinghamshire church where Thomas Gray wrote "Elegy Written in a Country Churchyard." Eaton added flower-filled side aisles and a singing canary for more cheer. The Wee Kirk o' the Heather, with stained glass windows telling the story of Robert Burns's faithful heroine Annie Laurie, echoes the church in Dumfriesshire, where Burns and Sir Walter Scott lived. The Church of the Recessional is a replica of Rudyard Kipling's parish church. In an alcove that the Builder "set apart for the youth of America where they may dream their dreams and find a guide for their tomorrow," Kipling's poem "If" is inscribed on stone, with a treacly bronze statue of a little boy reading it positioned in front.

When a bride-to-be named Cora Wills asked to be married in the Little Church of the Flowers, in 1923, the Builder was surprised and delighted. More than sixty thousand people have been married in Forest Lawn's churches since then, including Ronald Reagan and Jane Wyman. Along with the usual cemetery services, Forest Lawn offers bridal consultants. People often exclaim at the California-style bizarreness of being

married and christened – that happens here too – in a cemetery, but this is one point on which Forest Lawn is, accidentally,
old-fashioned. The real village church, surrounded by its
graveyard, was as a matter of course the scene of funerals, wed-
dings, and christenings.

Forest Lawn's celebrity, or notoriety, has been focused on
its marketing innovations: the one-stop funerary and burial
shopping that Eaton invented, and its resemblance to a theme
park. But its turning away from the fact of death is at least as
remarkable. Creating a cemetery with many lengthy inspirational messages and 380,000 graves where death is rarely
mentioned and frequently unnoticed is no mean feat. Forest
Lawn often seems to be, like the proverbial "*Hamlet* without
the Prince," a cemetery without any dead.

The chief way this is accomplished is through the use of
small bronze memorial tablets set level with the ground. Not
only do they make maintenance far cheaper, they rid the place
of the "misshapen monuments" and gravestones that so
depressed Eaton. It was not easy to detach mourners from these
morbid reminders of their loss. Tombstone makers and granite
suppliers were predictably outraged, but Eaton's toughest sell
was the customers themselves. Telling them how beautiful the
park was going to be, he assured them, "You wouldn't want to
mar it with tombstones. It would spoil everything."

Finally, he hit on the right persuasive tactic. Customers
who surrendered their "monument privileges" (the right to
erect an upright stone) saved 10 percent. Later, tombstones
were simply outlawed. Families with enough money could
memorialize their dead, but only in statuary approved by Forest
Lawn and in the Great Mausoleum's stained glass.

The most striking thing about Forest Lawn is that, until
you are quite close to a slope full of bronze tablets, you can
hardly see them. The visitor is conscious of green hills, towering
trees, and the occasional statue. The tablets themselves look like
basting stitches set in the grass, arranged sometimes in curving

lines, sometimes in straight. Occasionally they glint in the sun, a Morse code announcing, to the initiated, hundreds of thousands of burials.

A fourteen-by-twenty-four-inch tablet, the most popular size, costs $595 (U.S.) in Forest Lawn's 2002 price list, not including a $190 "setting fee." That allows very little space for biographical information, usually something the length of "Beloved Mother," with name and dates. (A rare sign of personality is glimpsed on Steven Tangalakis's stone. Below his name and dates, 1953–1995, there is the single word "Bitchin'." One wonders what his next-grave neighbor, Mary MacInnis, who died in 1994 and has a picture of Jesus engraved on her tablet with "Lo I Am With You Always," would have thought of that.)

Although Forest Lawn's former clergy relations director, the Reverend Ronald Beams, told me, "We want to mourn the beloved but celebrate life," grieving here is an almost clandestine activity. Good cheer and a secondhand contact with the high points of Western civilization are so prominent at Forest Lawn that jagged, wracking grief would seem inappropriate. The garden at the Wee Kirk o' the Heather is intended, a sign reads, "for those of you who want to draw apart and rest awhile in silent meditation and prayer." That is about as close as Forest Lawn comes to acknowledging the harsh pain of bereavement.

Unlike Mount Hope and the other rural cemeteries, which were designed for strolling, Forest Lawn is a quintessential Los Angeles place, planned for cars, with no sidewalks. You can park by the relevant section and negotiate the slope with the grave you mean to visit, but I saw no one doing that on the two pleasant spring days I spent there. The terrain and the rows of uniform tablets do not invite lingering.

The oldest section, populated before the ban on tombstones, is the most human part of Forest Lawn. There is space on the stones for more information; the choice of monument – a standard headstone, a Celtic cross, an urn, a classically inspired mausoleum – allows some scope for individuality. Frank L. Baum, the author of *The Wizard of Oz*, happens to be buried here, but in general there is nothing particularly distinguished about this section. It simply looks like a cemetery, a place to spend time remembering particular dead people, and that makes it unusual.

Forest Lawn is the reductio ad absurdum of the rural cemetery: more literally and more grandiosely than the 19th-century cemeteries, it is an art gallery, a school of patriotism and morality, a museum of architecture, a splendid park. But unlike the rural cemeteries, which grounded their secondary functions in the constant presence of death, Forest Lawn regards the dead as a necessary evil. If it had been possible to erase them entirely, Eaton would probably have been happy.

Forest Lawn's great days were the 1920s and '30s, when its lower-middle-class, Anglo-Saxon sensibility and soft-focus Christianity suited and flattered its clientele. At a time when transatlantic travel was uncommon, its copies of European art constituted something close to a genuine cultural experience. And its sunny, euphemistic philosophy accorded perfectly with 20th-century southern California. Four other Forest Lawns were created in the Los Angeles suburbs, and after World War II, during another of America's periodic revulsions from the idea of death, the memorial park idea spread around the country.

Its heyday is over – European immigrants in particular resisted memorial parks, wanting individual headstones – but Forest Lawn is still beautifully maintained. About ten thousand families make use of its services every year, through either burials or cremations, the latter now accounting for more than a quarter of its business. And Forest Lawn is adjusting to different times. Although it remains a largely WASP preserve, more than 10 percent of its customers in the last two decades have been Armenians. The number of Asians and even African-Americans (Forest Lawn was originally closed to blacks) is growing. "We Anglos have a lot to learn from the ethnics,"

Ronald Beams said, mentioning that African-Americans expect two-to-three-hour funerals. The Forest Lawn standard service lasts about forty-five minutes, but the memorial park is willing to accommodate almost anything – mariachis, videos, jazz, a horse-drawn hearse.

In line with the outreach programs now common for cemeteries and funeral homes, Forest Lawn's grief support coordinator conducts two two-hour seminars, called "Living Through Life's Losses" and "Making It Through the Holidays." They provide a leaflet guide to the mourning process. But more of the memorial park's energies are spent on community programs, "for property owners and visitors alike," as its newsletter puts it. They include pumpkin decorating contests, concerts, a staged visit from "Michelangelo," Mother's Day card-making events, and an Easter sunrise service held in Spanish.

Forest Lawn's optimism is still in place, expressed in a contemporary idiom. In 2000, its ad campaign was called "Celebrate a Life." Radio spots featured a good hit of Dixieland jazz, followed by the briefest admonition: "Celebrate a Life. Forest Lawn. Call us when the need comes."

Celebrating a life is an excellent idea. As long as that includes, when the need comes, mourning a death.

⌘

Mount Hope bypassed the fashion for memorial parks, but it too changed with the times. More than a hundred acres was added to the cemetery in the 19th century, and after the turn of the 20th, the flat area at the southern end of the property, called the New Grounds, was developed. Organized in straight, broad avenues, partly because of the terrain, partly because the picturesque style was no longer fashionable, the new section is a recognizably modern cemetery attached to a Victorian one. Modern or not, Mount Hope has remained steadfast to the idea of the individual raised gravestone or monument, as desired by the plot owner. With driving mowers unusable on awkward sites in the original sections (which occasionally demand the old-fashioned hand sickle), it is an increasingly expensive policy. But, for $1,230 a plot ($1,600 for one in the old sections), it is still possible to commemorate your dead with a standing stone or statue.

Today there are 350,000 permanent Rochesterians buried in Mount Hope, on 196 acres connected by 14.5 miles of roads. The cemetery remains "operational," as its director, Nancy Hilliard, says proudly. Which means that burying traditions at Mount Hope stretch from the first years of Victoria's reign to the 21st century. Cremations, which were first done at Mount Hope in 1912, will soon account for 20 percent of the total. The cremated remains can be buried in a special section or in family plots, or they can be scattered. There are plans to add community mausoleums to the two chapels. The cemetery's popular Memorial Day and July 4th ceremonies are things of the past, but Hilliard favors the new Christmas and Easter commemorations being held for relatives: "It starts to bring families back."

As do volunteer societies at other historic cemeteries, the Friends of Mount Hope (founded in 1980) adopt graves, sponsor talks, repair monuments. They conduct general and specialty tours of the cemetery's flora, fauna, and architecture, visiting the graves of the abolitionist Frederick Douglass, Susan B. Anthony, and other famous inhabitants. Their efforts have borne fruit, for the cemetery is in better shape than it has been for many years, and in 2001, about twenty-seven hundred visitors toured Mount Hope under the Friends' auspices.

Other visitors came individually, but even a total of four thousand a year would be a far cry from the six thousand or more *a week* reported in 1909. On a temperate weekday afternoon now in Mount Hope, there are walkers, joggers, bicyclists, and the very occasional visitor to a plot, bringing flowers, tidying a grave, standing lost in memories. The mourner is more likely to be male than female, cemetery visiting being one of the few mourning activities in which men outnumber women. Hilliard, who also points out that men are more extravagant than women when it comes to buying a coffin or headstone, thinks she knows why: "A man is like a child. He needs to *see* something to connect. A woman can grieve at home."

Walking in the New Grounds is an even more multicultural experience than a turn in the old sections. There are Chinese graves with small urns for burning facsimile money and Ukrainian ones with permanently lit lanterns. There are headstones so full of biographical details, down to the years degrees were granted, that they have been called resumé stones. A few headstones are whimsical, such as the one that orders, "Bloom!" (On the back, which is embellished with some musical notes, it becomes clear that the stone honors Joel Bloom, 1963–1996.)

The 18th century favored slate for headstones, the 19th century marble, and the material of choice for the 20th century was polished granite, often with a rose, a lily, or a crucifix cut into the pinky-grey surface. Late in the century, the occasional truck, automobile, airplane, violin, or pair of dancing shoes appears on the stone, indicating a hobby or occupation. The feelings inscribed onto those stones are not necessarily more florid than in the 19th century, but they are expressed in distinctly 20th-century ways. There are photographs and facsimile signatures. Graves are decorated with artificial flowers that spell Mom, Dad, Beloved, or Baby. Sometimes it is important for the mourners to inscribe the dead's relationship to them in letters as big as or bigger than the name of the dead – Sister, Husband, Mother.

The New Grounds has a children's corner where, at the end of a long Rochester winter, sodden teddy bears and other stuffed animals, their fur matted, lie helter-skelter, like stones heaved up in a field. These gravestones, like the 19th-century ones dedicated to children, are the most poignant of all. The modern ones use more words, and they are surrounded by mementoes, china ornaments, toys, balloons, and flowers real and plastic. Marlon Javon Edwards, who was born in 1990 and lived less than nine months, is buried beneath a granite stone in the shape of a teddy bear. A black-and-white photograph of Marlon is affixed to the stone. Yolanda Smith, who died at eighteen months in 1991, has a stone in the form of a drowsy cherub. Paris Johnson, who died at two in 1982, has a heart-shaped stone, a wooden cross, and a statue of a dog.

The inscriptions are similarly unaffected. "Gone to be an Angel," declares the stone for Mary Louise Smith, who died at four in 1982. Jorel Charles Hassail's stone promises, "Someday I'll hold you in Heaven." The inscription that I always linger over in this section is the one for Naem Akins Holmes, who lived from August 28, 1982, to May 21, 1983. His small stone says, "Benevolent Brave Boy." The idea of someone less than nine months old with those qualities is at once improbable and convincing. The thought of the parent or parents who chose those words is heartbreaking.

Like most cemeteries, Mount Hope has rules: artificial flowers are allowed only between November 1 and March 1; no balloons (they kill birds and clog sewers), no glass (dangerous to groundskeepers), no monuments that may be offensive to other plot owners. They're prepared to turn a blind eye to infractions, especially in the last category, for a while, occasionally. After all, Mount Hope began as a cemetery willing to accept diversity and individuality. And "offensive" is a subjective term.

The Fingland family put Mount Hope's tolerance to the test. When their twenty-six-year-old son, Tom, drowned in 1981, Marjorie and Ernest Fingland erected a standard granite stone. What followed was not standard. Over the stone, Ernest Fingland built a hand-hewn, rustic arch of white cedar. Painted reddish brown, it stands over five feet high, and its top is a planter filled with real and artificial flowers. The words "Son Tom" are roughly carved on one side of the arch. Around the grave and arch, the parents planted two evergreens, rosebushes, tulips, hyacinths, and daffodils. Tom was a farm boy who loved animals, so his parents added statues of a rooster, a rabbit, and other animals to their small garden. His father came twice a day to Mount Hope, about half an hour from his house, to tend the plot. Marjorie Fingland decorated it with Easter bunnies, Thanksgiving turkeys, Halloween pumpkins, birthday cards. Tom was the eighth of twelve children, and each year the family decorated a Christmas tree on his grave, with each of his siblings hanging an ornament in his memory.

About a year after Tom's death, Mount Hope officials began asking the Finglands to remove the arch, saying that wooden monuments weren't permitted in that part of the cemetery. The Finglands resisted. Ernest pointed out a large wooden monument near the cemetery gates. When he was told that it wasn't comparable because it commemorated two prominent Rochester families, he countered that he would remove his arch as soon as that one came down. After that, the superintendent backed off, according to the Finglands. Today the gravestone is marked "Mother" and "Father" as well as "Son." Ernest Fingland died in 1986, five years after his son. Marjorie Fingland, who had become blind, was taken to the grave by her daughter two or three times a week until her death in 1992.

In 2000, bearing a blurry photocopy of a newspaper photograph of the plot, I asked the first Mount Hope groundskeeper I met if he knew the location of the Finglands' graves. In a cemetery of 350,000 interments, he recognized it immediately. There is still nothing like it at Mount Hope. In addition to the perennial flowers and the evergreens, there are artificial flowers, in hanging baskets and in the ground, a ceramic chicken, a statue of the Holy Family, a cross, a plaque of Our Lady, and a family picture of a man with two children at a swimming pool.

What does it mean, this idiosyncratic, homemade mélange organized around religion, holidays, and family? Nancy Hilliard sees it as a social or aesthetic problem. It was her predecessor who objected to the display, and she agrees: "What is necessary to some is offensive to others." For her, a grave is a fine but not entirely private place. Ernest and Marjorie Fingland, on the other hand, regarded their plot as thoroughly private property. They believed their son was conscious of their care, and that it was a natural extension of their pride and joy in him in life. Aware that some people found their constant attention morbid, they were unshakable. "We're not crackpots," Ernest Fingland said. "My son meant the world to me. He still does. Being in a cemetery hasn't changed the way I feel about him."

Many modern people would see a psychological problem here, a case of excessive mourning. Arthur Schmale, a psychiatrist, was consulted by a Rochester newspaper reporter when the controversy was at its height in 1984. He conceded that the Finglands' behavior sounded "a little dramatic." But, he continued, "who's to say that's abnormal or pathological? It speaks to the importance of this person, how much they want to keep his memory alive and how much they miss him now that he's gone."

That sounds right to Ernest Fingland Jr., Tom's oldest brother. "Probably six or seven of us stop in there all the time," he says of the family plot. He doesn't believe that Tom knows about their visits, nor that he is conscious of their prayers. With the exception of one sister, he says, they're not a particularly religious family. But they are a close family, and they've always visited their dead. Even a grandmother who was buried more than an hour away was visited a few times a month. Dead or alive, as his late father pointed out, they're still family and still beloved. Nor does the Finglands' care for the family graves seem likely to die out with Ernest Jr.'s generation. Grandchildren are among the regular visitors, and recently one of them restained the arch and repaired one of its posts.

FIVE

AFTER GREAT PAIN

They sat with Job on the ground seven days
and seven nights. None spoke a word to him
for they saw how very great was his suffering.
   – Job 3.13

After great pain, a formal feeling comes –
The Nerves sit ceremonious, like Tombs –
   – Emily Dickinson

Emily Dickinson, that expert in grief, put her finger on it. After the hurt of death and burial, a "formal feeling" often does come, a mood of apparent apathy, a wish not to be shocked any more, a desire not to have to improvise but to rest in the comfort of known formulas and practices. Unfortunately, in most of the Western world today the formal feeling meets with a vacuum. Typically the burial or cremation signals the end of ceremony, even the end of the informal gathering of friends and family. A reception may follow the disposal of the body, but then the world returns to business as usual, and the mourners are left more or less to fend for themselves.

When two Oregon psychologists set out to investigate the relationship between grief and rituals in 1987, their checklist of "post-funeral rituals" was thin indeed. The possibilities included receiving and acknowledging flowers, cards, and money; sorting and disposing of the dead person's personal effects; notifying distant connections by letter of the death; visiting the grave. Except for the last, these are not really rituals in the usual sense of a repeatable activity charged with a special, un-mundane meaning and a particular protocol. They are chores, and bleak chores at that.

Other cultures cushioned the mourner's return to the world. A gradually diminishing series of customs and ceremonies attempted to ease his loneliness and aimlessness. Age-old practices offered an implicit promise: "Over hundreds of years, your people, in mourning, did this. In time, they found comfort. So will you."

After the burial and, often, a solemn meal came a time of protected seclusion for the mourners. Many cultures happened on two periods, the first one of seven or eight days, followed by a lighter period of some weeks. The bereaved in Japan mark the seventh day after death, the one-month anniversary, and the forty-ninth day, when the dead person's translation to the spirit world is thought to be completed. Jewish mourners sit shiva for seven days, followed by a less restricted period called *sheloshim*, which ends thirty days after the death. The Muslims' period of heaviest mourning ends after forty days.

These times are a combination of indulgence and prohibition. The mourners have company and a relaxation of their normal duties. At the same time, normal grooming, joyful pastimes, finery, and even foods associated with good times are frequently forbidden. Many Muslims do not sugar their coffee during the mourning period. In the 1920s, the Bedouins gave up coffee completely and symbolically overturned their cups and pot, as a mourning song lamented:

> Oh, thou coffee pestle
> It is long since I heard thee pounding.

The cups were weeping over the coffee-pot
And the coffee-pot cried until it could no more!

⌘

Of all Western cultures, the Jews have preserved the fullest repertoire of post-burial customs. They underscore the perplexity of
the first days and weeks of mourning: something is irrevocably
finished, while something else, the adjustment, is beginning.

When they return from the cemetery and before they enter
the house of bereavement, Jewish mourners wash their hands
to indicate that they are leaving the pollution of death behind
them. Then they sit down to the "meal of consolation," a meal
the mourners must not prepare for themselves. The community provides it, and it features round foods – often hard-boiled
eggs, sometimes lentils, bagels, peas. Spanish Jews eat olives.
Their symbolism has been variously explained. Roundness
echoes the cycle of life and death, goes one theory. The multi-
plicity of lentils is a metaphor for life and fertility, says another.
The imperfectly rounded foods suggest the imperfection of
life. Hard-boiled eggs signify endurance. These are all foods
with no mouths, because grief at this stage is inarticulate. Take
your pick: all the interpretations offer a sympathetic echo of
the mourners' situation.

After the meal, shiva begins. Shiva is a time and a space
designed for the mourner. The time is seven days (*shiva* is
the Hebrew word for seven), and the biblical precedent comes
from the story of Joseph, who "made a mourning for his father
for seven days" (Genesis 50.10). The space is the shiva house,
the home of the dead person or a close relative. For a week, the
main mourners as defined by Jewish law – parents, siblings,
children, spouse – spend at least their waking hours in this
house, being visited by friends and family.

As the phrase "sitting shiva" indicates, shiva is also a position. A halfway point between the alertness of standing and the

surrender of lying down, sitting suggests a combination of inertia and, perhaps, a willingness to be comforted. (How apt that the nerves in Dickinson's poem also "sit ceremonious, like Tombs.") Traditionally the mourners sit on special low chairs, immobilized by sadness, exhaustion, or simply custom, and the community comes to them.

The modern shiva looks like a subdued version of an open house, in which visitors express their sympathy to the mourners, take coffee and cake, and become engaged in conversation with other shiva-goers. The time is sometimes shortened to three days, or even to one.

The traditional shiva is a strikingly different thing, in which normal social roles are suspended. When her father died in 1990, Joyce Slochower followed most of the rules for a traditional shiva. The door to her Upper West Side apartment in New York City was left slightly ajar, and the visitors let themselves in. The mirrors had been covered. Joyce sat on a low chair or a couch without cushions. Her blouse had been torn above the heart, in the ritual called *keriah*, and she wore that blouse for the entire shiva. She did not wear makeup or leather shoes, and if she had been a man, she would not have shaved for the week. She may not have had the "rumpled look" of shiva, as it has been approvingly called, but she did not look like her usual self.

The visitors familiar with shiva protocol did not greet Joyce or extend condolences. When she acknowledged their presence, they took their cue from her. If she spoke about her father, so did they; if she had chosen another topic, they would have replied to that. It is also perfectly permissible for the mourner never to acknowledge a visitor. Paying a shiva call is a mitzvah, or good deed, in itself, and the visitor would have left with the confidence that his presence alone had been a support.

Strictly speaking, no refreshments are offered to visitors. At Joyce's apartment, food was available in the dining room for shiva callers, but there was none in the room where she sat. (On the other hand, the mourning family's meals, which they took in private, were all provided by the community.) When the visitors left, they did not say goodbye, but either the traditional farewell, "May God comfort you among the mourners of Zion and Jerusalem," or some other form of good wishes, such as "May we meet again at a *simchah*," a joyous occasion. Joyce was not supposed to respond to that, and the visitors saw themselves out.

It is a most peculiar kind of interaction, and an essay on shiva etiquette is well titled "Who's the Host? Who's the Guest?" A traditional shiva has an almost surreal look. There are rules, but none where the mourners' behavior is concerned. They sit close to the ground, unresponsive or openly weeping or in conversation, as the spirit moves them, while one by one the visitors, always physically higher, hover sympathetically nearby. It is a subject for Edvard Munch, perhaps as close to a genuine picture of grief as any social situation allows.

Beneath the shiva's apparently indulgent surface lurk darker elements. As with the Jewish "wailing time" before the burial, anthropologists believe that the prohibitions for the bereaved – against sexual activity, normal grooming, work, even reading the Torah except for certain sad texts – sprang from the ancient sense that the close mourner was somehow guilty or polluted or dangerous. Added to that was the wish to confuse evil spirits, so they would do no further harm. To that end, Jewish mourners in Talmudic times overturned their beds and couches and sat on them or on the ground, with a cloth over the head and most of the face. Couches are no longer overturned, evil spirits are no longer feared, and the bereaved are no longer considered guilty, but Jewish mourners continue to sit and act differently during shiva.

Joyce Slochower is a psychoanalyst, and she observed her own mourning with a professional eye. She notes that sitting

close to the ground concretizes the mourner's feeling of close-
ness to the dead as well as her depression. We talk about "feeling
low." Sitting lower than those not in mourning takes the
expression literally. In the same spirit, when the rabbi cut
Joyce's blouse, she felt there was "something raw" and true to
the experience of bereavement about it. The tear was her
badge of loss.

Aside from her profession, she brought a fresh scrutiny to
her shiva experience for another reason: she was at the time
fairly new to observant Judaism. Her childhood had been
almost completely secular, and she had never paid a shiva call.
Her closest bereavement had been the death of her grandmother, ten years before her father's death. That shiva, in the
modern style, lasted a single afternoon. Her mother served
food and the guests talked politics. Joyce found it "unbearable."

By 1990 she had joined an egalitarian, observant Jewish
congregation. A diverse group that included a healthy sprin-
kling of Jewish scholars, psychoanalysts, and rabbis, it became
her extended family, her village. When her father died, the
congregation did nothing without her consent, but they were
prepared for every aspect of Jewish mourning, from the
washing of the body to the posting of the shiva rules outside
her door.

Her strongest memory of that week is the grateful realization that she was supported by a sheltering web larger than
close friends and family. Joyce has always had trouble with the
Jewish formula of condolence, "May God comfort you among
the mourners of Zion and Jerusalem." She thinks the Hebrew
words themselves, the concept they express, and the strain of
the moment of departure when they are meant to be uttered
are all "awkward" and more ritualistic than humanly comforting. "But," she adds, "if there's something that's meaningful in
it, it's the phrase 'among the mourners.' The feeling of being
alone in death is so horrible that to have that link with other

people feeling this way too is very powerful." As the only child of parents who separated when she was two, she sat shiva alone. But she was always "among the mourners," and that was her congregation's great gift.

When the shiva began, Joyce took her place on a low chair in her living room more or less innocently. Sitting shiva was the custom of her community, and she was willing to give it the benefit of the doubt. At the least it would give her time to begin to assimilate the fact of her father's death. As a therapist, she believed that the mourner in the first days has "a powerfully diminished capacity to be involved in the world of real relationships or activities." He needs time to sort through his complicated feelings about the death, to experience and express his loss, to be angry with the dead for abandonment, to long for the dead, to endure a temporary depression. Ultimately his task will be to accept that his living relationship to the dead is over, while he builds a new, internal relationship with the beloved.

Rather to her surprise, Joyce found the traditional shiva a "brilliant structure" within which to begin these tasks. Freed from domestic and work responsibilities for a week, she had few possibilities for distraction. The prohibitions against normal greetings and farewells, the insistence that she *not* play the role of hostess, made it difficult to evade the shiva's raison d'être: the fact of her father's death. Shiva is, as she says, a situation "perhaps unique in its social discomfort," and with good reason. The sheer oddness of a woman in her own house who does not greet or say goodbye to guests, offers no refreshments, and wears torn clothing and no makeup constantly reminds visitors and the mourner herself that this is not an ordinary social event.

So the mourner has little choice. She must address her loss. In the case of Joyce Slochower's father, as in most deaths, there was considerable unfinished business. An analyst himself as well as a professor, Harry Slochower had been an adoring, moody, difficult father. His daughter's embrace of Judaism had enraged his secular soul, although he had begun to make his peace with it. She had kept a recent serious illness from him and was feeling guilty about that. He had died on the Sabbath, when she did not answer the telephone, and she worried that she might have saved his life had she allowed herself to be contacted. He died three weeks before his eldest grandchild's bar mitzvah.

All these roiling feelings of anger, regret, and love could be expressed over the seven days. As many people do for a shiva, Joyce put out photographs of her father at various ages, to serve as props for memory. She remembers that she often wondered aloud with visitors how he would have reacted to the shiva itself, part of the observant Jewish world he had decisively rejected as a boy. With her father's students and patients, she tended to discuss his accomplishments. The closer she was to a visitor, the more ambivalence she described.

Certain that the essence of shiva is its radically unsocial concentration on mourning, she was content to break some of its rules. In particular, Joyce disregarded the prohibition against washing one's body and one's clothing. "I was not interested in having body odor," she says. "But it would have felt bizarre, really bizarre, to put on makeup. One had to do with being in my own skin, and the other was about putting on a face." Similarly, she never fretted when people forgot the protocol or did not know it and greeted her normally, or when she would approach a friend and forgetfully sit on a regular chair.

As the week went on, she began to realize that the visiting community members, one by one, were fulfilling a therapeutic function in which she had a particular interest. The British psychiatrist and pediatrician D.W. Winnicott called it the "holding function." Unlike the more glamorous task of analysis, holding refers to the sympathetic environment created by the therapist. Judgment and interpretation are withheld so that the patient has permission to think thoughts and express feelings, some of them hitherto unthinkable and inexpressible.

Joyce had long thought of the holding function as a more complex therapeutic task than interpretation, so her surprise on seeing that untrained people were effectively performing it during shiva was considerable. It was another of the shiva's topsy-turvy elements. In the same room that functioned as her office, where she mustered her professional skills to provide a holding environment for her patients on the analytic couch, she was being "held" collectively by her community. On her low chair, she poured out her heart, she reminisced, she resented the ways her father had failed her, she regretted the ways she had failed him, she retreated into commonplaces at moments when feeling was too difficult or fatigue overtook her. And her visitors simply accepted whatever she wanted to say or not say, however upsetting or raw or false it may have sounded to them.

Ideally, the shiva caller does not corroborate the mourner's emotion from his own experience of bereavement. Nothing should compete with the mourner's preoccupation with her own grief. As an analyst Joyce Slochower believed that staying "emotionally present but not intrusive" communicates confidence about the patient's ability to survive his most painful feelings. Now, as a mourner, she was benefiting from the same generous neutrality on the part of her visitors.

She recognized that the community providing this shelter has its own protections, much as the therapist is "allowed" weekends, holidays, and the termination of a session. Since the community shoulders the responsibility collectively, it sits lightly on individuals, who often make a single shiva visit of perhaps half an hour. Because the group's need to celebrate the Sabbath takes precedence over the mourner's need for support, the shiva is suspended for twenty-four hours beginning at sundown on Friday. That can be hard on the bereaved, she acknowledges, but the break "may actually begin to draw the mourner back into life," in the way that a therapist's holiday or other disruption in holding may strengthen a patient.

The only point where Joyce believes the rules fail the mourner is the unhappy coincidence of a major Jewish holiday with the week of bereavement. Shiva ends abruptly on the eve of the holiday, not to be resumed, leaving the mourner "traumatically unprotected," possibly interfering with the resolution of grief. She described these mourners to me as "ripped off . . . it doesn't make psychological sense." With this exception, and in the presence of a cohesive community (an important requirement), she sees shiva as a superb "prepsychoanalytic adaptation to a universal human need," a structure that meets a mourner's "intense regression" while safeguarding the needs of the larger community.

⌘

As I listened to Joyce Slochower, a remark made at the time of Scott's death resurfaced. Cindy Klein Roche, Scott's sister-in-law and a Jew, had been comparing the Roches' activities before and after the funeral with the bereavements in her family. The Roches, with their usual effectiveness and energy, were going out into the world and doing what they saw as needing to be done. What Cindy was familiar with was a period of retreat and inactivity, where the world came to the family. Hannah, she said, by sequestering herself in my sister's house and leaving it only reluctantly, came closest to sitting shiva.

At the time, I nodded and acknowledged the justness of the comment. I had paid three shiva visits in my life and knew nothing about the traditional version. Hannah had probably scarcely heard of the custom. But the more I learned about it, I realized that an old-fashioned shiva would have suited her perfectly.

In the first weeks after Scott's death, Hannah resented any conversation that was not about him – resented it bitterly, but had no words to express it. When well-meaning friends came to visit and, partly out of awkwardness, began talking with and about my sister's little girls, Hannah bridled inwardly. It was for that reason that, when she returned to Vancouver, she tried to be with no more than two people at a time, because a larger group would inevitably choose its own topics. Had she been sitting a traditional shiva, where she would have led the conversation or sat in silence, the dilemma would not have arisen.

In addition to everything else, Marilyn and D'Arcy Roche faced the problem of selling Scott's house. On the Wednesday, Thursday, and Friday of the funeral week, we met at his house and began the sad work of cleaning and clearing it out, distributing clothing and other possessions to people who wanted them, taking the rest to Goodwill. Hannah and Scott's brothers divided up his sweaters, shirts, and T-shirts. I remember Marilyn reminiscing as she packed some placemats she and D'Arcy had brought Scott from a trip to Ireland. I remember, as we went through his books, the stricken look on her face when someone handed her Scott's marked-up copy of John Kennedy Toole's novel *A Confederacy of Dunces*. It had been the subject of his senior thesis.

Rather like the custom of shoveling dirt on the coffin in the grave, clearing out Scott's house drove home the reality of the situation. It would have to be done at some point, and it allowed us to be together, to share memories inspired by Scott's things, and to have some feeling of accomplishment. But it was not for Hannah, who recalls it as "the last thing I wanted to do." For a while she would sort kitchen utensils or towels, and then she would disappear, usually to Scott's bedroom with one other person. One afternoon, she spent a long time there with Matthew Roche. While other people waited to clear out that room, the door remained closed. I was embarrassed at what looked like inconsiderate behavior, but I was missing the point. I had not yet encountered Joyce Slochower's description of the mourner's profoundly diminished ability to be involved "in the world of real relationships or activities."

On some evening during that week, I insisted that we go to a family-style restaurant in my sister's neighborhood. I felt a certain hostess responsibility for Hannah's college roommates, Jessie Janowitz, Jenny Martin, and Ashley Magargee, and some forlorn hope that a little red wine and pasta might lift our spirits. Another mistake. Hannah ate almost nothing and could hardly wait to get back to my sister's. As people who know shiva could have told me, food comes to the mourner at home, who eats or not, as she wishes, in private.

Hannah was sullenly miserable as well as shocked that week, and one of the privileges shiva gives mourners is the ability to have things their way. What Hannah wanted to do was to sit on the couch, sometimes with her young cousin Kate's warm body leaning against hers, which she remembers as an important, wordless comfort, and almost always with her roommates. Disturbed by their inertia, my brother-in-law tried without success to get them out for a short walk. When he accepted that they were not going to leave the couch, he took some pictures. In them, four handsome young women either ignore the camera or stare at it without much interest; above all, they do not smile. Documents of a hard, bittersweet time, the photographs have a gravitas more like the 19th century than the late 20th.

Sybil and I felt slightly rebuffed by Hannah in those days; she clearly didn't want our company as much as that of her friends. Her explanation, months later, was that we were concerned and sad about *her*, but she wanted to be sad about Scott, which is what she could be with her roommates. In Joyce Slochower's terms, they were providing the sympathetic environment that Hannah needed.

I doubt that a seven-day shiva would have suited Marilyn and D'Arcy, but Hannah seemed to suffer the regression that the custom indulges. Out of necessity, as Cindy Roche observed, she created her own shiva. And although she could occasionally be wheedled off the couch, it was where she wanted to be until we left for Vancouver, seven days after Scott died.

⌘

When it came to sitting shiva for her father, Joyce Slochower says, "I was it." That compounded her loneliness, but she admits that it also simplified things, eliminating conflict and competition. Gordon Pape did not have that dubious luxury. A Toronto architect in his early forties with a mobile mouth and a dryly comic turn of phrase, he has become sadly adept at sitting shiva or helping others to sit shiva. Five close relatives – his sister, father, two grandparents, and mother-in-law – died in a period of three and a half years in the late 1990s. Although he has an ideal shiva in his mind, most of his actual shiva experiences have been at least as frustrating as successful.

Gordon's most traumatic loss was the death of his sister Paula from a brain tumor at the age of thirty-eight. She was a year older than Gordon, and the brother and sister were close friends. As her condition deteriorated, he curtailed his architectural practice so that he could spend two days a week at her bedside.

While Paula was ill, he was becoming interested in the traditions of his wife's Conservative Jewish family. He loved the "complete mayhem" of the Conservative service, the uninhibited body language that suggested people were genuinely moved by the prayers, the spontaneity of worshipers coming and going, as compared with the formality of the Reform service with which he had been raised. He began going more frequently to morning services on his way to his sister's house, looking for solace in the rhythms of a liturgy he barely understood.

When Paula died, and Gordon and his sister Sky went with their parents to the funeral home to make arrangements, it was clear that they were all going to mourn differently. The funeral director asked if they wanted to rent the traditional low chairs for mourners (regular stacking chairs with the legs cut short). No, said the parents. Yes, said Gordon, and his sister agreed, in solidarity more than conviction. Did they want the cut ribbons that substitute for torn clothing in many Reform bereavements? Yes, said his parents and Sky. No, said Gordon.

So it went at the shiva. One of the upside-down aspects of a shiva is that the synagogue comes to the mourners, instead of vice versa. Services are traditionally held three times a day at home, which is what Gordon wanted. His parents preferred the Reform custom of one service only, in the evening. If Gordon wanted a morning service, they told him, he could go to synagogue. Hating to be with people other than his family at the time, he drove to the synagogue early in the morning, then returned to the shiva house. It was, he admits, "a bit of a clash," where his parents "weren't there for me." On the other hand, he realizes that "a morning service would do nothing for them."

The week-long shiva was held at his parents' house. Unlike Joyce Slochower, Gordon's mother assumed her normal hostess function, seeing to the food, making sure that the right china was being used, trying to introduce her bafflingly uncooperative son to various visitors. Gordon was, in his words, "a bump," seated on his low chair, sorrowing for his sister, "just wondering what's going on with the world and wallowing in self-pity." For the first few days, he was "almost totally shut down," and his description of his state of mind accords with the self-absorbed, non-social behavior that the traditional shiva indulges.

"You're as small as you get within yourself, and you're not ready to open yourself up to the outside world. You don't have to look at anybody, you don't have to address anybody, you don't have to do anything for anybody, you don't have to be nice. And why should you? You've just been uprooted in a very dramatic and traumatic way."

Conscious that his mother's conventionally polite behavior was irritating him and that he must be at least as puzzling to her, Gordon embraced what he calls "the element of selfishness" possible in a shiva. Since he was unwilling to talk in the first few days of the shiva, would he have preferred that people didn't come? Not at all, he answers, because that would have meant they didn't care. All he objected to was having to talk before he was ready, or to talk about things other than Paula: "I just wanted to focus on memories of her."

Gordon's kindred spirit was an uncle, an ultra-Orthodox Lubavitcher from New York City and "a burr in the side of my parents" for much of the shiva. At one point, as Gordon was sitting "staring at my toes" – he acts out the scene, bending over, his hands resting on his cheekbones, muffling his ears – his uncle pulled up a chair next to him. He assumed a similar position, and the two sat in complete silence for perhaps twenty minutes. Finally Gordon said something, they had a short conversation, and his uncle got up and went away. That, for Gordon, was a proper shiva encounter.

Midway through the week, Gordon felt a shift in his feelings. The recurring memory of Paula's funeral and the thud of the earth on her coffin – a "filmy nightmare," as he describes it – began to recede. That was the point at which he could allow people to provide some consolation. In the second half of the week, a cousin walked in whom Gordon and his sister hadn't seen in years. Something about him – some indication that he was willing to be used however they wanted – moved them to talk and talk and talk about Paula and her death. "For about forty minutes he just looked kindly," Gordon remembers, "and then he wished us well and left. We both said that was the best experience we'd had." Joyce Slochower would probably regard the cousin's behavior as a good example of the holding function.

People frequently say that one of the best things about a shiva is the way a family comes together to cover over the gaping hole in its fabric. Gordon Pape is too candid to claim that for his family. Not only did they have a disparity in their commitment to ritual, but the differences that had emerged during Paula's illness persisted after her death. He and Sky were still optimistically looking for cures months after his parents accepted that Paula's death was imminent. So her death was more truly a shock for her siblings than for her parents. Gordon sees that just as Paula's death was something different for each member of the family, grieving for her was a solitary experience. His parents couldn't understand what it was like for him to lose a close sibling and dear friend. He could imagine his parents' grief only if he imagined losing one of his children, "and I couldn't go there . . . You want to be there for the other person, but sometimes you just can't."

For Gordon, shiva's most reliably consoling aspect is the daily services held in the house of mourning, followed by the occasional meaningful exchange with family or visitors. And simply to have a cushion between the dreadful day of the burial and the rest of life is essential, as he discovered when his father died. Mr. Pape was buried the day before the holiday of Shavuot, which meant that the shiva lasted one day and was not resumed. Like Joyce Slochower, Gordon has "a major dispute with the great sages" on this point: he feels he was robbed of his transition, forced back to the world before he was ready. With the shiva for Paula, time unfolded and there was a marked difference between the beginning of the week and the end. With his father, a structure designed to last a week was abruptly dismantled after a day and the inhabitants scattered. It felt wrong at the time and still feels unresolved.

An ideal shiva such as Joyce Slochower's is fortuitous and rare. Like most other mourning customs, it probably mirrors a family's fissures as often as it repairs them. Every Jew knows stories of rival shivas, where the "first family" and the "second family" mourned separately. I met a widower who sat shiva at home with his young children during the day and joined his difficult in-laws in the evening for their shiva. Many veterans of modern shivas will complain about their falsely social atmosphere, but when they hear about a traditional one, they are shocked by what they imagine is its strained oddity.

On the other hand, even mourners who had a short, modern shiva remember with feeling the stories they had never before heard about their father, their sister, their wife. (Typically, the visitors talk about the dead person's life, and the mourners tell and retell the story of the death – a good thing, since even the most distressing story becomes more bearable when told often enough.) What most people agree on is that a shiva is a breathing space even when it is a trial, a place to start to absorb the unabsorbable. Even those most critical of shivas will say, "I can't imagine how people can go to work or resume their old life without something like this."

On the seventh day of a shiva, it is traditional that someone, often a rabbi, comes to "stand up" the mourners. A verse from Isaiah (66.13) is recited, the same verse used in the Anglican funeral service: "As a mother comforts her child, so shall I the Eternal comfort you . . . and the days of your mourning will come to an end."

For people a week into bereavement, that must often sound overoptimistic, even bitterly so. But a first stage has undeniably come to an end. In what is typically a powerful moment, the family leave the house for the first time together and walk around the block. Weakened and diminished, they rejoin the world and walk a short but real distance.

SIX

HOW TO MOURN

> One writes, that "other friends remain,"
> That "loss is common to the race" –
> And common is the commonplace,
> And vacant chaff well meant for grain.
> – Tennyson, *In Memoriam*

One of the things we had taken with us when we left Harborview Medical Center was a manila envelope. Inside, along with leaflets from local bereavement support groups, was a book called *Letting Go with Love: The Grieving Process*, by Nancy O'Connor. The same package was given to every family that had a death in the hospital. Hannah handed me the book. "You read it. If there's anything I need to know, underline it." I read it, and I did some underlining as instructed. It was my first "how to mourn" book.

⌘

Mourners have rarely lacked for guidance, if not rules. Often the rules were unwritten and unspoken, simply embedded in customs. The fact that in various societies, women held their heads while wailing their loss, or men scratched their cheeks and pulled their beards, or women hid their presumably tear-stained faces behind crape veils meant that, in those cultures, that was how a mourner was supposed to behave. More than that, the correct action presupposed the correct feeling.

Some cultures expect the mourner to grieve extravagantly. A few, but not many, aim to suppress feelings almost entirely. In Java, as described by the anthropologist Clifford Geertz, the desired state for mourners is what the Javanese call *iklas*, a condition of inner freedom and calm where emotions quiet into detachment. Their ritual requires a close mourner to hold the dead on his lap while the body is being washed, and one must do this with equanimity. Geertz tells of a young girl who was "crying slightly" after her father died suddenly. Relatives told her that unless she stopped weeping she would not be allowed to wash the body. She stopped.

More often, a culture attempts to moderate the mourner's feelings, neither denying grief nor luxuriating in it. The Romans officially urged such a middle way, with laws that limited funeral excesses and prescribed set periods of mourning for different relationships (twelve months for a child over the age of six, one month for a child under six). Unofficially, literate Romans crafted the condolence letter, a minor literary form that spoke volumes about their expectations for the mourner.

In 45 B.C. Cicero's daughter, Tullia, who was about thirty, died from complications of childbirth. Inconsolable for months, Cicero isolated himself in a remote region. "In the morning," he wrote to a friend, "I hide myself in the dense, impenetrable forest and don't emerge until nightfall." Even his reading, he reported, "is interrupted by fits of weeping." Cicero received many condolence letters, one of which came from his friend Servius Sulpicius Rufus, an orator and jurist then serving as governor of Greece. Sulpicius's carefully wrought composition, mingling sympathy with calls for stoicism, is a fascinating piece of advice to the mourner.

He begins warmly and personally, recalling how overwhelmed he was when he heard of Tullia's death. Relatives and friends such as himself, he says, are poor consolers because they themselves are so hurt that they can only attempt comfort while in tears. Then he turns to some instances of how reason can lessen sorrow. Ideas like these, Sulpicius writes, will not be new to Cicero, but he may be too distracted by grief to recall them on his own. Sulpicius begins with a trip he had made past the once vibrant towns of Aegina, Megara, Piraeus, and Corinth, now lifeless and abandoned. When whole towns lay corpse-like, the folly of mourning a single human death struck him sharply. "Please pull yourself together, Servius," he had admonished himself at the time, "and remember that you were born a mortal man."

In a similar vein, he mentions the recent civil war and the end of the republic, in which Julius Caesar had vanquished Pompey and his aristocratic supporters, including Cicero. Compared with "so serious a weakening of the power of the Roman state" and the death of many celebrated men, Sulpicius affectionately reprimands Cicero, "are you moved by such deep sorrow if we lose the frail little soul of one frail little woman? Even if she had not died at this time, she must nevertheless have died a few years from now because she was born a mortal. Take your mind and your thoughts away from these things and reflect instead on things which are worthy of the person that you are."

Sulpicius reminds his friend that Tullia enjoyed most of life's blessings. She saw her father become a praetor, then a consul, finally an augur. She had been married to three men from noble families. She lived "as long as it was necessary, that is, she lived while the republic lived . . . And she departed from life when the republic died. How, then, can you or she complain about fate on this account?"

He ends with a call to self-discipline: "We have, on a number of occasions, seen you sustain good fortune very decorously and thereby gain great glory. Now act in such a way that we may know that you can also sustain bad fortune just as decorously."

How likely is it, I wondered when I read this letter, that Cicero — or any parent — would be comforted by the thought that his child's life overlapped that of the republic? Sulpicius's counsel struck me as breathtakingly wrongheaded. But we don't know how Cicero reacted. He was a Latin father, undone by Tullia's death, but he was also a Roman male, keenly conscious of self-control and duty.

To modern eyes, Sulpicius's effort to give Cicero some distance on his daughter's death probably looks callous and futile. In another light, it's an attempt to get the bereaved to reframe the situation so that its pain is less cruel. Whether that ever works is questionable, but mourners through the ages have been urged to "look at it this way" — "this way" being some species of abstraction that puts the particular death in a larger perspective.

In China, in the 3rd century B.C., the Taoist mystic and philosopher Chuang Tzu claimed that such thinking helped him. He suffered a loss, and at first he grieved. Then he calmed himself by reflecting that his beloved had originally been lifeless, formless, even lacking substance. In death, she had simply returned to her former state, as the seasons pass from one to another. "And while she is thus lying asleep in the Great House [the universe]," he wrote, "for me to go about weeping and wailing, would be to show myself ignorant of Fate. Therefore I refrain."

Buddha offered a slightly different remedy, in the well-known story about the woman whose child had died. Crazed with grief, she went everywhere with the dead child in her arms, beseeching people for a cure. Finally she went to Buddha, who told her he needed some poppy seeds to heal the child, but from a very specific source: "Go and beg four or five poppy seeds from some home where death has never entered." After she tried vainly to find such a house, she went back to Buddha in defeat. "In his quiet presence her mind cleared," the story goes, "and she understood the meaning of his words.

She took the body away and buried it, and then returned to Buddha and became one of his followers."

Again I asked myself, when I read these accounts, would you miss your wife or child less because you reminded yourself that death comes to all, or that life and death are part of a great cycle? I couldn't imagine it. It might quench self-pity, or a feeling that you had been specially singled out for misfortune, but it would not begin to make up for the loss of that dear, particular person. But while advice such as Sulpicius, Chuang Tzu and Buddha offered struck me, in Tennyson's terms, as vacant chaff rather than grain, there is no denying that similar consolations have been the staples of philosophies and religions in many times and places.

Christianity believed it had solved the problem of mourning. As the Victorian critic John Ruskin asked, "Why should we wear black for the guests of God?" Not only were those in heaven happy, mourners could look forward to an eventual reunion – a more hopeful outcome than the cold comfort of "Death comes to all" or "To everything there is a season."

For a time, the dying came in for special attention, as treatises on the making of a good death, called *ars moriendi* (Latin for "the art of dying"), multiplied from the 15th to the 17th centuries. As William Caxton's subtitle – "The Arte & Crafte to Know Well to Dye" – for the *Ars Moriendi* he wrote in 1490 indicates, these books were self-help manuals for the end of one's own life.

But until the 19th century, there were few extended Christian counsels for the bereaved. Mourners, when they received any attention, were simply expected to see their lot as a test of faith and to rejoice that their dead were with God. The 17th-century American poet Anne Bradstreet lost three grandchildren and a daughter-in-law in a four-year period. She marked each death with a poem, which begins in sorrow. Of her granddaughter Anne, who died at the age of three, she writes "with troubled heart and trembling hand." Of her daughter-in-law

Mercy, whom she compares to a tree, she says, "My bruised heart lies sobbing at the root." But in each case she moves quickly from sadness to rejoicing at their happiness in heaven and trusting that God's ways, however mysterious, are just.

To her grandson Simon, who lived only a month and was predeceased by two sisters, she writes:

> Go pretty babe, go rest with sisters twain;
> Among the blest in endless joys remain.

And to her son, whose wife and four children had died, she counsels:

> Cheer up, dear son, thy fainting bleeding heart,
> In Him alone that caused all this smart;
> What though thy strokes full sad and grievous be,
> He knows it is the best for thee and me.

⌘

> The admonition not to mourn is misplaced.
> "Jesus wept." Is not this a sufficient sanction for
> the mourner's tears?
> – Lydia Sigourney, *Letters to Mothers*

Had Anne Bradstreet lived two hundred years later, her mourning poems would almost certainly have had a different emphasis. It is not that her orthodox Christianity was out of date, because the belief in an afterlife and in the unknowable rightness of God's decisions persisted. Rather it was that by the 19th century, the pathos of the dying and the mourner's grief had become more interesting than the religious resolution. Gradually over the century and a half that followed the poet's death in 1672, the mourner's plight, which she acknowledges briefly, took center stage.

The disciplined neoclassical attitude, which bore death with as firm an upper lip as possible, first softened noticeably in the mid-1700s. The poets of the so-called Graveyard School, discovering the pleasures of melancholy while wandering in English country churchyards, were harbingers of a new sensibility. As the Romantic movement flowered, with its interest in the ordinary lives of ordinary people and what Keats called "the holiness of the heart's affections," the emotion of loss became increasingly fascinating. Ahead of the 19th-century Christian, the carrot of eternal life still bobbed, but now he was allowed – no, expected – to mourn and mourn heavily.

Out of this climate was born a category known as consolation literature. It took various forms – novels, poems, biographies, devotional manuals – but its purpose was to sympathize with and ease the mourner's distress. At the same time, inevitably, the attitude to mourning and the descriptions of it found in consolation literature set a standard of behavior and feeling for the bereaved.

Occasionally a great piece of literature was incidentally consoling. Tennyson's long poem *In Memoriam*, published in 1850, became a runaway success, as hundreds of thousands of readers found comfort in his account of his grief for his friend Arthur Hallam and its eventual lightening. Queen Victoria considered *In Memoriam*, along with the Bible, her greatest source of solace after Prince Albert's death. But more often, consolation literature was the work of ministers, amateurs, and less-than-eminent professional writers.

Lydia Sigourney, sometimes called the "Sweet Singer of Hartford," was not a good writer, but she was an astonishingly popular and prolific one, turning out more than fifty volumes between 1815 and 1865. As well, the Connecticut writer was a voluminous contributor to the poetry annuals and the popular magazines of the day. She turned her hand to non-fiction and fiction as well as poetry, and in all of them death made frequent appearances. Sigourney's *Letters to Mothers* (1845) reads like a

19th-century Dr. Spock, but overlaid with frequent intima-
tions of mortality: after chapters on "Infancy," "Schools," and
"Health," she concludes with "Loss of Children," "Sickness
and Decline," and "Death."

Lydia Sigourney's advice to mourners in those chapters
comes from the standard arsenal of Victorian Christianity. The
happiness of our children, she writes, is never more secure
than when they are in heaven. Death is the end for which we
were designed, "the consummation of our highest hope," and
a child in heaven properly directs his mother's attention to the
next world.

Where she differs from Anne Bradstreet – and this is the
side of her I find most sympathetic – is in her insistence that it
is right to grieve. "He who appoints such discipline," she writes
of Jesus and death, "never intended that we should be insensi-
ble to it, or that we should gird ourselves in the armour of
pride to meet it, or seal up the fountain of tears, when he
maketh the heart soft."

The fountain of tears was a rich source of poetic inspiration
for Sigourney. Strangers wrote her with requests for obituary
poems, one wanting a poem for a mortally ill wife and their
baby – could she write one that would serve as a memorial for
the two of them, if they both died? Another begged for a poem
about his dead child which could be hung over the mantel.
With or without commissions, the 19th century offered plentiful instances of deaths. Volumes of poems by Sigourney, filled
with titles such as "Burial of Two Young Sisters," "African
Mother at Her Daughter's Grave," "Death-Bed of the Rev.
Dr. Payson," and "Baptism of an Infant at Its Mother's Funeral,"
appeared regularly.

Her poems typically follow a pattern, beginning with
happy memories, progressing to a description of the death and
finally resignation to God's purpose. "The Lost Darling," for
example, opens boldly: "She was my idol." Then the grieving
mother catalogues her toddler's charms in prosaic, poignant

detail. She thinks back to her voice, "like some tiny harp that yields / To the slight fingered breeze," as it talked to her doll, soothed her kitten, "or with patient care / Conned o'er the alphabet." Now the mother sits alone, weeping over the tiny dresses she has made or imagining that a restless sound comes from the empty crib. After remembering her child's death in realistic detail, down to "the ghastly white / Settling around her lips," she commands her heart to "be still": the girl is in heaven.

No doubt the resolution is sincere, but it is more brief (three lines in a thirty-eight-line poem) and much less touching than the homely memories of the child's life and death. Mawkish and clichéd as Lydia Sigourney frequently is, she almost always gives her mourner, imaginary or real, a space in which to grieve. While most of Bradstreet's attention went to acceptance, most of Sigourney's is firmly fixed on sorrow.

One of the most popular and most appealing full-length works of consolation is called *The Empty Crib: A Memorial of Little Georgie*. Facing the title page is a picture of two sturdy toddlers dressed for an outing, their caps set smartly on their long curls. The author, Theodore Ledyard Cuyler, was the prominent minister of the Lafayette Avenue Presbyterian Church in Brooklyn, New York. He and his wife had twin sons, Georgie and Theo. When they were four and a half, in 1867, Georgie contracted a virulent case of scarlet fever that took him from health to death in a single day. The condolence letters his parents received were so touching that Mrs. Cuyler suggested printing them, in "the hope that they might be equally comforting to other people in affliction," particularly bereaved parents. The Cuylers planned a private distribution, but the printer was so moved when he read the book that he urged publication.

It was a typically 19th-century idea that reading the Cuylers' correspondence would help others. The Victorians enjoyed perusing collections of model letters on a variety of subjects, for use as patterns – a proposal of marriage, a letter of apology. The Cuylers did not intend theirs as model condolence letters, but it was a familiar form and a way into a favorite subject. His father prefaced the correspondence with the story of Georgie's life and concluded with additional thoughts on loss, but the heart of the book is the letters they received from friends, acquaintances, and strangers.

"That simple story of a sweet child's life," as Cuyler described the result, published in 1868, "travelled widely over the world and made our little 'Georgie' known in many a home." Some of those homes were grand ones. The prime minister of England and Mrs. Gladstone read the book and reminisced about their own dead child. Dean Arthur Stanley read it aloud to his wife in the deanery of Westminster Abbey, and when he visited the Cuylers in Brooklyn, he asked to be taken to Georgie's grave in Greenwood Cemetery. He was one of many thousands of readers of *The Empty Crib* who made Georgie's tomb a place of pilgrimage.

The Victorians who traveled to the grave of a little boy they had never met would have been hard pressed to imagine a world unmoved by Georgie's story. But, a century later, the American historian who found *The Empty Crib* self-indulgent, exhibitionistic, and morbid probably spoke for a sizable number of her contemporaries. The shift in feeling is reminiscent of the intellectuals who sobbed at the death of Little Nell when Dickens's *The Old Curiosity Shop* appeared in 1841, to be followed a half-century later by Oscar Wilde's famous witticism, that one would need a heart of stone not to laugh at the death of Little Nell.

When it comes to *The Empty Crib*, I side with the Victorians. Not that the book is pleasant reading; the story is sad, after all. Baby talk rarely travels well, and it must be admitted that Georgie talks his share. But aside from that, this is the unpretentious biography of a normal little boy, followed by a bundle of eloquent letters.

The narrator, a sophisticated clergyman who happens to be Georgie's father, addresses his story to "the largest household in the world," the household of the sorrowing. Cuyler, who spoke at his son's funeral on "the sustaining grace of God in trial," believed that religion offered the ultimate consolation. But first he writes as a father, proud of Georgie's beauty, his quaint sayings, the "fine vein of poetry in his nature." The little boy who went out to the garden to see the strawberries sleeping and who prayed, "Oh God, please to make Georgie a good boy, *right away!*" is skillfully drawn. So is the imp who, playing horse too roughly, refused to answer his mother's objections because, as he later explained, "horses never talk."

In the winter before Georgie died, when he would rest his head on his father's shoulder and repeat the hymns he had learned in Sunday school, Cuyler "felt a secret tremble at the thought that so much treasure was intrusted to so frail an earthen vessel." Georgie's words on going to bed after his last day of play, "My little footies are tired at both ends," may sound insufferably cute, but four-year-olds say such things. Cynics will raise their eyebrows at a preschooler who recited a hymn on his deathbed and then asked about meeting Jesus, but it was unremarkable in a 19th-century Christian household.

What makes the Cuylers' grief and their friends' sympathy so recognizable is that, like Lydia Sigourney, they never pretend that something terrible has not happened, nor do they shrink from unmanageable feelings. Georgie's twin, Theo, who often hid his face and "seemed to be mourning his other self," was the most outspoken. When he complained, "I think God was real *mean* to let Georgie die; I won't have anybody to play with," his father comments, "Older people have *felt* quite as rebelliously as the bereaved child; only they were not willing to say it as bluntly." When his mother held Theo on her lap and talked about Georgie's enduring spirit, he refused to be comforted: "I knew Georgie's *body*; but I don't know his *soul*."

The Cuylers and their friends knew that leaping first to faith, however sincerely felt, would not work. First the harrowing loss and the sense of having been cheated needed recognition. "It would be an impertinence to remind you of any of the trite arguments of consolation," a minister friend writes to Georgie's parents. "It is all very well to be told how he has been saved from the sorrows and perils of earth. You wanted to see him *upheld amid* the perils of God's grace, doing a brave, true-hearted man's work in *this* life, and then receiving his reward up yonder. It is easy to say that he has 'only gone on before.' You wanted him as a companion *here*. It *is* a grief, – a terrible loss, – which I can only imagine."

The psychological acuity of this letter strikes a modern note. Much of the advice and encouragement the Cuylers received would not be out of place in a 21st-century self-help book about mourning. One thing their correspondents know above all is that grief must find expression. One writes, "Had you or had I kept silence, the very stones would have cried out." An old friend, the pastor of the American Chapel in Paris, anticipates a common reaction: the overwhelming sense of insecurity that makes the mourner fear for the safety of his surviving family. These feelings are distressing, he writes, "but they do not render any thing we love the more unsafe."

Underpinning all this human sadness is the conviction that Georgie was happy in heaven. At its most childlike, it appears when Georgie's Sunday school class troops by the Cuylers' house after his death, wearing mourning badges and singing the hymn he sang on his deathbed:

> Jesus loves me; He has died,
> Heaven's gate to open wide;
> He will wash away my sin,
> And bid his little child come in.

It's there, at a more complex level, when Cuyler and his clerical friends meditate on human pain and God's purpose. At his most unflinching, Cuyler asks himself why God causes suffering and writes, "My only answer is, that *God owns you and me*, and He has a right to do with us just as He pleases. If He wants to keep His silver over a hot flame until He can see His own countenance reflected in the metal, then He has a right to do so." It is an image with a stoic grandeur. One may find the idea repugnant, attractive, provoking, or quaint. But it undeniably informed the Cuylers' world, and they expected it to bring a measure of peace to the bereaved.

When Georgie died, a neighbor kept the print of his little hand, left on her parlor window the day before his death, as long as it lasted. His father ends his memoir in a similar spirit, sitting in the nursery where all Georgie's things are arrayed, down to his velvet cap hanging on a nail. He asks, "Has that bright sunny boy – whose brief biography we have tried, with trembling hand, to write – lived and died for naught?" Quite the contrary, he answers. "No bereavements are commonly so fruitful in spiritual blessing as those which, at once, empty our cribs and fill our hearts with Jesus." He and his family have learned "the sweetness of sympathy . . . We have been admitted to the sacred circle of the sorrowing."

None of it will restore his son, at least in his human form, but he has a poignant confidence that something of Georgie remains: "As I look at all the playthings, and at the precious little slate on which he tried to mark, with feeble hand, on his dying day, I cannot believe that he is dead. He must be somewhere in my dwelling yet."

⌘

Every society has developed some way of marking the solemn fact of death, and even the most primitive has usually evolved a pattern for the behavior of the family of the dead.
– Millicent Fenwick,
Vogue's Book of Etiquette (1948)

> Nothing in our country is more undecided in
> the public mind than the etiquette of mourning.
> – Mrs. John Sherwood,
> *Manners and Social Usages* (1897)

Etiquette books address the mourner from a different angle. Unlike consolation literature, they describe how mourning should look, not how it feels. The occasional etiquette writer, of course, does forget herself and ventures into the realm of feelings but, strictly speaking, the rules of etiquette point to the behavior that is owed to the dead, to society, and to the mourner. Reading the chapters devoted to bereavement in standard American etiquette books from the 1890s to the 1990s reveals one of the most dramatic changes in attitude in the history of mourning.

The Victorians believed that ceremonial respect paid to the dead and the bereaved were important components of a good society. Gradually, in the 20th century, people began to think otherwise. The astonishing idea took hold that there was something morbid and even antisocial about mourning. The Victorians thought that grief required time, that it involved a slow and stately progression of feelings, which was echoed by the step-by-step resumption of color in women's dress. The modern world differed profoundly: the sooner the mourner returned to society and the more unremarked the loss, the better for everyone.

The chapters devoted to mourning in M.E.W. Sherwood's popular *Manners and Social Usages*, first published in 1884 and updated in 1897 and 1912, are a mostly sensible map through the Scylla of overwrought, unhealthy mourning and the Charybdis of frivolous disrespect for the dead. In Sherwood's day, an American widow generally restricted her social life for eighteen months to two years, and a widower did the same but for less than one year. Resumption of social life always corresponded with the return to normal clothing, after a period in mourning garb. After three months, a woman might go to a concert, but not to the opera or a dinner or a party – those required a minimum of six months. Behind Sherwood's schedules is a theory. She believes that mourning customs ensure a respect for the dead, which is an absolute necessity so "that all society may move on in decency and order." Without rules about when to resume dinner parties, shiny jewelry, and stationery without black borders, chaos would come again.

But Sherwood's concern is not only for the dead and society as a whole. She is quite modern in her belief in pleasure and recreation for the bereaved. "The more the heart aches," she writes, "the more should one try to gain cheerfulness and composure, to hear music, to see faces which one loves: this is a duty, not merely a wise and sensible rule." The condolence letters that urge a mixture of pleasure and duty are the best: "To advise a mourner to go out into the sun, to resume his work, to help the poor and, above all, to carry on the efforts, to emulate the virtues of the deceased – that is comfort."

World War I is often cited as the great calamity that drew down the curtain on traditional mourning, but signs of change were apparent in America even in the last decade of the 19th century. Almost casually, Sherwood mentions something that would have been unimaginable a generation earlier: the respectable person who decides not to adopt mourning clothes. "If one chooses, as many do, not to wear mourning," she writes, after six months "they can go unchallenged to any place of amusement, for they have asserted their right to be independent."

Marion Harland, whose *Complete Etiquette* was published in 1914, goes further. Granting a surprising authority to the individual and his impulses, she allows that the mourner must, "to a certain extent, be a rule unto one's self" when it comes to withdrawing from society. The sorrowing person will shrink naturally from going into social life: "To such a one we need suggest no rules. To those less sensitive or less unhappy, it would be well to say deep black and festive occasions do not form a good combination."

Harland ends on another contemporary note: don't judge the behavior of the newly bereaved. "The heart knoweth its own bitterness," she writes, "and if that bitterness can be sweetened by some genial outside influence, let others hesitate to condemn the owner of the heart from seeking that sweetness. Those whom we have lost, if they were worth loving, would be glad to know that our lives were not all dark."

That commonsensical advice, a long way from the Victorian assumption that a mourner would shun pleasure for years and still radical in many quarters in 1914, became much more usual as the century progressed. By the 1940s, the old rules about clothing and social life were largely relics of a bygone era. Millicent Fenwick, writing *Vogue's Book of Etiquette* in 1948, makes it clear that few people still choose to wear black. She has less trouble relinquishing mourning clothes than she does in seeing the mourner make a hasty return to society, but for an unexpected reason. It is not out of respect for the dead or solicitude for the bereaved that she disapproves of the mourner who goes to night clubs or cocktail parties; it is out of concern for those who are not in mourning. Those at a big dinner party attended by a recently widowed woman have two choices, she says: they can overlook the widow's situation, enjoy themselves, and be callous, or they can allow their mirth to be dampened. In either case, "the whole evening becomes a painful and difficult situation which could easily have been avoided."

This is a new and very 20th-century attitude: the bereaved should not make other people uncomfortable. The Victorians, who regarded the mourner as an absolutely normal and unembarrassing member of society, would have been astounded by this idea. No doubt, as early death became rare in modern times, people felt more awkward when faced with a bereaved person. Being a mourner in the 19th century made you one with the full tide of humanity; being one in the mid-20th century made you a social pariah.

Millicent Fenwick's solution to the discomfort question was that the mourner should absent herself from felicity for a while. By 1965, Elizabeth Post, who had revised *Emily Post's Etiquette: The Blue Book of Social Usage*, was urging that everyone, including the mourner, should return to "normal life" as soon as possible. Admiring the Eastern peoples who rejoice in the rebirth of a loved spirit rather than "selfishly mourning" a loss, she admits this philosophic calm is rarely possible. But the implication that mourning is selfish remains. The important thing is to keep occupied, she advises, and "avoid casting the shadow of our own sadness upon others. The sooner that we can overcome our grief and turn our thoughts to the future, the better."

Her no-nonsense attitude extends to a subject that went ignored in earlier etiquette books: dating for widows and widowers. In the 19th century, courting for a widow was impossible until two or more years of serious mourning was completed, and many people believed that a widow best commemorated her husband by remaining one forever. A widower could begin courting much earlier, partly because he often had to find a mother for his children. But Post is marching to a hastier drummer. Either the widow or the widower "may start to have dates when he or she feels like it," she writes, but for a few months they should be rather quiet – an evening at the movies or at a friend's house.

Amy Vanderbilt, whose *New Complete Book of Etiquette* was published in 1967, is in agreement that "the lonely widow or widow who wishes to face realistically the problem of deep personal loss" is soon ready for quiet dating – after about three months, in her opinion. "Modern men and women approve such emotionally healthful reaching out for reassurance."

Vanderbilt's rather clinical terms hint that mourning is something of a lapse in mental hygiene. Most mourners, she writes admiringly, resume their normal social lives within about a week of the funeral "as an aid to regaining our ability to function normally." She notes, "We are developing a more positive social attitude toward others, who might find it difficult to function well in the constant company of an outwardly mourning person."

No doubt it is good for the bereaved to feel they can begin dating when they wish, but calling those who do so quickly "realistic" and "emotionally healthful" suggests that those who take longer are not. The feeling is strong in these mid-20th-century etiquette books that mourning is not entirely acceptable. The healthy person with an appropriate measure of social responsibility stops it as soon as possible, with the least possible ado.

The prevailing rules never suit everyone. A sizable number of Victorian mourners, particularly women, probably felt confined and stifled by their society's expectations. Conceivably, large numbers of bereaved people in the 20th century felt hurried and ignored by their contemporaries' ideas of how to mourn. Fortunately for them, if they realized it, there was a notably different stream of advice available, beginning in the last quarter of the century.

⌘

What you should be doing is taking care of yourself, following your own pace. What you should not be doing is feeling drained or discouraged by the expectations of others.
— Elizabeth Mehren, *After the Darkest Hour the Sun Will Shine Again*

Need 1. Accept the death.

Need 2. Let yourself feel sad.

Need 3. Remember the person who died.

Need 4. Accept that your life is different now.

Need 5. Think about why this happened.

Need 6. Let others help you, now and always.

       – Alan D. Wolfelt, *Healing Your Grieving*
Heart: 100 Practical Ideas for Kids

About the time that the Posts and Amy Vanderbilt were coun-seling mourners to carry on with the minimum of fuss, a contrary trend began to make itself felt. The pendulum that in the 19th century had swung to one extreme, that of compul-sory deep mourning, and then to the other, of severely minimal mourning in the mid-20th century, was moving again. In the 1960s, the expressiveness and emotionalism that marked the decade surfaced at every level, from political protests to encounter groups to tête-à-têtes between friends. Once people were encouraged to talk about their feelings, losses of all kinds were going to be part of the conversation.

More particularly, the publication in 1969 of Elisabeth Kübler-Ross's book *On Death and Dying* was an important turning point in attitudes toward mortality. Kübler-Ross's interviews with mortally ill cancer patients brought dying out of the closet and returned to it something of the social accept-ability it had lost. When it was permissible once more to think and talk about dying, it became possible to do the same about mourning. Out of this new-again spirit came a kind of book addressed only to the mourner, concerned neither with duties to the dead nor with obligations to society. The modern incar-nation of a genre as old as Jeremy Taylor's 17th-century treatise *Holy Living; and, Holy Dying*, it is the self-help manual applied to grieving.

Not all self-help books originate in the United States but most do, and there is something peculiarly American about their optimistic, self-reliant, let's-fix-it approach. From Benjamin Franklin's advice on how to be healthy, wealthy, and wise in *Poor Richard's Almanac* to Dale Carnegie's counsel on winning friends and influencing people, self-help books suit a country where God helps those who help themselves and a boy born in a log cabin could grow up to be president. The earliest, like Samuel Hardy's 1673 *Guide to Heaven*, concentrated on the soul. Beginning in the 18th century and continuing to the present day, more worldly matters – usually, how to acquire money and power – predominate. With the 20th century came a new reliance on psychology and an emphasis on emotional well-being.

In *Oracle at the Supermarket: The American Preoccupation with Self-Help Books*, Steven Starker identifies the winning formula behind a phenomenon like Norman Vincent Peale's *The Power of Positive Thinking* (1952). A successful self-help book relies on simplification, copious anecdotes, and the promise of "technique": the twelve easy steps, the ten rules, the worry-breaking formulas, the practical guidelines that will bring the reader whatever it is that he wants. But, as Starker writes, the particular technique is unimportant compared with the inspirational, motivating message of the self-help book, "which temporarily makes the reader feel more in control, less helpless, less despairing."

More in control, less helpless, and less despairing are precisely the feelings that mourners desire, and self-help books about bereavement multiplied astonishingly in the last decades of the 20th century. In 2001, Amazon.com listed more than twenty-five hundred books about grief. A small number are scholarly works or essays of various sorts, but the vast majority fall into the self-help category. Without our package from the hospital, it wouldn't have occurred to me to read such a book in the first days after Scott's death, but it interested me that Sybil made a point of going to a bookstore and choosing a few books on mourning, to help her understand her sister's plight.

In the spring of 2000, I visited the Barnes & Noble bookstore near the University of Washington in Seattle and asked for self-help books about mourning. I was directed to the Addiction/Recovery section. In the subsection called Death and Grieving, I found 125 separate titles. Some were about dying, but most dealt with mourning. They included books about mourning in general, books about specific kinds of deaths (murder, suicide), and books about specific kinds of bereavements (spousal, parental, etc.). I counted fifteen books about the death of a child, twelve about the death of a parent, six about the death of a spouse. (Judging from these books, most dead parents seem to be mothers and most dead spouses are husbands.)

Self-help books run the gamut from formulaic and pat to thoughtful and subtle. They are addressed to children, like Alan Wolfelt's booklet *Healing Your Grieving Heart: 100 Practical Ideas for Kids*; to adults past middle age mourning a parent, like Edward Myers's intelligent book *When Parents Die*; and to every other age. In length they range from a six-page pamphlet available in a rack at a funeral parlor to the 338 closely printed pages of Therese Rando's *How to Go On Living When Someone You Love Dies*. Some are self-published, by people whose only expertise is that they have been bereaved, but many are written by therapists and brought out by the largest mainstream publishing companies. They are big business, with revenues in the millions and multiple printings. And although there are no required credentials or regulatory standards for self-help books, they have achieved an undeniable respectability. Steven Starker reports that 58 percent of American psychiatrists have recommended self-help books to their patients, as have 88 percent of psychologists.

Most self-help books on mourning follow the familiar recipe that mixes a description of the problem with case histories and advice. Variations and additions arise, as a book's particular focus dictates. After Bill Jenkins's son was murdered, for example, he wrote and self-published *What to Do When the Police Leave: A Guide to the First Days of Traumatic Loss*. In addition to chapters on mourning in general, there are sections devoted to dealing with the police and the justice system, the media, with sudden and unwanted fame and its equally abrupt withdrawal.

Often most of the help in a self-help book comes from a description of the rich variations in "typical" mourning. In general, the more sage and sophisticated the book, the more space is given to such description and the less to rules. *The Grief Recovery Handbook: The Action Program for Moving Beyond Death, Divorce, and Other Losses*, by John W. James and Russell Friedman, is at one end of the spectrum in being highly directive, action-oriented, and geared to a quick resolution of grief. Therese Rando's book, written by a psychologist who specializes in mourning, is at the other end, a wise, comprehensive map of bereavement that is long on understanding and short on specific advice.

Mixed in with the self-help books in the Death and Grieving section I found the occasional mourner's memoir, the story of one particular loss. There were a few anthologies, collections of poems, essays, and passages about mourning. And out of the modern conviction that feelings must be expressed has come a subgenre, the mourning workbook, which functions as a kind of guided journal. Amateur or professional, manual or memoir or workbook, these books say to the bereaved at the turn of the 21st century: this is what mourning is like, this is how to mourn.

There is a striking unanimity in their accounts of mourning and their counsel. Flippantly, you could say that the overarching rule in these books is that there are no rules. Again and again, readers are told, "Don't let anyone dictate what you should feel or do, or for how long. Your mourning is yours alone. Do it your way." Elizabeth Mehren is a good illustration of this laissez-faire approach. After her baby daughter died of an intestinal infection, she wrote a book called *After the Darkest Hour the Sun Will Shine Again: A Parent's Guide to Coping with the Loss of a Child*. It's an unusual hybrid of literary quotations and stories of children's deaths intermixed with sharp little essays on such subjects as time, courage, the "normal pathology of grief," the friends who say the wrong things. Mehren writes from "the club that no one wants to join." As she says, there's no strict code of conduct, no dress rules, and no one has been asked to leave for failure to adhere to the guidelines.

The guidelines, such as they are, are all about the club members doing as they please. Good grief, Mehren says, means surrendering to the pain, crying when you feel like it, sobbing if you choose and, if you are so inclined, pounding your pillow while sobbing. "And you do not have to make amends for this kind of behavior," she continues. "The way our club members look at it, it's your grief and you can cry if you want to."

In this vein, Mehren endorses the mourner's craving for solitude (or, as one club member calls it, "the Garbo factor"), for support ("Take it where you can find it"), and for what she calls cleaning house. The last refers not to dusting and vacuuming but to ridding your life of friends who expect you to "snap out of it" or not talk about your grief. Under "Timetables," she writes crisply, "Grief is a process, and it has no timetable. End of subject."

Mehren's edgy wit is singular on the Death and Grieving shelves, but her permissiveness is not. Behind the prevailing leniency, however, there actually is a central rule in these books. It is that mourning is compulsory. You may put it off or deny it, but eventually you must do it. Often the rule comes with a threat, implied or explicit: failure to mourn will make you sick, emotionally and probably physically. (Studies support this claim, although not with the one-to-one correlation you might imagine from reading some of these books.)

Not only is grieving necessary, the self-help books contend, it is active labor. As the current mourning mantra has it (a variant of Hannah's saying that grieving heals), "Time doesn't heal, but healing is work that takes time." Although the term "grief work" has a late-20th-century ring, its originator was none other than Sigmund Freud. The original title for his magisterial 1917 essay "Mourning and Melancholia" was "*Trauer Arbeit*," or "The Work of Mourning." The task, as Freud saw it, involves an acceptance that the beloved person is no more, and a slow, piecemeal, and above all effortful withdrawal of the mourner's attachment to that living person. This bit-by-bit labor – which entails a mental if not literal poring over keepsakes of the dead, each memory, each dashed expectation – is carried out, as Freud says, at "great expense" of time and emotional energy. While it takes place, "the existence of the lost object is continued in the mind." Although Freud could not explain why this process, which we take for granted, is "so extraordinarily painful," he did not doubt its effectiveness: "When the work of mourning is completed the ego becomes free and uninhibited again."

Invoking Freud in the context of self-help books sounds incongruous. So it seemed to the writer Francine du Plessix Gray, who turned from a recent crop of grieving guides to "Mourning and Melancholia" and likened it to moving from Mantovani's Strings to Beethoven's Grosse Fugue played by the Emerson String Quartet. But even the most simplistic of the self-help books owes something to the theories laid down by Freud and the analysts who came after him. So thoroughly have their notions permeated the subculture of mourning that they are visible even in Alan Wolfelt's child-size version of the mourner's checklist.

Freud's beliefs that mourning cannot be shirked and that it is long, hard work are two of the cornerstones of the modern understanding of grief. But Freud devoted relatively little attention to mourning, and the work of John Bowlby, whose three-volume opus titled *Attachment and Loss* appeared from 1969 to 1980, has had a greater impact in this field. For Bowlby, a British psychotherapist strongly affected by Konrad Lorenz's work with animals, the paradigm of loss is the baby, whether monkey or human, separated from its mother. His model of grief begins with numbness or a difficulty in processing information, followed by the child's protesting and searching for the mother, then a period of disorganization and despair, ending in detachment.

Bowlby's work stresses the disturbance in the mourner's environment more than in her psyche, and his definition of success is that the bond with the dead person has been severed. His theory of bereavement was refined and enlarged upon by influential therapists such as Colin Murray Parkes, Beverley Raphael, and William Worden. When Parkes investigated adult grief, he adapted Bowlby's catalogue of behaviors, describing "a succession of clinical pictures which blend into and replace one another" – torpor, pining and searching, chaotic hopelessness, and finally reorganization. His theory of mourning has recently been described as a preprogrammed course cued by a particular stimulus, "like nest-building behavior in birds." Parkes contends that the sequence he and Bowlby present is at best "a rough guide," and that mourners move forward, backward, and sideways through it as their impulses dictate, not necessarily in a straight line.

Certainly you do not have to be a confirmed Bowlbyite to recognize the stages he reports. I remembered Hannah's initial blankness and, after a few weeks, what Bowlby and Parkes would call her pining and searching phase. In her case, she pored over her sympathy letters and cards as aids in pining. A reluctant crier but with a sixth sense that she needed to do it, she found that rereading her condolence mail always triggered tears. (As they did mine, whenever I visited her in Vancouver. There was something heartwrenchingly natural and graceful in those letters from people in their early twenties about the death of a friend.)

Sometime in the first month, when she was still stonily withdrawn and taciturn, Hannah put together a vast photograph album of her six years with Scott, arranged chronologically. She called it the Scott album, and she took it with her every Sunday afternoon to Scott's favorite Vancouver coffeehouse, a place near the university called Bean Around the World. She also took a thick green candle, which she lit at her table. Her friends knew that, from four to five o'clock, they could go there to drink coffee and chat about Scott as well as other things, sometimes looking at the album, sometimes not. It was a fixed point in the week to remember the most gregarious of men in company. Both the album and the Scott coffee, as Hannah called it, sounded like Parkes's searching phase, where the mourner revisits old haunts, old images of the dead, even their clothes. So did her investigation of Scott's electronic notebook; there she found a touchingly detailed chronology of their romance – part of his proposal strategy.

In those same months, Marilyn Roche, also in a searching mode, meticulously combed through and settled Scott's financial affairs, marveling at the evidence she found of his prudence and foresight. She collected favorite pictures of Scott, along with letters and other mementoes, and kept them in a large bowl. Early each morning, when she would "spend time with Scott," she sifted through the contents of that bowl.

The behaviors detailed by Bowlby and his followers surface regularly in self-help books, usually as reassuring descriptions of typical grief. Their view of the end of mourning is more problematic. For Bowlby's disciples, recovery was equated with detachment from the dead person and, often, with the forging of a new attachment. When I first heard that one of the tasks of mourning was to "reinvest" the emotional energy that had gone into the relationship with the dead person in a new relationship, I bristled. The financial metaphor struck me as mechanical and callow, as did the implication that there was a finite amount of energy, or love, that had to be diverted from one object to another. The apparent belief, typical of these analysts, that a widow's remarriage meant that her relationship with her dead husband could be neatly bundled up and labeled "over, finished," seemed facile.

It was Freud's followers rather than Bowlby's who pointed to a way to continue the relationship with the dead while returning to a full, vivid life. They developed the idea that healthy or successful mourning entails an evolving tie with the dead, an internalized connection that could ultimately enrich the ego. At the same time, the mourner is available for a new life – perhaps with another person, perhaps with the remaining family, perhaps involved in a cause or calling. As Therese Rando says, "Death ends a life, but not a relationship." Interestingly, the idea of "continuing bonds," to borrow the title of a 1996 book on the subject, is rather new in the field of bereavement, but not so new in the self-help books. Probably that is because self-help books, although often written by professionals or making use of their findings, stay close to the ground in their reliance on real mourners' anecdotes and reports.

And mourners, whether or not the experts approve, tend to stay in touch with their dead. A man I know whose close friend died suddenly a few years ago lunches regularly with mutual friends, and they always spend considerable time talking about Michael. It's their way of perpetuating their relationship. Another friend who was widowed twenty years ago often remembers her husband in her car. He taught her to drive in the early 1950s, overcoming her youthful timidity, and in traffic she frequently thinks, "Thank you, Harold." The relationship can continue to be strenuous, as the writer Anne Brener's is with her mother. In life she was difficult, and at times Brener struggles with her mother's spirit; at others, their connection flourishes. During one of the thriving times, her husband commented about his long-dead mother-in-law, whom he never knew, "You know, she hasn't been so bad lately."

⌘

"Bereavement is complex," Dennis Klass, a psychologist and specialist in mourning, writes, "for it reaches to the heart of what it means to be human and what it means to have a relationship." It follows that the more inclusive and nuanced the model of mourning in a self-help book, the better. That was what I liked about Therese Rando, whose 1988 book *Grieving* was given the more upbeat title *How to Go On Living When Someone You Love Dies* in subsequent printings. Drawing on ideas from Freud, Bowlby, Melanie Klein (who believed that mourning for one loss rekindled older griefs), and others, she has developed her own generous, humane theory of mourning.

For Rando, "recovery" should be understood as in quotation marks, because in many ways a serious loss never stops being a loss. But even the most searing bereavement can eventually be integrated into an ongoing life. To accomplish that, in Rando's model, the mourner must acknowledge and understand the loss, experience the pain and the fact of the separation, and finally move "adaptively into the new life without forgetting the old." Each one of those steps may involve many parts, both emotional and cognitive: from recognizing and mourning the so-called secondary losses (financial security, grandchildren who will not be born, the family home that must be sold) to adjusting one's "assumptive world" (rethinking beliefs about justice or religion, for example) to achieving a healthy connection with the dead.

These are all what Rando considers appropriate goals. Among the inappropriate goals are being the same person as before the death, having the same life as before the death, either letting go of the dead completely or focusing exclusively on the loss, "getting over it," or achieving "closure" (a word I rarely encountered in the thirty-some mourning guides I read). Mourning is lifelong and never easy but, to borrow the title of Rando's first chapter, "Knowing More Can Help."

It's not always easy to predict which, if any, self-help books will strike the right note. Marilyn Roche, who seemed to know what she needed to do, was annoyed by their platitudes. I sent her *Good Grief* by Deborah Coryell, not a self-help book as such but a series of eloquent essays on grief as a teacher and as an inescapable part of life. Marilyn commented, "It was the only one that made sense to me."

D'Arcy Roche, on the other hand, is less psychologically oriented than his wife. Like many men, he had returned to work and a hectic traveling schedule within a few weeks of the funeral. His instincts were for "putting this behind us" and "getting on with life," while Marilyn felt stunned and unable to think of anything but Scott. They were nearing an impasse common to bereaved parents, where their different styles of grieving were becoming problematic, when D'Arcy's sister sent him three standard self-help books. They taught him a great deal, he says, particularly about the varied forms grief can take, about how his more stoic approach looked to Marilyn and even how normal (but isolating) it was that two parents had separate relationships with and separate bereavements for the same child.

My own favorites included Therese Rando for her soundness, Elizabeth Mehren for her wit. Unexpectedly, one that appealed to me strongly was a workbook, a form I associate with the primary grades in school. *Mourning and Mitzvah*, by Anne Brener, is no ordinary workbook but a learned companion to the intricacies of Jewish mourning and the psychological truth that informs them. In and around some sixty guided exercises, I found all kinds of information and wisdom, for Jew and non-Jew, mourner and non-mourner.

But I found many of these books difficult to read. Partly, I suspected, it was because the subject was painful and the writing and ideas were often banal. A friend happened by while I was reading one and smiled superiorly at "the kind of book that puts the author's academic credentials" on the cover. (The American self-help books do proclaim the author's degrees whenever possible; it is Therese Rando, Ph.D., Nancy O'Connor, Ph.D., Alan Wolfelt, Ph.D. The English edition of *Bereavement: Studies of Grief in Adult Life,* on the other hand, makes no mention of Colin Parkes's M.D. or F.R.C.Psych. on the cover.) Self-help books may not be for the ultrasophisticated, but I did not think that was my problem.

Nor did I find them sentimental or self-indulgent. It's true that Wolfelt's colorful "My Grief Rights" poster, emblazoned with ten rights of bereaved children ("I have the right to show my feelings of grief in my own way") struck me as possibly mawkish or over the top. And I wondered how many children would actually hang it in their room. But, I reminded myself, it was no more bizarre than the mourning pictures and embroideries that decorated 19th-century parlors and work aprons.

Most often, I think, I found self-help books hard going because by the time I read them, the mourner who chiefly concerned me seemed to have figured out the central wisdoms of these books by herself. In March 1998, a kind friend took Hannah to a lecture by the same Alan Wolfelt responsible for the children's grief rights poster. She and the friend agreed that while the presentation was hammy, the content – the standard advice that mourning was hard but compulsory work – was good. But Hannah had been operating on that assumption almost since Scott's death, without benefit of books or lectures.

When I asked her how she had grasped the necessity of wholehearted mourning, her first answer was that she had no choice. Unlike Scott's brothers, who lived far away and could go for months without seeing him, "my entire calendar was wiped out." She talked with him every day and spent every weekend with him; he died a few weeks before he was due to move to Vancouver. Apart from school and a choir rehearsal once a week, she had spent her time with Scott, and now it seemed inevitable that she would use that time to mourn him.

At odds with her sense that mourning was unavoidable was a contrary feeling, which she describes as "paranoia about denial." To my surprise, she connected Scott's death with her childhood sorrow about her parents' divorce. She had never cried about that, never wanted to talk about it until, ten years later, when she was nineteen or twenty, the distress returned, compounded. This time she was determined to avoid a delayed, complicated reaction. "I wanted to do the work," she says, "and have the worst part over."

Again to my surprise, Hannah seems not to have doubted that as long as she grieved, she would eventually feel less miserable. About ten days after Scott's death, she, her friend Ashley, and I were in a pancake house in Vancouver. Hannah was drawn and expressionless; she looked dreadful and ate a fraction of her pancake. Suddenly she said matter-of-factly, "Chances are, I will marry someone else. But Scott's parents have lost a child." My heart leaped. Not only did she have some kind of profound optimism that her life would proceed (a feeling I wasn't sure I shared at the time), but she was not so engulfed in her own tragedy that she could not pity the Roches' appalling loss. Of course, she was not out of the woods. She had barely entered the forest, and months and months of sadness followed. But it was a start.

When I asked Hannah about her favorite reading that first winter and spring, her choice was unexpected: C.S. Lewis's *A Grief Observed*. The English writer and scholar's record of his mourning after his wife's death from cancer is not a self-help book, although it is now shelved in the Grief/Recovery section. It is a diary, and an argument with God about why He permits suffering. Hannah liked the brevity of the diary entries, the day-to-day permutations in Lewis's mood, and, especially, "that he was mad at God."

She did ultimately read the book given to her by Harborview Medical Center, Nancy O'Connor's *Letting Go with Love*, but without much enthusiasm. Three years after I first read it, I returned to it, noting the parts I had underlined. A digest of most of the current thinking on mourning, O'Connor's book sometimes rides roughshod over its complexities, and I frequently found her advice rather glib. On the other hand, the book sets out to speak to all kinds of mourners – and at a time when they are not likely to be reading dense or subtle material.

Although my memory of *Letting Go with Love* was that there wasn't much content there, I saw that I had underlined a fair bit. There were two places where I'd written "Nonsense" in the margin: where O'Connor describes a widow wearing her wedding ring as "a form of denial" ("The ring must go eventually – the sooner the better") and where she predicts that few of the widow's married friends would maintain the friendship. But mostly I had underlined parts that struck me as significant information for Hannah, for me, or for both of us. Generally my underlinings fell into a few, now-familiar categories. The first can be summarized as the assertion that grief is long and painful, but that way lies life. Urging the reader to feel all of the fear, pain, and anguish as they occur, O'Connor promises, "This is the choice that eventually allows you to go on with your life." The second category of underlinings was her reassurance that grief has a progressive course that eventually ends: "*You will survive* and, in time, once more experience joy in living." Those must have been powerfully hopeful words for Hannah's mother, if not for Hannah, in the first weeks after Scott died.

I also underlined descriptions of the different faces of grief: the numbness, the confusion, the anxiety, the fatigue, the sense of physical shock. Occasionally, I would note a piece of advice – the relief that tears bring, the value of keeping a dream log – but more often it would be a description that rang true. There is something salutary or at least confirmatory about the right words in the right order, even when they illustrate something sad. When O'Connor writes of the early weeks after the death of a partner as "a state of acute emotional deprivation," I felt the shock of recognition. That was what I saw every time I looked at Hannah's face. It was terrible, and knowing that someone else understood it enough to describe it accurately was, strangely enough, a help.

At their best, self-help books provide knowledge, and knowledge can allay panic, anxiety, the mourner's conviction that she is losing her mind, and the despairing sense that this pain is endless. At less than their best, they still provide a warming sense that someone comprehends the mourner's turmoil. Even well-intentioned family and friends may become impatient or bored or frustrated with the trajectory of grief. Self-help authors do not. Nor do the authors of memoirs, such as C.S. Lewis, which shows that Barnes & Noble is correct to class *A Grief Observed* with the self-help books. Mourning is an extreme of loneliness, and these disparate books keep the mourner company, even if only briefly, on her long, solitary path.

SEVEN

THE GENDER OF MOURNING

And you over there, yes, *you*, tell me the
story of your Chinese grandmother's duties,

How after seven years she must dig the bones
of her husband's father out of the ground

And wash them one by one in the clear
rain water and lay them to dry in the sun,

While her son's wife kneels down beside her
in the patient air, learning how it's done.

> – Nell Altizer, "The Widow Teaches
> Poetry Writing"

The grandmother in Nell Altizer's poem exhumes, cleans,
and dries her father-in-law's bones, while her daughter-
in-law kneels "in the patient air," learning the important work
of the second, and final, burial. The grandfather and his son,
whose family is being cared for, do not figure in the little scene.

At an Akan funeral in Ghana, women have three serious
functions. In trance, they may become possessed by the dead
person's spirit, walking, talking, or dancing like him and convey-
ing his messages and commands. They sing the memorial dirges,

accompanying them with tears, gestures, and occasionally steps. Less formally, they wail and cry – a significant obligation, since such signs of distress are believed to indicate the worthiness of the dead person, and men are not supposed to weep in public. The Akan female lamenters have counterparts all over the world. Few cultures have male lamenters.

The most extreme discrepancy between male and female bereavement is seen in the Hindu custom of sati (or suttee), in which a widow immolates herself on her husband's funeral pyre. The rationale for sati is that, as the Shuddhitattva, a guide to tantric practice, explains it, a wife should be the same as her husband: "If her husband is happy, she should be happy, if he is sad she should be sad, and if he is dead she should also die." There is no comparable custom for a widower.

Men, of course, are not absent from mourning rituals and customs. The vast majority of ministers, rabbis, pundits, and priests who perform funerals, burials, cremations, and commemorative ceremonies are male. There are cultures where the duties and prohibitions involved in bereavement are fairly equally shared, or where male mourners have particular onerous responsibilities. In Judaism, until recently, only men were obliged (and permitted) to say Kaddish, the prayer of mourning recited daily for roughly a year.

But much more often than not, women are the designated mourners. Until the 20th century in the West, they were the ones who were – depending on your point of view – most tenderly protected or most heavily restricted in bereavement. Nor is it only that women have been more fenced in with rules. At least superficially, it might be said that women are gifted amateurs when it comes to mourning: amateurs in the obvious sense that they have mostly been excluded from the priestly class but, more important, amateurs in the sense of an affectionate inclination. Women, for whatever reason or reasons, appear to have a penchant for mourning.

In North America today, women buy self-help books about grief, attend bereavement support groups, and participate in Internet mourning sites and discussion groups in far larger numbers than men. Bereaved women report greater sadness, more frequent ruminations about the dead person, and a longer period of grieving than men. They accept the idea that grief is a hard, slow process, but one they must not abandon. When I told people what I was writing about, the reactions split dramatically on gender lines. Women would typically respond, "What a wonderful topic." Men were much more likely to express distaste or a wish to distance themselves from the enterprise, often saying sarcastically, "Oh, that's a cheerful subject!"

⌘

> Man's love is of man's life a thing apart,
> 'Tis woman's whole existence.
> – Byron, *Don Juan*

Some of the theories about why mourning is a strongly feminine activity in so many cultures and times are speculative. That people in the earliest societies should have presumed a connection between women and the end of life is plausible. Woman was essential for birth, so why not for death? The gate between life and not-life swings in both directions. Female powers of fertility were revered, and perhaps women possessed other, related gifts: the custom of female keening in Ireland has been linked to a primitive belief in the restorative potency of women's tears.

Other links between women and mourning are less remote. For most of the world's history, death, like the life of a woman, was intensely domestic. It still is in some parts of the world. The body was prepared, waked, and mourned at home, in the heart of the feminine sphere. More than that, death strikes at one's personal relationships. The ancient division of male and female labor had kept women focused on private life, and the loss of someone in the family circle was an affront to a traditional woman's raison d'être.

E.M. Forster eventually grasped something of that when he wrote the biography of his maiden aunt Marianne Thornton. He had chosen her as a subject because she had lived a wholly personal existence, in the bosom of her family, which suited Forster's philosophy of life – or so he imagined. It was when he began reading his aunt's voluminous descriptions of her parents' deaths, which occurred in 1815 when she was eighteen, that he saw a chasm open between her and himself. Stitched into a notebook, the story of the Thorntons' deaths filled over sixty pages in their daughter's tight handwriting – twice as long as a separate memoir, written at age sixty, of her entire life to that point.

It is "not merely wordy," Forster sighs over the account of the father's death, "it is far removed from us in spirit. He was ill. He died. His family and friends were with him. Why cannot his daughter leave it there – keeping the rest in her heart?" Forster's short, declarative sentences and the final bewildered question encapsulate a central divergence between male and female when it comes to grief.

Marianne Thornton could not "leave it there," so Forster combines lengthy (and absorbing) excerpts with paraphrase. Writing in 1956 about a woman who had died in 1887, he attributes his aunt's verbosity to the temper of her time. "On goes her sad narrative," he complains, "gently, relentlessly, as if the spirit of the age, which adored death beds, was speaking through her lips. Nothing is insincere, nothing strained or in bad taste, but on it goes, on . . ."

Forster is right to mark the divide between the 19th and 20th centuries, the first enthralled by death and the second determined to ignore it as much as possible. But there is another divide here, one of gender. Stereotypically, a 19th-century woman and a 20th-century man would not find each other the most kindred of spirits when it came to death. For the most part, Forster runs true to stereotype.

On behalf of Marianne Thornton, it must be said that for an eighteen-year-old with eight younger siblings, the youngest aged five, to lose both parents within a year is no small thing. These deaths were absolutely the most significant events of her long life. Even without the attendant financial and custodial worries, they surely warrant sixty pages of close handwriting. But Forster frets anew about the "super-abundance" of Marianne's description of her mother's death: "The bereaved and their comforters all write enormous letters, symptoms are dwelt upon, dying speeches and death-moments repeated and extended, the Will of God is bowed to again and again, sorrow is so persistently exhibited as joy that both become meaningless. The twentieth-century observer has to remind himself that inside all this cocoonery of words there was love, there was pain. It was the technique of the age and of a section of the middle class; it lasted, as far as my own family were concerned, into the 1850's. After that the tech-nique of mourning shortens, it is now very brief and some sensible people cut out mourning altogether."

Up to that point, Forster voices the rationalist, modernist view of the evolution of mourning. Then, without warning, he veers off that well-trodden path into something more per-ceptive. Of those "sensible people" who eliminate mourning, he continues, "With it they cut down pain, which has practical advantages, and with pain they cut down love. People today love each other from moment to moment as much as ever their ancestors did, but loyalty of soul, such as the elder Thorntons possessed, is on the decrease."

Still chafing at his aunt's prolixity and obsessiveness, Forster grasps the connection: there is no continuing love (or "loyalty of soul") without pain, and eliminating mourning, or pain, means diminishing that kind of love. His aunt's lifelong devotion to her family came with its price, which she paid.

It was a price paid by many women more modern than Marianne Thornton whose lives were circumscribed and defined by their families and intimate friends. Writing about the experience of widows in the mid-20th century, the British psychiatrist Colin Parkes summarizes bluntly, "Husbands occupy a larger part of the life-space of their wives than the wives do of their husbands."

It reads like a clinician's restatement of Byron's line about love, "'Tis woman's whole existence." Parkes's "life-space" has a practical as well as an emotional component. A widow who was economically dependent on her husband, as the great majority of widows have been, could be forced to leave her home, to become dependent on the goodwill of her children, to sink into destitution.

Her chances of remarrying were much smaller than those of a widower of a similar age. In Ludlow, England, in the first half of the 18th century, 40 percent of widowers remarried, compared with only 10 percent of widows. A study of elderly men in 16th-century Norwich, England, indicates that only 5 percent lived without women. Then as now, women outlived men, which meant that the older the age range, the more unequal the sex ratio when it came to remarriage. Elderly widowers often married considerably younger women, which further increased the disparity.

A husband, even an impoverished one, was a desirable commodity in the 19th century, but, while poverty impelled some widowers to remarry, in a widow it was a serious detriment. Age was another drawback for women, as tables of remarriage in 19th-century Britain demonstrate. Widowers over thirty remarried at almost three times the rate of widows of the same age; widowers over fifty remarried at five times the rate of widows over fifty. To Pat Jalland, who studied the letters and diaries of fifty-five middle- and upper-class English families in the Victorian and Edwardian eras, it was clear that widowhood fell much more heavily on a woman than on a man. In a society where girls were brought up to be wives and mothers only, a widow ranked higher than a spinster on the social scale, but much lower than a wife. As Jalland writes, "Widows lost husband, status and occupation simultaneously."

Aside from the greater likelihood of remarriage, the typical widower had another crucial advantage: he had work that supported him financially and occupied his attention. As a rule, Victorian widowers were urged to return to work as soon as possible. When his wife, Therese, died in childbirth in 1863, William Harcourt, a thirty-six-year-old barrister, was utterly forlorn. "Indeed I do very badly without her," he wrote to his mother. "The desolation of this house is quite unbearable to me. I find I am quite unable to form a concise plan of the future. My existence was so mixed up with hers."

For three weeks he stayed at the family's country house, visiting his wife's grave daily, until he looked so ill that his mother-in-law, Lady Lewis, called in the family doctor. His recommendation, as reported by Lady Lewis: "That he should be got into harness and be forced to work in his profession as the *only* remedy or rather palliation to his present state." Therese's brother concurred, writing to Harcourt that staying in the country might encourage "your learning to love your sorrow instead of bearing it . . . We have in this world to rub so much against our fellows that we must get our wounds healed as quickly as we can."

The counsel Harcourt received (which he took, returning to his law practice a little more than four weeks after his wife's death) is a good example of the differing expectations for women and men. Jalland observes, "Victorian widows were never advised to 'get our wounds healed as quickly as we can,' nor warned of the danger of 'learning to love your sorrow instead of bearing it.' Widows were usually advised to pray, to rest, and to resign themselves to the will of God; if that prescription took many months of sad contemplation and grave-visiting, their families did not find it necessary to sound the alarm. What was considered self-indulgent for men was required therapy for women, for many of whom it seems to have been more helpful than not."

Faced with a society in which almost half of marriages would end with one spouse's death within twenty-five years, in which satisfying work outside the home was virtually unknown for women and remarriage for a widow unlikely, and in which bereaved women were encouraged to dwell on their losses, small wonder that mourning became a notably feminine province. The situation of the 19th- and early-20th-century English women Jalland describes was paralleled in many other times and places, and not limited to widows. For a traditional woman whose life centered on her family, to mourn, and mourn deeply, was often an eminently sensible reaction.

⌘

The particular shape of a woman's life made intensive mourning a predictable outcome, but feminist historians suspected something less neutral and potentially sinister. They saw in mourning customs an attempt to control women, particularly their sexuality. It is true that, as mourning practices and schedules became heavier in 19th-century Europe and its colonies, they were accompanied by a growing discomfort with the idea of widows remarrying. It was most often expressed by praising the "loyal" widow who remained one forever, with, after 1861, Britain's Queen Victoria as the most exalted example.

Etiquette books stressed that, even when it was officially permissible for a widow to move from lusterless crape to something with a hint of shine, or from black to grey, white, and lavender, it was more seemly if she delayed for some days or weeks. The woman who had truly loved her husband, it was believed, clung to her mourning clothes. The thought of signaling by her clothing that she was available for courting filled her not with alacrity but with dismay. Shrouding the widow in a thick, malodorous fog of crape and hampering her way out of mourning with numerous niceties of timing and attitude must have encouraged some of them to think that it would be far simpler and more "natural" to live forever secluded and in black.

From the innuendos and social pressure, however stifling, of 19th-century Britain to the most horrendous of fates for the widow – sati – seems a great leap, but it was not necessarily so for the Victorians. Sati was much on their minds, since it had been outlawed in Bengal only in 1829, after much public agonizing, by Governor General Lord William Cavendish Bentinck. It remained a grisly low point in the treatment of widows, and it became almost commonplace among 19th-century progressives to criticize the excesses of mourning garb as a "symbolic" sati.

India is not the only place where widows perished as part of their husbands' funeral ceremonies. Sometimes they died, as did slaves and pets, so that the husband would not be deprived of his pleasures in the next world; sometimes so that other men would not enjoy the widow; sometimes so that the widow would not enjoy other men. There are records of widow sacrifice in the dim past in Scandinavian countries and in Egypt; in New Zealand, Africa, the Fiji Islands, and among the American Indians before the missionaries came. In China, widows who remarried were considered unchaste, but if they committed suicide, honorary gateways were built to commemorate them.

But sati holds a special place in the Western imagination, partly because the British in India enumerated and closely observed widow burnings, and partly because the custom stubbornly persists. The first Westerners to record it were

Alexander the Great's soldiers in the Punjab in the 4th century B.C.; twenty-five hundred years later, there are still sporadic reports of sati.

Although its advocates claim it as a doctrine of Hinduism, there is no scriptural authority for sati that is not negated by an equally valid edict. What can be traced with more clarity, beginning about the 5th century B.C., is a tragic narrowing of possibilities for the Hindu widow. The rise of Buddhism with its stress on asceticism, unrest in Indian society, and foreign invasions all played their part. The greater the upheavals, the more instances of sati. By 700 A.D., the orthodox view, expressed by the sage Angirasa, was: "For all women, there is no other duty except falling into the funeral pyre when the husband died."

The motives advanced for sati are plentiful, almost bewilderingly so. The husband benefited enormously, because his wife's act was believed to atone for his misdeeds. Even if he had committed the sin of sins, killing a Brahmin, the wife who immolated herself purified him. Conversely, according to Angirasa, failure to perform sati carried a grievous threat for a woman: "As long as a woman does not burn herself on the death of her husband, she is never free from rebirth as a woman." Sati allowed a woman to atone for her own sins as well as her husband's. That was important because a widow had clearly committed a sin in a previous life that merited this heaviest of punishments – the death of her husband, her God on earth. Other, less exalted motives included protecting vulnerable Hindu women from so-called lawless Muslims and deterring wives from poisoning their husbands. Even less highminded was the fact that sati enabled the widow's children or in-laws to keep her dowry or inheritance or, at least, save the cost of her upkeep.

Another incentive, for a woman, was the knowledge that the life of a Hindu widow was miserable in the extreme. Completely at the mercy of her eldest son, often limited to one meal a day and deprived of a bed, she shaved her head and wore clothes of penitential white. As an inauspicious person, her presence was unacceptable at a family celebration or ritual. She was not permitted to leave the house, not even to draw water. A woman might well prefer the temporary pain of sati to a lifetime of unhappiness.

It seems safe to say that most women who indicated their intention to die on their husband's pyre were not interviewed about their motives by Indians. The few whose comments were recorded were typically questioned by Britons, and the women tended to reiterate the prevailing belief in atonement and the pointlessness of life without a husband. One such interrogator was Richard Hartley Kennedy, the surgeon to the British residency – the colonial administration – at Baroda. In 1825, he witnessed the cremation of a Brahmin businessman he had known and the immolation of his wife, Ambabai.

The British resident had already failed to dissuade Ambabai; although she was tired from attending her dying husband and from the required day-long fast before sati, she walked steadily to the place of execution. Kennedy made one last attempt to change her mind, but "her look of reply was quite sufficient; she had not come without counting the cost . . . She looked forward, without a doubt, to secure for herself and her husband, by the sacrifice, a new life of happier existence." Even jesting at one point with Kennedy about the curiosity with which he surveyed the scene, Ambabai impressed him with her sublime "loftiness of manner" and the "glowing enthusiasm of her mind." As the flames overwhelmed the pyre, Kennedy retreated as slowly as he could, looking for any sights or sounds of agony: "I do not think that either took place." Ambabai's round, amiable face had looked to Kennedy as if it was designed for mirth. She was about thirty years of age.

But all these reasons – noble, ignoble, addressed to men or addressed to women – did not loom large when the Indian opponents of sati presented a "Hindoo Congratulatory address" to Governor General Bentinck after abolition. The Hindu gentlemen left no doubt about the real motive for widow burning, as they saw it. "Excessive jealousy of their female connections," they wrote, "operating on the breasts of Hindu princes rendered those despots regardless of the common bonds of society and of their incumbent duty as protectors of the weaker sex." Determined to "prevent every possibility of their widows forming subsequent attachments, they availed themselves of their arbitrary powers and under cloak of religion introduced the practice of burning widows alive under the first impressions of sorrow." In other words, sati was, as the Indian writer Sakuntala Narasimhan puts it, "the ultimate chastity belt."

The spectacular pomp of the funeral procession had several deliberate parallels with the wedding ceremony. Dressed in bridal luxury, the sati (the term refers to both the deed and the woman who performs it) signified her decision to die by dipping her hand in the red or yellow stain used to decorate brides' hands and leaving an eloquent handprint on the lintel as she left her house. (The prints decorated houses for years, a source of pride for the family. In 1879, there were thirty-seven in the Bikanir palace still plainly visible, with many more faded or otherwise indistinct.) As she proceeded to the pyre, the sati, already considered a deity, distributed food or coins to the onlookers. Because it is bad luck to hear the sati cry out in panic or pain, once the pyre was lit, the crowds screamed "Victory" to drown out any less joyful sounds. In the same vein, the sati's flailing arms were regularly interpreted as blessing the crowd rather than imploring for rescue.

The advocates of sati insisted that women eagerly volunteered for the privilege. Its opponents, Indian and Western, amassed stories of drugged women and of restraints, often made of bamboo scaffolding, used to prevent women from leaving the pyre; when these measures failed, critics said, families forcibly returned a terrified woman to the pyre. But whether a sati perished stoically or in hysterical fear hardly matters. They were all, as a writer in the *Calcutta Review* put it in 1867, "morally if not physically drugged."

Even in its heyday, sati never affected more than a tiny minority of one country. But, although the 7,941 women burned to death in Bengal from 1815 to 1829 represented a small percentage of the population, the number is staggering. (The figure is not comprehensive, representing only those satis the British were able to record.) The death of one woman by sati, in fact, is appalling. Although the real numbers will never be known, it is estimated that at least forty satis have taken place since India became independent in 1947.

The excitement and satisfaction that sati brings to some persists, as the story of Roop Kanwar demonstrates. What was unexpected in this case was its rapid and long-lasting glorification. Roop Kanwar was an attractive eighteen-year-old woman who had been married to a twenty-four-year-old university graduate, Mal Singh, for eight months. They lived in the village of Deorala, in the state of Rajasthan; he died suddenly on September 3, 1987, apparently of gastroenteritis. On September 4, attended by a crowd that numbered in the thousands, his wife climbed onto his funeral pyre and died in the flames that cremated him.

The site of the sati, in the middle of the village, almost instantly became known to villagers as the "temple." Within ten days, news of the sati had spread as far as New Delhi. Ten thousand pilgrims arrived daily in anticipation of the ritual that takes place thirteen days after cremation, called the *chunari*, while souvenir sellers hawked incense, coconuts, toys, snacks, and a composite picture of the couple. Made from photographs taken in life, it showed a beatifically smiling Roop Kanwar holding her dead husband's head on her lap, encircled by flames. The same image was used to produce posters and statues. The couple's house, especially their bedroom, was transformed into a secondary shrine.

Roop Kanwar's parents, who lived two hours' drive from Deorala, in Jaipur, learned of their daughter's immolation only after it was over, in the local Hindi newspaper. Nevertheless, they apparently joined in the general exaltation. A relative declared, "She has blessed the family for seven generations before and after." The *Jansatta*, a large-circulation newspaper, dismissed the storm of protest from India's feminist movement. "Out of hundreds of thousands of widows perhaps one would resolve on a sati. It is quite natural that her self-sacrifice should become the centre of reverence and worship. This therefore cannot be called a question of women's civil rights or sexual discrimination. It is a matter of a society's religious and social beliefs."

The question of Kanwar's intentions is now impossible to settle. The official story, told by her in-laws and seemingly accepted by her parents, is that, despite their attempts to dissuade her, she willingly chose to die, dressing as a bride and ceremoniously bestowing bits of her finery on the crowd on the way to the pyre. An opposed version has her hiding in a barn when she heard about the plans for sati and frantically thrashing her arms as the flames engulfed her. The historian Veena Talwar Oldenburg has compiled a plausible "counternarrative" in which Mal Singh's parents engineered a sati that made them the inheritors of their daughter-in-law's quite substantial dowry. If Kanwar had not immolated herself, it would have returned with her to her parents' house after the death of her husband.

But, as Oldenburg and other Indian feminists note, even if it could be proved beyond a shadow of a doubt that Roop Kanwar went knowingly and deliberately to her death, she was at most a puppet of an internalized ideology, not an agent. That ideology remains dismayingly robust. It is alarming that in 1987 a schoolteacher – Mal Singh's father – could be part of a sati, or that his fifteen-year-old son could light a pyre that held his living sister-in-law; alarming that Roop Kanwar's parents, an urban businessman and his wife, acquiesced so mildly in their eighteen-year-old's fate.

For every anti-sati article that appeared in an Indian paper or magazine in the months-long controversy, a pro-sati piece was published, usually couched in terms of traditional Hindu values. In 1990, three years after Kanwar died, the site of her death was attracting about a hundred visitors on ordinary days and five times as many on special days. Women in traditional Rajasthani attire regularly prostrated themselves before the platform, asking for the benediction of Roop Kanwar, the *sati mata* (Mother Sati).

The silver lining in the Roop Kanwar case was the mobilization of India's feminists. United as never before, women's groups organized rallies and marches, insisting that Rajiv Gandhi's government intervene in the Roop Kanwar cult. These women were instrumental in the arrest of Kanwar's father-in-law and two brothers-in-law and in the passing of new legislation that prohibits the glorification of sati as well as sati itself. Unfortunately, the Kanwar case stalled, probably for ever, and the new statute is far from perfect. But the celebration of sati does seem, for the first time, hemmed round with genuine difficulties, and Indian feminists are unlikely to keep silent in the event of a similar case.

Sati is the extreme example of a mourning practice foisted on one sex by the other. But the extreme is worth thinking about, since it can shine a bright light on the ordinary. The motive for sati may be sexual jealousy, but the rationale advanced for it has to do with the nature of true womanhood, true wifely affection, and true mourning. It is a repellent, distorted ideal, but it has had an insidious staying power.

The kindly 19th-century Englishman who hoped in his secret heart that his widow would not remarry would have been horrified at being compared to a murderously jealous Hindu despot. The lengths they were willing to go to varied tremendously, but under the skin, the Hindu and the Anglican might each have understood the other's wish not to be replaced.

And because it is hard even for the most sophisticated to distinguish between what society tells them they should feel and what they really feel, the English widow enveloped in bombazine and the Hindu widow in her wedding sari might each have had an inkling of what the other was going through. The first was at worst cribbed, cabined, and confined by the expectations of the other sex, while the second lost her life. The distance between their fates was vast, but they were on the same continuum.

⌘

> A man must partly give up being a man
> With women-folk . . .
> . . . .
> Let me into your grief. I'm not so much
> Unlike other folks as your standing there
> Apart would make me out. Give me my chance.
> I do think, though, you overdo it a little.
> – Robert Frost, "Home Burial"

Most people before about 1950 would have had no difficulty with the title of this chapter. Of course "the gender of mourning" referred to women, they would have said. Theirs is the tender-hearted sex, which takes human connections more seriously than men. "Woman is more compassionate than man," Aristotle wrote, "more easily moved to tears." Clearly she was designed by Nature to mourn more than a man.

Lately, many Westerners have been at pains to disbelieve if not disprove that notion. They see accepting that stereotype as another impediment to women taking their place at the head of board tables, or men taking their place at a baby's changing table or a kitchen counter. The sooner we see most if not all emotional differences between males and females as the result of misguided socialization, their thinking runs, the sooner we can live in a non-sexist world. In that spirit, the self-help books about mourning, which began appearing in the late 1970s, mostly assume that men and women go about grieving in the same way. Sometimes the books include a few paragraphs, a section, or even a chapter about masculine tendencies or problems (excessive use of alcohol being a common one). But by and large, there is one way to mourn, and it is an expressive way.

In 1991, *Men and Grief* appeared, by a writer and bereavement consultant named Carol Staudacher. Although she had been inspired by a bereaved father who insisted, "Men don't grieve the same way women do," Staudacher describes the work of mourning in the same terms as other self-help books: "Simply put," she writes, using italics for emphasis, *"there is really only one way to grieve.* That way is to go through the core of grief." Going through the core of grief means "thinking about, talking about, crying about, and often writing about the reactions and emotions provoked or unveiled by the death."

At the same time, Staudacher describes the male mourner as someone who typically doesn't want to talk about the loss, wants to be alone, takes physical or legal action, or becomes otherwise immersed in activity. But, given her theory, this behavior is a problem. Underneath the stereotypic strong, silent male mourner, Staudacher sees a feeling person who needs encouragement to express his emotions. Work and other activities are avoidance tactics; venting and pining are the roads to healing.

Tom Golden's *Swallowed by a Snake: The Gift of the Masculine Side of Healing*, published in 1996 and revised in 2000, makes many of the familiar distinctions between the male and female ways of grieving. But Golden, a Jungian psychotherapist, stresses that everyone has both a masculine and a feminine side. For him, the masculine way – again, focused on cognition, action, and looking to the future rather than verbalizing, seeking support, and dwelling on the past – is not a predicament. It's simply the masculine way. In the tradition of Robert Bly and

Sam Keen, Jungians who concentrate on a man's special vulnerabilities and powers, Golden wants to channel a mourning man's strengths into ritual, which is a focused and heightened kind of action.

Terry Martin and Kenneth Doka approach the male mourner from a different and ultimately revolutionary position. In the course of their work in bereavement (Martin is a psychologist and Doka a professor of gerontology and a Lutheran minister), they began to suspect that the prevailing model of grief was doing a disservice to men, effacing their natural inclinations and compounding their loss. Probably because it is not a domain in which men have taken much interest, the characteristically feminine way of mourning has become the gold standard, one of the very few instances in our society where the female pattern prevails.

In *Men Don't Cry . . . Women Do*, which appeared in 2000, Martin and Doka describe two styles of mourning. The "intuitive" way is emotional, expressive, and prone to seek support from others. The "instrumental" style is cognitive, non-verbal, active, and private. The first describes the typical female mourner; the second the so-called masculine pattern. But some men react to loss in the intuitive style, and some women in an instrumental way, so the labels refer to mode rather than gender. It remains true, however, that the majority of women are intuitive mourners, and most men are instrumental mourners.

Controversially, Martin and Doka don't see either of these modes as more effective than the other. The mourner who weeps copiously, retreats into inactivity, and dwells on the past is no more guaranteed a successful outcome than the mourner who doesn't talk about the loss and concentrates on the headstone or setting up a scholarship fund or simply returning to work as soon as possible. Although this belief is heresy to the pro-expressive writers of self-help books, bereavement counselors and educators, as well as the relatively limited research done on the subject, corroborate Martin and Doka's stand. Each style has its potential pitfalls (health problems, including alcohol abuse, and so-called complicated, or frustrated, mourning for the instrumental mourner; depression and chronic mourning for the intuitive griever), but most mourners of whatever stripe eventually return to normal functioning. Trouble comes, in Martin and Doka's experience, with societal expectations that you should mourn one way, when your inclinations run in a different direction. Trouble also comes, sadly, when two people mourn the same loss so differently that they alienate rather than console each other.

Robert Frost wrote "Home Burial" in 1913, inspired to some extent by the death of his own little boy in 1900. A vivid dramatization of a couple's grief for their child, the poem has an added dimension in Martin and Doka's terms: it pits the intuitive mourner against the instrumental. Told largely in dialogue, "Home Burial" is set in a farmhouse where a baby boy has recently died. The wife stands brooding, as she frequently does, at the upstairs window. Her husband comes upon her and suddenly realizes why she stands there so often — the window overlooks the family plot where their baby lies buried.

She cries out that he is "blind" not to have noticed this, and he agrees ruefully, "My words are nearly always an offence." But he plows on, trying to break through her sullen misery and only making things worse. Clumsily he asks: "What was it brought you to think it the thing / to take your mother-loss of a first child / So inconsolably."

In her turn, the wife upbraids him:

> If you had any feelings, you that dug
> With your own hand — how could you? — his little grave;
> I saw you from that very window there,
> Making the gravel leap and leap in air,
> Leap up, like that, like that, and land so lightly
> And roll back down the mound beside the hole.
> I thought, who is that man? I didn't know you.

Unable to comprehend his purposeful activity at such a time, she watched in horror as he returned to the company in the kitchen, "with the stains on your shoes / Of the fresh earth from your own baby's grave," and talked about everyday affairs.

> I can repeat the very words you were saying,
> "Three foggy mornings and one rainy day
> Will rot the best birch fence a man can build."
> Think of it, talk like that at such a time!
> What had how long it takes a birch to rot
> To do with what was in the darkened parlour.

It is the classic chasm between grieving parents: she feels he doesn't care, and he feels she cares too much. She, the intuitive griever, is baffled and hurt by her husband's ability to function and to control his feelings in public. He, the instrumental griever, does what needs to be done – digging the grave, continuing to support the family – and sees his wife as melodramatic and self-centered.

When the wife begins crying, the husband says (infuriatingly but probably not inaccurately), "There, you have said it all and you feel better." As she goes to the door, seeking a sympathetic ear, he tries to stop her because someone is coming down the road. She accuses him of caring most about what the neighbors think, and the poem ends a stalemate. Each is isolated in a solitary grief, the wife angry, the husband puzzled and resentful. The title "Home Burial" suggests the death of their marriage as well as their child.

Frost's poem is a particularly detailed look at two modes of responding to loss, but once the distinction between intuitive and instrumental has been raised, examples will occur to everyone. Inundated by her feelings in the early days of her widowhood, Queen Victoria was an intuitive mourner. So, as Martin and Doka note, is Wilbur, the pig in E.B. White's book *Charlotte's Web*. When he learned about Charlotte's oncoming death, Wilbur "threw himself down in an agony of pain and sorrow. Great sobs racked his body. He heaved and grunted with desolation. 'Charlotte,' he moaned, 'Charlotte! My true friend!' "

Dave Eggers follows a different path. *A Heartbreaking Book of Staggering Genius,* one of the most talked-about literary debuts of recent years, is a memoir of the aftermath of his parents' deaths. He was twenty-one when his mother and father died within thirty-two days of each other. After moving accounts of their illnesses and deaths, I expected that Eggers, an expressive, occasionally manic narrator, would describe his feelings as a mourner. He doesn't.

In the family division of labor, he becomes the caretaker for his seven-year-old brother, Toph. His sister, Beth, a law student, is "always pulling out old photo albums, crying, asking Toph how he feels," but Eggers concerns himself with the antic, haphazard business of keeping his little brother clothed, fed, educated, and amused. A friend described the book as more about the life of a single parent than about a mourner. But I was frustrated, wanting to learn more about the narrator's bereavement. In fact I was learning about it: Eggers's mourning is his raising of Toph. He is a classic instrumental griever, adapting to his new reality by focusing on activity and the present, not on emoting or the past.

Fred Alger sounds like another instrumental mourner. On September 11, 2001, he was living in semiretirement in Switzerland, and the business he had founded, Fred Alger Management, was located in the World Trade Center. Returning to New York to pull his company together after the disaster, he described his situation later in September: "I lost my younger brother. One grieves. There are moments when you stop to reflect on it. Your eyes well up with tears. But those moments pass, and you get back to doing whatever it is you do. We call it the Alger Way of Doing Things: Knowing your job and doing it as well as it can be done."

Even Alger's use of the impersonal pronoun – "One grieves" – and of the word *reflect* – instrumental mourners are more comfortable using cognitive words like *think* and *reflect* rather than *feel* – points to a man who mourns by "doing whatever it is you do."

Presumably, Freud's belief in the necessity of separating slowly and deliberately from the dead applied to grievers of whatever style, although more might be evident with an intuitive mourner. When his father died in 1896, Freud reacted to what he called "the most important event, the most poignant loss, of a man's life" with distraction, inattention, and a sense of being uprooted – reactions that sound like those of an intuitive mourner. But when his dearly loved daughter Sophie died suddenly of influenzal pneumonia at twenty-six in 1920, he responded with activity. Resuming his long hours of work quickly, he wrote to a friend that he was "grateful for the distraction . . . As for mourning, that will no doubt come later." To another friend, he reported, "Apart from feeling rather more tired I am the same. The death, painful as it is, does not affect my attitude towards life."

True to the profile of the instrumental mourner, who tends to think about the meaning of the loss rather than surrender to uncontrollable waves of feeling, Freud mused:

> Since I am profoundly irreligious there is no one I can accuse, and I know there is nowhere to which any complaint can be addressed. "The unvarying circle of a soldier's duties" and the "sweet habit of existence" will see to it that things go on as before. Quite deep down I can trace the feeling of a deep narcissistic hurt that is not to be healed. My wife and Annerl are terribly shaken in a more human way.

Although he points to the "more human" grief of his wife and daughter Annerl (Anna), Freud did not escape lightly.

His inkling about his own deep hurt proved to be correct. Nine years after Sophie's death, he wrote that the loss had left him inconsolable: "And actually this is how it should be. It is the only way of perpetuating that love which we do not want to relinquish."

As might be expected, few people fit completely into the intuitive or instrumental category; most exist at some point on the spectrum, closer to the affective or cognitive end. Those who balance emotional and intellectual reactions most evenly are called blended mourners, which is how Marilyn Roche struck me. Marilyn missed and longed for and idealized Scott. She cried easily and often about him. At the same time, she oversaw the details of readying Scott's house for sale and selling it; she dealt with the complications of estate and insurance and made sure that some of Scott's funds paid Hannah's tuition, as he would have wished. It was Marilyn who supervised the funding and planning of the Scott Roche water polo tournament to be held annually at her son's high school.

D'Arcy Roche and their four sons fell, with variations, more clearly into the instrumental camp. They returned quickly to their work and regular lives and resisted much talk about their sorrow. Marilyn could feel piercingly lonely when she wanted to talk about the loss of Scott and they were willing to remember him fondly and with amusement, but apparently without pain.

The Roche family survived their sometimes dissonant styles, probably because they knew they all loved Scott. Marilyn had to adjust her natural bent more than the others, but, having lived with six males, it wasn't the first time she had done that. D'Arcy had to temper his wish that those he loved would not brood overmuch. It was D'Arcy who had pointed out to me after the funeral that the six years Hannah and Scott had been sweethearts represented a quarter of her life. And yet, when I talked with Marilyn and him that first Easter, he asked affectionately about Hannah, "Is she putting this behind her?"

I can't remember whether I or Marilyn or both of us breathed in exasperation, "D'Arcy!" And the good-natured man, already on his way to being colonized by the intuitive grievers in his midst, said immediately, "I put that very badly. I meant, is she coping with medical school?"

True to his instrumental bent, D'Arcy found an active and symbolically apt way to remember his son. When Scott climbed Mount Rainier, he accomplished it as he did most things, with minimal training and youthful luck. For a man in his sixties, Mount Rainier is a significant challenge, but in late 1999, D'Arcy began the arduous training to climb the mountain in honor of Scott. His ascent, in the fall of 2000, as close as possible to the date of Scott's climb, was made in hazardous weather. The younger men dropped off, but D'Arcy did not.

D'Arcy is not the only male in the family with a gift for the symbolic gesture. When Matthew Roche got married in the fall of 1999, he asked Hannah to be in the wedding party. But not as a bridesmaid – he wanted her to stand in for Scott, as one of the groomsmen. Guests who did not know her wondered why Hannah, wearing the same slim, silvery grey outfit as the bridesmaids, ushered people to their seats and took her place with the surviving brothers, Sean, Jamie, and Stephan, by the groom's side. It was an off-kilter, haunting sight, and one Scott would have relished.

The Roches bought a weekend beach house in their son's memory. Marilyn sometimes calls it the "Scott house," which it is in more than one sense. The group that gathers there as often as possible now includes several grandchildren, and each brother has named at least one child after the uncle who died before they were born: Alexander Scott Roche, Courtenay (one of Scott's middle names) Roche, Caroline Scott Roche, Samuel Scott Roche, and Scott Emerson Roche. Scott's brothers may not feel comfortable dwelling on their loss, but their children who carry his name are a powerful consolation for

Marilyn. In Martin and Doka's terms, this family has found a harmony between the expressive and the active, the emotional and the cognitive.

Probably few readers would quarrel with Martin and Doka's description of mourning styles, although their belief that successful grieving does not need to be expressive cuts against the grain of current thinking. But Martin and Doka have another bombshell, perhaps more shocking because they express it quietly. Their portrait of the instrumental griever includes the belief that his or her feelings are "simply less intense" than those of the intuitive mourner. Using a color metaphor, they write that the intuitive mourner typically feels grief in intense, rich colors while the instrumental mourner experiences sadness in pastels. The emotion is more tempered, which makes the instrumental mourner more distractible and more capable of mastering his or her moods.

Martin and Doka state it matter-of-factly, but it is nonetheless startling. In other words, contrary to what you read in the self-help books, the strong, silent type doesn't need to learn how to express his feelings; he may not have many intense feelings that demand expression. Calmly, Martin and Doka voice one of women's deepest fears about men – that they don't care as much – and confirm it.

It's important, though, to understand that for Martin and Doka, grief is not necessarily feeling. For the intuitive griever, the experience of bereavement *is* largely about feelings, but in Martin and Doka's understanding, grief is an energy, a task, and a process of adapting to an unwanted reality. Feeling may figure in that more or less prominently. To say that the instrumental griever doesn't feel as intensely doesn't mean he doesn't grieve. He may do it cognitively (trying to understand what the death has meant to the family, for example), through activity (which often involves taking over some of the household responsibilities temporarily abandoned by the intuitive mourner), or through spirituality.

What he or she can't do very often is cry, dwell on the past, or talk about feelings, especially when they aren't very prominent. Kenneth Doka is the author of another important book, *Disenfranchised Grief: Recognizing Hidden Sorrow*, about the circle each society draws around the "true" mourners, leaving others – adulterous lovers, gay partners, friends, for example – out in the cold. Doka believes that a mourning style can also disenfranchise the griever, particularly the instrumental style. Both male and female instrumental mourners have difficulties in our communicative society: the woman with a stiff upper lip because she is an oddity, the man because he is unfairly supposed to be strong and expressive at the same time.

What makes one person an instrumental mourner, another intuitive, another blended? Individual personality is an obvious determinant. Sometimes the nature of the loss is a factor, as with Freud, who mourned intuitively for his father, more instrumentally for his daughter. The emotional tenor of a culture influences mourning styles. It would be sensible to expect more intuitive grievers in the openly emotional Mediterranean world than in the relatively self-contained societies of northern Europe.

But the "feeling rules" of a culture can shift over time, and human emotions are more malleable than sometimes supposed. English men in the 17th and 19th centuries were floridly emotional. It was more than possible to weep and talk at length about one's feelings; it was admired. In the 19th century, when a man had to leave a concert of sad songs, retreating to sob in another room, it was not considered strange. In between these peaks of emotionalism, in the 18th and 20th centuries, a cooler, drier, more understated Englishman was in vogue. No doubt the prevalence of instrumental versus intuitive mourners waxed and waned according to the currents of the age.

Clearly social conditioning has favored male instrumental mourners and female intuitive mourners. When a team of psychologists and students of the family surveyed the grieving practices of sixty societies in the 1970s, they found that slightly more than half of the societies expected that the sexes would weep to the same extent. The remainder (twenty-eight out of sixty) allowed women more leeway than men when it came to crying. They did not find a single society where men were expected to cry more than women.

Even so, the change in permissible behavior, especially for women, has been enormous in the last half-century. Ruth Harley, the mother of my late friend Sandra Gwyn, is a case in point. When Ruth's first husband died, in St. John's in the 1940s, Newfoundlanders still adhered to the old-fashioned belief that women were too frail to attend funerals and burials. Sandra always remembered staying home with her mother on the day of her father's funeral.

In time, Ruth remarried, and when her second husband died, in Ottawa in the 1970s, she attended the funeral. Tragically, her son Nick Fraser died in the late 1990s, when Ruth was in her late eighties. I watched her at the funeral, sitting in front of her son's coffin, and thought that this woman had seen too many bereavements. When her daughter-in-law Danielle Fraser mounted the pulpit, something else impressed me: how strikingly the definition of what a widow can bear has changed in Ruth Harley's lifetime. Wearing a dramatic black picture hat, Danielle described a well-loved and difficult husband who had never achieved what he hoped to. She ended with a line from Eric Clapton: "He was smooth, he was rough / He was more than enough."

Far from being too delicate to attend the funeral, Danielle wrote and delivered a eulogy no one who heard it will ever forget. Ruth Harley, who acquiesced to her society's convictions about "human nature" when her first husband died, lived to see quite another possibility. The feeling rules do shape us, but they and we are capable of change.

Mourning styles may also owe a lot or a little to biology. Noting the higher rates of depression in women after a death or divorce, a Toronto psychiatrist named Barbara Dorian has speculated that women's brains may be hardwired to take attachment and the rupture of attachment more profoundly than men. It makes obvious evolutionary sense for a sex traditionally charged with child-rearing and would plausibly lead to high numbers of female intuitive mourners. Similarly, instrumental men who could control their feelings and continue fighting while their mates and family fall in battle, or return to the hunt after a death in the family, would have a clear survival advantage.

On the face of it, since our frames, voices, and reproductive systems are different, it should not seem surprising that our emotional makeup might be too. Some suggestive brain research has been done on the subject, although so far without very compelling findings. But speculating that male and female brains are designed differently makes educated 21st-century people uncomfortable, raising, as it does, worrying political consequences. A few tentative voices are beginning the discussion, and it remains an intriguing possibility.

Ironically, although Martin and Doka are at pains to dismantle gender stereotypes, the effect of the book, for me at least, tended to confirm them. Reading it, I thought of a couple whose very close friend died. The wife reported, "I went into the bathroom and cried and cried. Bob went to his computer and began writing the eulogy." I remembered a psychological study of boys in Grade Five that concluded they considered talking about problems or worries in relationships simply "a waste of time" – not painful, not hard, not frightening, just beside the point. Of this research, a friend with a ten-year-old son said, "Yes! I've partially indoctrinated my husband, who now reluctantly accepts that we have to talk about our relationship occasionally, but Max is still unreconstructed male. He can't think of anything less interesting than feelings." I recalled my father's description of the funeral of a good friend's wife. The husband, children, and several grandchildren all spoke, and tears flowed. It sounded emotional, sorrowful, cathartic. My father, the warmest of family men, chose another word: "draining."

Counterexamples sprang to mind, too – the acquaintance who returned to her busy law practice within days after her mother's death, because "my mother brought me up to be responsible, and attending to my responsibilities is honoring her memory"; her husband, who still devotes considerable time to thinking and talking about the loss of a sister, now some years in the past. But overall, Martin and Doka's thesis reminded me of the Bara in Madagascar, who divide mourners into two buildings, the women to weep over the body in the "house of many tears" and the men to receive restrained visits of condolence and to make the funeral arrangements in the "house of men." Or of the Old Believers in Russia, who assigned the male mourners to make the coffin and tell stories, while the women cried and lamented.

My generation assumed we could dismantle those rigid divisions of labor, and it is humbling to acknowledge that the foundation looks sturdier than we supposed. Which doesn't deny that some men do want to stare at a wall and weep, while some mourning women would love to get their hands on a hammer and nails. And even if the majority of men and women run true to type, Martin and Doka have done a valuable service in concentrating so even-handedly on mourning style and its ineluctability. Will it help a mourner bewildered if not alienated by a partner's differing response to realize that it's probably as difficult to shift as eye color? Perhaps, a bit. Would it remove a cruel burden if an intuitive griever didn't have to hide his tears, and an instrumental one wasn't constantly being nudged by her friends to talk about her feelings? Absolutely.

Besides, mourning is not a single thing; it is a whole constellation of reactions and behaviors and tasks. The Bara may have been on the right track with their idea of houses, but there's no need to stop at two, and no need to separate them by sex. There's more than enough work here for two genders.

EIGHT

SAD CLOTHES

My poor sad face & garb *must* tell its tale.
— Queen Victoria (1864)

As a small boy in Edwardian England, Geoffrey Gorer identified those who had lost a loved one by their clothes. Whether the woman swathed in dull black or the man wearing an armband waited on him in a shop or was a guest in his house, the boy knew that he was to be particularly quiet and not fidget in their presence. "As children we learned that mourners were in a special situation or state of mind," Gorer writes, "and had to be treated differently from others, with more consideration and more respect." When his father died on the *Lusitania* in 1915, the ten-year-old boy had bands of crape sewn on his sleeves and was given black ties to wear at his school. He felt, as he says, distinguished: "I was set apart, and this was somehow fitting and comforting."

The distinguishing of the mourner by an altered appearance — whether with special colors, garments, or hairstyles or with specially painted or mutilated faces or parts of the body — was something the adult anthropologist Geoffrey Gorer came to know as part of virtually every human society. "Ma's sad cap" was how Queen Victoria's youngest child, Princess Beatrice, described her widowed mother's tulle headgear, and sad caps and other such distinctive attire have marked the griever all over the world and for a long time.

At one level their variety is enormous. On his first voyage to New Zealand, Captain James Cook noticed that Maori widows wore wreaths of rushes and bird feathers, sometimes decorated with birds' bills and heads. Mourning women in ancient Greece sometimes wore a man's mantle, presumably to indicate a disregard for their appearance. Palestinian women cover the bright coins in their headdresses. Bereaved men in New Caledonia stop cutting their hair and wear turbans made from bark.

Even the color of mourning varies. "We mourn in black," the Duke of Exeter says in *Henry VI, Part 1* – largely but not entirely true in the West until recently. White, the color of grief in many Asian and peasant cultures, was still being worn for mourning in southern Hungarian villages in the 1970s. Twentieth-century Chinese mourn in coarse, undyed hemp. Red is the mourning color for some Gypsy tribes.

Beyond the variety, there are a few crucial generalities about mourning garb. The first is that it must be noticeably different from the ordinary. The Haya people in Tanzania shave their heads in mourning and only in mourning; otherwise, it would look like wishing for a death. In Europe and the Americas, no one wore crape, a scratchy, odorous, and punitive material, except when in mourning. Mourning wear is a short-hand that signals: "This person is in a particular, vulnerable state. Take care."

Mourning clothes are most often plain, sober, even humble. Thus the unsewn hemp garments of the 20th-century Chinese mourner, which are simply torn and arranged on the body. Observant Jews in mourning are forbidden costly leather shoes; they wear slippers instead, and beards, symbols of distress and sometimes penitence. That mourning clothes should express a lack of vanity, even an unkempt look, is understandable. Why they should convey humility and penitence is less obvious.

Originally, wearing black or poor or old garments was another attempt to avoid exciting evil spirits, a way of saying, "You've done enough to this house now" or "Not me!" By darkening and dulling yourself into near invisibility, you risked less harm.

A third generality points not so much to the mourning garb itself as to its importance. When Vatinius appeared at a funeral banquet wearing his dark mourning toga (suitable for the burial) instead of the white toga prescribed for the banquet, Cicero saw this "fit of lunacy" as a bad omen for the state as a whole. Everyone who witnessed this outrage, he claimed, "grieved for the plight of the commonwealth." Think of *Gone with the Wind* and the gasps that went around the ballroom when Scarlett O'Hara flicked open her mourning fan, accepted Rhett Butler's audacious invitation, and actually danced in her black widow's dress and veil. No matter what the rules in a particular community, to breach them is to be callous about the feelings of individuals in pain and reckless about the shared assumptions that bind a society together.

⌘

If your daughter is about to die, her father will
sharpen his big knife. He says, "I am watching my
daughter. When she closes her eyes, I am going to
do what I wish." He means that he is going to cut
himself. She died, he cuts the lobe off his ear. I, her
mother, will cut off the tip of my finger, the little
finger or the fourth or middle finger, perhaps all
three. Both of us, her father and I, cut off our hair . . .
After we return from the grave, we, her parents, cut
our arms and legs, making horizontal slashes. We
slash our clothes, too . . . For a year or more we dress
poorly. Nowadays we dress in black . . . The missionaries told us not to cut ourselves. It displeases Jesus.
— Elsie Clews Parsons, *Kiowa Tales*

Many traditional cultures mourned by cutting their clothing, their hair, and themselves. In Sappho's lyric on the death of Adonis, girls ask the goddess Kythereia, "What can we do?" Her answer is, "Beat on your breasts, my girls, and tear your dresses." Red was a mourning color for the ancient Romans because it suggested the blood produced when women scratched their faces at funerals. Indian tribes before and after contact with missionaries gashed their hands, arms, legs, faces in grief, the men as well as the women. All that cutting is suggestive – of a torn heart, anger, remorse, propitiation, probably other things as well.

One of the most spectacular cases of large-scale, histrionic mourning in late medieval Europe took place in 1491 in Evora, Portugal. Eight months after marrying the infanta Isabel of Spain, Alfonso, the prince of Portugal, fell from his horse and died. The Portuguese people went into mourning, wearing coarse white cloth. Men cut their hair and beards; women scratched their faces until they drew blood. The court wore black. Princess Isabel cut her hair and did not undress for forty days, eating only a little soup. Wearing sackcloth, with her cloak pulled over her face, she refused to go to bed for three months. After the king, João II, and his queen had a bed set up for her, she would use it only without sheets. Feverish, she closed her window, lit her room with one candle, and wept most of the time. Finally she covered her shorn head with a black hood and returned to Spain.

There are several notable things about this tragedy in a relatively remote part of Europe on the eve of the Renaissance. The common people still mourned in humble, white clothes, while the aristocracy adopted black, the newly pan-European color of grief. Ordinary Portuguese women still scratched their faces, in the time-honored custom of southern Europe, but not apparently the princess or members of the royal household. Presumably the aristocracy was more "modern," more amenable to the teachings of the Church ("It displeases Jesus," as the Kiowa woman said of self-mutilation), while ancient customs lived longest among the folk. The princess expressed her grief by mortifying her flesh (barely eating, living in near-darkness, refusing to go to bed) and by embracing humility, perhaps penitence (wearing sackcloth, the traditional garb of repentance; refusing bed linen; cutting her hair).

Cutting or completely shaving off a widow's hair has an obvious meaning in cultures where a woman's hair symbolizes her sexuality: Hindu widows in Bengal and Madras formerly had their heads shaved, as did Igbo widows in Nigeria. But many societies, including dozens of North American tribes, express sorrow by cutting the hair of both sexes, even the men from tribes such as the Crow, who pride themselves on their elaborate hairstyles.

Cutting the hair has a double significance. Immediately it points to vulnerability, misery, a lack of care about one's appearance. But eventually it is a reminder of regrowth, a promise that what has been roughly shorn will be luxuriant again; that ragged, new grief will not last forever. Sometimes haircutting is explicitly tied to the end of mourning. A widow of the Wintun Indians would once have had her hair cropped and covered with pitch; when it had regrown, she was free to marry (but only her husband's brother). In the 19th century, the Pomo Indians used to mingle a dead man's ashes with pitch and apply it like a chaplet on the widow's skin at the edge of her shorn hair; the growing hair that eventually obscured the ashes and pitch was a graphic sign of time passing, of recovery.

Some societies take the opposite route and forbid the cutting of hair during mourning. Bereaved men in 15th- and early 16th-century Venice, Milan, and Florence grew their beards, normally a sign of shame and misery. In the Qing dynasty, Chinese men were prohibited from shaving their heads for a hundred days after the emperor's death. Again, this is the requisite differentness of mourning. When a trim, coiffed appearance is the norm, hair goes long and unkempt. When hair is valued for its plenty, mourning demands it be shorn.

One of the things that made the Jews unusual in the ancient world was the commandment forbidding them to cut themselves during mourning (Deuteronomy 14.1–2). All the more reason, then, to tear their garments – not their skin, but the thing closest to it. When Joseph's brothers brought his bloodied coat of many colors to their father, Jacob, he "rent his clothes, and put sackcloth upon his loins, and mourned for his son many days" (Genesis 37.34). David tore his clothes on hearing of the death of Saul (2 Samuel 1.11).

Jacob and David rent their clothes immediately on hearing of the death. This is still a possibility, but *keriah*, as this ritual is called, is now usually performed by observant Jews in the funeral chapel just before leaving for the cemetery; it can also take place at the cemetery. Eloquent and powerful, *keriah* mimics heartbreak by tearing that which covers the heart. Like other peculiarly resonant customs, it conveys a myriad of not always articulated or even understood feelings. Various commentators have seen in *keriah* a defiant anger, whether at God, the deceased, or oneself. In *Kaddish*, his account of the year after his father's death, Leon Wieseltier suggests something of that inchoate rage: "All this tearing and cutting. Life rips you up, so look ripped up. Flaunt your disintegration." Anne Brener points to two additional "uses" of *keriah*. It affirms "the sense of strangeness" felt by the mourner and, like other customs that date from Talmudic times, it was designed to heighten the sense of tragedy, so that mourners could weep.

A similar custom exists in Palestine, where women tear the embroidered chest panel of their dress to express grief, then wear it torn for the forty-day period of mourning. When making a present of a dress, the giver says, "God bless thee and the dress! May it not be torn or worn for mourning!"

Keriah is reserved for the closest relatives of the dead person: son, daughter, father, mother, brother, sister, and spouse. The cut – never on a seam because it is not to be mended – is often begun by the rabbi with a razor or knife, then finished by hand by the mourner. Sons and daughters wear the torn garment throughout shiva. To preserve her modesty, a daughter may baste her garment after the funeral, a son only after thirty days, but in neither case should they be permanently mended. A wound closes, but the scar remains. For other relatives, the tear need not show, nor is it necessary to wear torn clothing throughout shiva.

The moment of rending is a keenly painful one. The family stands, in the traditional Jewish posture for suffering, exposed before the congregation in the fullness of their sorrow. Even the choice of the clothing to be sacrificed can be fraught with ambivalence, expressing something of the survivor's relationship to the dead.

When his elderly father died in the 1990s, Al Green was a Toronto family practitioner in his sixties. His wife, Sabina, described him on the morning of the funeral: "Al doesn't spend a lot of time primping; a GP is a fast dresser. But that day he spent the whole morning not getting dressed. I started asking him what he was wearing, and he didn't want to talk about it. What normally takes five minutes took hours. Finally he emerged in a good sports jacket and a wonderful tie. Most people wear something old, because you have to wear it damaged for a week and then you throw it in the garbage. I said, 'Are you sure?' And he said, 'My father was always so nicely dressed, I want to look nice for this, for his sake.'

"When the moment came, the rabbi slit Al's jacket straight across the lapel and cut his tie nearly in two. It hung by a thread. Later that night, Al, who has been to many funerals, said, 'I might have worn something else if I'd remembered what was going to happen, because that was my best tie.'

"I could hardly believe what I was hearing. I said, 'But you did know what was going to happen.'

"'Maybe I did,' he admitted."

Ruining good clothes must always have posed problems for Jews of modest means, but life in North America, where both men and women worked alongside Gentiles, made it even more awkward. When the mother of Sara, the heroine of Anzia Yezierska's early 20th-century-novel *Bread Givers*, dies, and the time comes for the family to rend their clothes, Sara protests. A schoolteacher in New York, she has only one suit: "Tearing it wouldn't bring Mother back to life again!" Family and friends are aghast at "the *Americanerin*": "Her face is washed. Her hair is combed. Did we care how we looked when our mothers died?"

Sara's reluctance became widespread, and in the 1930s, American funeral directors devised a clothes-saving alternative to *keriah*: the black ribbon that is simply torn and pinned over the heart. Although dismissed as trivial and evasive by traditional rabbis, the ribbon is now the North American norm for Reform and many Conservative Jews. Yes, it bypasses the ancient, destructive (and somehow comforting) impulse, but it remains an unmistakable sign of loss.

⌘

In the costume storage area of the Strong Museum in Rochester, I am looking at American mourning clothes with the curator of textiles, Mary Ellen Perry. Wearing cotton gloves to protect aged cloth, we carefully lift from tissue paper pointed widow's caps in the Mary Stuart style, hoods and shawls the color of night. There's even a turn-of-the-20th-century black veil inset with a yellow isinglass rectangle to allow the widow to see, minimally – a surreal garment that suggests a World War I aviator crossed with a nun.

Finally we take from its box a long, deeply hemmed veil of Courtauld's crape, the premier mourning material that distinguished middle- and upper-class Western widows until the 1920s. I have read about crape (occasionally spelled crepe or crêpe), a crimped and dulled silk so prized that Courtauld's employees had to take an oath before a justice of the peace not to reveal its secret formula. I have seen pictures of it, covering widows' heads and skirts, tortured into flowers and other decorative effects in the later stages of mourning. I have read about its rusty smell, about the lengths widows went to in order to clean and reblacken it (Mrs. Beeton's *Household Management* advised the use of a camel's-hair brush and black ink).

But nothing has prepared me for the feel of it. Thick and harsh, it's the sartorial equivalent of an abrasive scrub, a Brillo pad for the face. Even through our gloves, we feel its meanness. Mary Ellen Perry sighs. "Imagine having to wear this, on top of your grief."

The development of Western mourning clothes began slowly, with few rules and plenty of regional variations. But, beginning in the 17th century, royal example percolated further and further down the social scale, gradually homogenizing European practice, until, exhausted by overindulgence and overelaboration in the 19th century, it died out more or less completely in the 20th.

The precedents in the pre-Christian world were sober, unostentatious garments. The ancient Greeks mourned in dark grey and black, the Romans in a dark brown or brownish black called *pulla* that by the middle of the republic connoted grief and humiliation. A Roman widow wore a square head covering called a *ricinium*, usually dark in color, for her year of mourning. By the end of the 2nd century A.D., Roman funerary laws urged mourners to forgo jewelry, white and purple clothing, and dinner parties. At that point, the constants of Western mourning were in place: dark colors, the all-important head covering for a woman, the restriction of finery, the connection between mourning clothes and social life, and a time limit for such expressions of grief.

Medieval mourners, who tended to wear loose robes like nuns and monks, were not exclusively committed to black. Monastic colors – black, white, grey, and brown – were also acceptable. Chaucer's widowed Criseyde wears both brown silk and black; the poor often wore a color called drab, a dull grey or brown also known as "sad color."

Black triumphed by the end of the 14th century in England, rather earlier on the Continent. As the darkest of the dark, black satisfied the mourner's old, superstitious wish for near invisibility. At the same time, the Catholic Church used black vestments for the penitential season of Lent and for masses for the dead, which were designed to atone for their sins. The penitential aspect dovetailed with the mourner's attempt to present himself as humble and unobtrusive, and black won the day.

But not entirely and not immediately. Women, children, and young people still had white funerals, which could extend to white mourning. Henry VIII had Anne Boleyn beheaded on May 19, 1536, and on the Feast of the Ascension (May 26) he wore "white for mournynge." (He married Jane Seymour in the next week.) Royalty often claimed distinctive mourning colors for itself, scarlet, purple, white, even blue. As late as the second half of the 16th century, Mary, Queen of Scots, the most trendsetting royal mourner until Queen Victoria, listed black, white, grey, and tannie (tan) mourning outfits in her wardrobe.

Called the White Queen because of her fondness for French *deuil blanc* (white mourning), Mary was frequently bereaved during her short life – of her mother, her father-in-law Henri II of France, her two husbands. She left her mark on the history of mourning gear with a small bonnet that came to a point in the middle of the forehead. Called a "Paris head" before Mary adopted it, it became known as the Mary Stuart cap and was the favorite headgear of European widows, most notably Queen Victoria, until the 20th century. (Hence the term "widow's peak" for the pattern of hair growth that resembles the cap.) The Mary Stuart cap's last royal outing was probably in 1952, when Queen Mary, aged eighty-five, wore one on the death of her son George VI.

Royal example gave cachet to lavish funerals, mourning gear, and etiquette: and aristocratic gatekeepers, such as the Court of Heralds in England, fought a long and ultimately unsuccessful battle to keep the bourgeoisie from mourning in the style of their betters. By the end of the 17th century, the new, striving middle class was free to follow a significantly rigidified code of mourning. No longer vaguely monastic, mourning wear now differed from ordinary clothes only in color, dullness, and certain telltale details. There was a schedule of appropriate materials, colors, and trimmings, depending on one's relationship to the deceased, with as many as three or four grades, from the so-called first mourning through second mourning, ordinary mourning, and half-mourning.

Mourning not only was the thing to do but could be very charming. In 1666, Samuel Pepys noted approvingly in his diary that Lady Falmouth was "now in second or third mourning and pretty pleasant in her looks." (Second or third mourning probably meant black silk, perhaps with fringed trimmings.) When Pepys's own mother died at the end of March in 1667, he put his family and servants into mourning and busied himself at various shops getting the required dulled shoes (often chamois rather than leather), bronze or black swords, and clothing: "To my shoemakers, cutler's, tailors, and up and down about my mourning." By no means immune to all this fine sobriety, within a week after his mother's death, he wrote, "I to church, and with my mourning, very handsome, and new periwig, make a great show." However, at the end of May, when his wife appeared prematurely dressed in second mourning, with a black moiré waistcoat and short petticoat trimmed with silver lace "which is too soon," Pepys was "horrid angry" at her lapse in decorum: "It vexed me to the blood."

Mourning dress descended ever further down the social scale. In 1731, the *Universal Spectator* sniffed, "Women of inferior Rank, such as Tradesmen's wives behind the Compter should make no Alteration in their Dress since it cannot arise . . . but from a meer Affection of the Mode at St. James." Nevertheless, tradesmen and their wives persisted in wearing mourning, despite its cost. Dying clothes was one way around the expense of an all-black wardrobe, and the records of 18th-century dyers indicate that people of all classes patronized them, with black the most popular color.

On the other hand, for the fashionable French, mourning represented an economy. Court mourning, which in 18th-century France could deprive the entire nation of color and jewelry for six months, was so frequent that a special newspaper, the *Annonce des Deuils*, provided details about the length and depth of each new bereavement. Noting how much money court mourning saved the Parisians, Sebastien Mercier noted in the *Tableau de Paris*, "Black clothing goes wonderfully well with mud, bad weather, economy and their dislike of spending time on their toilette!" So much black was bad for the textile industry, and the manufacturers' petitions for a reduction in official mourning were finally heard in 1789.

Mourning for all but the poorest classes was by now fairly standard across Europe and extended to colonists in North and South America, Australia, and South Africa. When a provident 18th-century Cape Town man ordered mourning accessories in advance from Holland, his list would have made good sense in Stockholm, Madrid, New York, or Caracas. It included crape to wind around men's hats and women's bonnets, mourning handkerchiefs, twelve pairs of black chamois gloves (leather being too shiny), twelve mourning fans, twelve half-mourning fans, two dozen matte shoe buckles, two dozen matte knee buckles, two dozen black shirt buttons, mourning ribbons, and black neck clasps for ladies' kerchiefs.

All this prepared the way for the heyday of mourning clothes, the 19th century. When Virginia Woolf's gender- and time-traveling hero Orlando is translated to that century and femaleness, she has a vision of objects draped around a huge cross: "widow's weeds and bridal veils; hooked on to other excrescences were crystal palaces, bassinettes, military helmets, memorial wreaths, trousers, whiskers, wedding cakes etc." It's an apt introduction to a highly sexualized culture where mourning is crucial, omnipresent, and massively assigned to women. Not only is she going to be a woman in this damp, fecund era, Orlando thinks resignedly, she is apparently going to be a woman in mourning: "Tomorrow she will have to buy 20 yards or more of black bombazine" for a skirt.

Orlando's assumption was reasonable, since mourning lasted longer and was more strict in 19th-century Britain than ever before, and most of its obligations lessened for men and deepened for women. A widower wore mourning (black suit, watch chain, tie, and buttons) for his wife for three months. A widow typically moved through four stages for a total of two and a half years. After a year and a day tented in plain, heavy crape, she spent nine months in only slightly less crape, then three months in black silk with jet ornaments, and finally six months in half-mourning: white, grey, violet.

The middle-class demand for "black goods," as they were known, called forth mourning warehouses beginning around the 1840s. The Grande Maison de Noir, near Charles Worth's couture house on the Faubourg St.-Honoré in Paris, provided all-in-one shopping for a bereaved household, supplying everything from the hearse to clothing to the all-important guide to behavior. London's best-known mourning warehouses, such as Peter Robinson's and the House of Jay, offered similarly extensive service.

Mourning clothes were considered so pressing and universal a need that two innovations developed as a result. "Everything, London" was the telegraphic address of the Harrod's mourning department in 1895, and the array of products and services supplied by the mourning warehouses gave birth to the department store. Speed was obviously essential (an Australian tailor in 1873 advertised "mourning orders five minutes"), and the mourning warehouses accustomed clients to almost-finished garments that required only minor adjustment. From there it was a short step to ready-to-wear clothes.

The chicken-or-egg situation of a population eager to mourn and new developments in merchandising and marketing that encouraged them made for ludicrous excesses. If there was a death in the family, some brides married in black. A man still in mourning for his first wife could marry again, but he returned to mourning wear the day after the wedding. Even more remarkable, his second wife went into mourning for her predecessor the day after the wedding, whether or not they had met. (She would also go into mourning for the parents of her predecessor.)

No class except the most destitute escaped mourning clothes. When Queen Victoria's daughter Princess Alice married in 1862, six months after her father's death, the queen allowed a white wedding dress but ordered an all-black trousseau, including black-trimmed lingerie, for her nineteen-year-old. After a visit from Emma, the widowed queen of Hawaii, Queen Victoria noted with approval that, although "a savage" in appearance, she wore proper mourning dress. The poor mourned as best they could, joining funeral societies that lent out a black dress and cloak when needed, dying clothes when possible. A 19th-century American cartoon shows a mistress meeting a former maid, now in mourning. The maid explains that she had been too poor for mourning clothes when her first husband died. Now her second husband is prosperous enough that she can afford to wear retroactive mourning for the first.

⌘

"See *me*, look at *me*, Mary!" said Topaz importantly,
revolving in black on the cutting-out table where
she stood because it was more convenient to fit one
so doll-like there. "I'm all in black, you see! I'm all

in black! I'm going to the funeral tomorrow!" as
the dressmaker tried a nice bit of crape on the body
of her dress ("the scraps will do for that,
Merriman"). There was silence. Topaz hearing the
silence, glanced from face to face, and saw the
looks. Her features puckered, she opened her
mouth wide and wept loudly. "Mother, Mother!"
she cried out loud in the face of those looks. But
Mother was not there.

> — Ethel Wilson, *The Innocent Traveller*

Before the 20th century, it seemed completely normal that even the smallest child would wear mourning. Children were dressed as miniature adults until the second half of the 18th century, which as a matter of course included mourning garb. By the 19th century, when the Romantic movement had popularized more free and easy, natural clothes for children, mourning dress had become too important for anyone, even the youngest, to avoid.

Poor "Mun" Verney, aged five, never got the blue satin coat his godmother had intended as an Easter gift. When his grandmother died in the spring of 1641, Edmund's godmother thought better of her present: "Now I know he is in mourninge therefore have sent him a porringer to ete his breakfast in." When George II, landgrave (count) of Hesse, died in 1661, an engraving of the funeral procession shows his small daughter Maria Elisabeth decked out like a Halloween spook, swathed from head to foot in veils of deepest black. Children from prosperous families observed court mourning as well as personal mourning, with permanent results in the case of the so-called Eton suit. Eton College went into mourning *en masse* when George III died in 1820, exchanging the boys' red or blue jackets for black ones, an order that has never been reversed.

Even babies wore mourning, often but not always white with black trimmings. Crib sheets were bordered with black or sometimes, as in 18th-century Switzerland, embroidered with black thread. M.M. Sherwood's two-year-old son died in 1808, at a time when women frequently did not attend funerals. Instead, she spent the burial day at home, decorating her three-month-old daughter's cap and dress with black ribbons. Sherwood was a minor novelist, and in *Lady of the Manor* (1825) she describes the mourning outfit, complete with black sash, straw hat, and ostrich plume, of a ten-month-old whose mother died at his birth.

Queen Victoria, a devotee of strict mourning observance even before she was widowed, recommended exclusively white and lilac mourning clothes for her daughter Vicky's five-month-old on the death of the baby's great-grandmother. Even quite distant relationships could rob a toddler's wardrobe of color. When her own mother's half-sister's husband died, the Queen decreed mourning for her three-year-old: "Darling Beatrice looks lovely in her black silk and crepe dress."

Clearly babies and very small children did not understand the significance of their black ribbons, nor presumably did many Eton boys grieve sincerely for a dead monarch – points often made by those who wanted to simplify or eliminate mourning dress for children. But older children were quite capable of grasping its meaning. When Edmund Verney (a younger relation of Mun) died in 1690, his grandfather hoped to cut corners on mourning dress for the boy's fifteen-year-old sister, Molly. Poignantly, she wrote him, "I know my mourning will cost a good deall of money, but I believe you wod have me morn hansomely for so deare a brother, and since ther is none left but myself to morn for him . . ."

In the last third of the 19th century, dress reformers and sensible souls were insisting that children not be consigned to lengthy and severe mourning. It takes an "innovator" in Staffordshire in the 1850s, where Ethel Wilson's autobiographical novel, *The Innocent Traveller*, begins, to protest that dressing a baby in black for her mother's funeral is a horrid idea and that she should be left at home. By 1875 in New England, when Louisa May Alcott published *Eight Cousins*, Uncle Alec – the hearty proponent of oatmeal, outdoor exercise, and bright colors – is adamant that his orphaned niece Rose must leave off her black dresses. Wearing mourning, even in the violet shades her aunts are planning for her, is seen as one of Rose's bad habits, like drinking coffee: unwholesome and upsetting.

By the end of the century, the waif in black and the strong-minded, unconventional adult who opposes mourning for children begin to appear with a certain frequency in children's books. Another "odd little black figure," the orphaned Mary in Frances Hodgson Burnett's *The Secret Garden* (1911), must also put off her mourning: her guardian says it makes the place even sadder than it is, and the maid Martha's commonsensical Yorkshire mother "doesn't hold with black."

⌘

After World War I, fewer and fewer Westerners were "holding with black," even for adults. Some of the reasons advanced for the demise of mourning clothes – Britain's disenchantment with Queen Victoria's prolonged mourning, the huge losses of the Great War and the decline in morale occasioned by mass mourning, the rise of funeral and mourning reform societies, the growth of large, anonymous cities – apply to the simplification of mourning customs in general. Others, such as the entry of women into the workforce, pertain more directly to mourning clothes. After 1918, the British middle classes lost interest in mourning clothes. The custom lasted longer among the working classes and the aristocracy, but even there it had diminished to the odd quaint exception by the 1950s.

Things proceeded rather differently in the United States, where the East Coast upper class largely gave up serious mourning wear in the 1930s. The American working classes, drawn from diverse ethnic backgrounds, did not look up the social scale for guidance and, with the middle class, gradually left off mourning in the 1920s, '30s, and '40s, as it became incompatible with modern life. This inexorable shift can be tracked in America's etiquette books from the late 19th century to the end of the 20th. Beginning with the dizzyingly complex clothing schedules of the Gilded Age, they proceed through decades where contradictory impulses of individuality and conventionality coexist and end in a world where changing your way of dressing because someone close to you has died is a bizarre idea.

In *Manners and Social Usages*, which guided readers from the 1880s until the eve of World War I, M.E.W. Sherwood positions the American widow midway between the lugubrious English ("Everyone who has seen an English widow will agree that she makes a 'hearse' of herself") and the light-minded French ("An American lady is always shocked at the gayety and cheerfulness of French mourning"). She cannot say enough against the crape veil, accusing it variously of abrading the skin, irritating eyes "enfeebled by weeping," causing catarrhal disease, blindness, and cataracts, and injuring lungs with the arsenic that permeated it. Her dislike of crape extends to its use on dresses: "a sort of penitential and self-mortifying dress, and very ugly and very expensive."

Modern enough to worry about the effect a mother's deep mourning would have on a sensitive child, Sherwood can also veer abruptly into the conventional (lace is never "mourning"). She reserves her deepest scorn for those who only dress the part, as in her story of the soldier's young widow seen dancing, like Scarlett O'Hara, in her long black veil, holding in her black-gloved hand a handkerchief "that looked as if it had been dipped in ink." Approvingly, Sherwood quotes a passerby: "She should have dipped it in blood."

By the time the New York Society of Self-Culture published Ella Wheeler Wilcox's *Correct Social Usage* in 1909, some relaxation was apparent. Only immediately after a death, "when the control of the emotions is uncertain," is it usual to cover the face with a long veil. A mother wears plain black for a year after the death of a young child, "and soon lightens it for the sake of her other little ones." Children under twelve wear mourning only upon the death of a parent, and white and grey mourning at that. After two years, a widow may discard her veil and wear lusterless silks. And, most important of all, "much is left to the option of the wearer."

The mourning band sewn on the left sleeve of a man's coat, an innovation seen in Edwardian and Georgian England, seems to have had a dubious acceptability in America. In *The Etiquette of To-Day*, published in 1913, Edith Ordway is firmly opposed, for it "has only the virtue of cheapness for those who cannot afford to show marked respect to the dead." Even more scathing was Emily Holt, who in her *Encyclopedia of Etiquette* in 1921 traced this growing "affectation" to liveried English servants whose masters were too stingy to outfit them in proper mourning. At a time when people still looked to mourning costume for clues about the nearness of the loss, Holt's greatest objection to the band is interesting: it is "unclassifiable," as men wear it for the nearest as well as very distant family.

Emily Holt's postwar book charts the conventional two-year schedule of mourning for a woman on the death of a husband, child, parent, or sibling, probably rather old-fashioned at the time. There are minor softenings of the rules: mothers mourning infants may elect not to wear black at all; mourning for relatives outside the immediate family is greatly shortened. But at the end of Holt's section on mourning wear for women comes the thin edge of the wedge: "Many ladies of unquestionable taste and discretion now content themselves simply with wearing clothes that are black in color and have given up the rather ostentatiously funereal crepe."

By 1948, the bereaved could read in Millicent Fenwick's *Vogue's Book of Etiquette* that not only were mourning clothes unnecessary, but one might very well have a "principled objection" to them. At the same time – perhaps because there was comfort in so recent a benchmark, perhaps because those who still cared about mourning cared passionately about being correct – Fenwick goes on to provide almost comically minute regulations for those few who wish to wear mourning.

The rules for sports clothes, in particular, are as arbitrary and unpredictable as anything at Victoria's court. Millicent Fenwick, who became a Republican congresswoman from New Jersey later in life, conjures up a world of East Coast bluebloods where mourning golfers attired themselves (properly) in grey flannels, white shirt, and black tie. Shooting required no special mourning clothes, according to Fenwick, except in the case of driven-bird shooting, when a black armband is necessary. Black armbands should also be worn for riding and hunting, except when wearing black riding habits or "hunting pink," which for some reason is considered correct for mourning.

Such arcane distinctions have no place in the modern, middle-class world of *Emily Post's Etiquette*, revised by Elizabeth Post in 1965. Mourning clothes, which the author regards as a self-indulgent delaying tactic, are fortunately becoming rare: each year more people "show the mourning in their hearts only by the quiet dignity of their lives." A woman may wear all black if she wishes, although not at her office. Men, she ventures, would not want to wear a black band on their sleeve because it is "an implied bid for sympathy." *Amy Vanderbilt's New Complete Book of Etiquette*, published in 1967, takes a similar attitude. Happily, Vanderbilt writes, mourning clothes are now rarely seen, although "those who wish to cling to rapidly passing tradition" can still find a few stores catering to their needs. At least as far back as the ancient Greeks, female mourners were distinguished by their head coverings. In the 1972 edition of *Amy Vanderbilt's Etiquette*, the author dismissed the wearing of veils and, almost as an aside, even the wearing of hats at funerals.

⌘

Queen Victoria clung to her black, reluctant more than four years after Albert's death even to wear the red velvet and ermine robe of state when she opened Parliament. Sidonie Colette also loved her husband, who died in 1904. But she had a different reaction to wearing mourning, as her daughter Colette recorded in "My Mother's House":

> We brought her back to the house, and there she promptly lost her temper with her new mourning, the cumbersome crape that caught on the keys of doors and presses, the cashmere dress that stifled her . . . "Oh, how hot it is! Heavens! The heat of this black stuff! Don't you think I might change now, into my blue sateen?"
>
> "Well . . ."
>
> "Why not? Because of my mourning? But I simply loathe black! For one thing, it's melancholy. Why should I present a sad and unpleasant sight to everyone I meet? What connection is there between this cashmere and crape and my feelings? Don't ever let me see you in mourning for me! You know well enough that I only like you to wear pink, and some shades of blue."

The question is a good one. What connection is there between special clothes and one's feelings? For some, the link was real. Clothing, the thing we wear next to our skin, is such an intimate expression of ourselves. The expression "to be in mourning" meant both to have suffered a loss and to be wearing mourning clothing. Queen Victoria, who said, "My poor sad face & garb *must* tell its tale," felt the connection. Sidonie Colette felt stifled.

Very few people now feel much of a relationship between their clothes and their grief, even for a funeral. I don't remember any close mourner at Scott's funeral wearing bright red, but there was a range of light, neutral, and dark colors. Marilyn and her daughters-in-law had flown to Seattle when they heard about the accident; no one had packed for a funeral, so clothes had to be bought. Marilyn refused to connect her new light blue dress with sadness – she had chosen it to celebrate Scott's life – and she wore it to a family wedding the following May. Hannah, too, had raced down to Seattle without good clothes, and some Vancouver friends arrived later with a few likely dresses from her closet. But my sister had a new black velour jumper, and we preferred that for Hannah, with a white blouse. Dressing her was like dressing a doll, she was so completely uninterested, and I think she would have worn whatever we put on her. By a sheer fluke, the one dressy outfit I had taken to Asia was a black suit, and as a result I was among the most soberly dressed at the funeral.

Hannah wore her own idiosyncratic mourning garb almost every day in the winter and spring after Scott's death – a vivid orange vest made of padded parachute silk that he had given her for Christmas. The very opposite of the letter of Victorian mourning in its brightness and shininess, it was absolutely correct in its spirit: it was Hannah's outward and visible sign of grieving for Scott. Part of its poignancy was its personal, eccentric character, but that was also its limitation. Only Hannah and her close friends knew what it represented.

I asked her if she wished she lived in a world where she could wear a universally understood mourning symbol, like an armband, and she said simply, "I would love that." It reminded me of Geoffrey Gorer's sense that his black band set him apart, and the goodness of that realization. Other mourners corroborate Hannah's feeling. A few months after her father died, the writer Barbara Gowdy was walking down a street, missing him. A stranger coming in the opposite direction took note of her woebegone face and jokingly ordered, "Smile!" Months later, she was still angry as she remembered the episode: "That never would have happened if I had been able to show by my clothes that I was in mourning."

Nobody expects the return of mourning gear, but every so often someone designs his own. Matthew Galleli is a teacher in Rochester. About a month after his wife died in 1997, wanting to counteract the assumption that his grieving was finished, he began wearing a black ribbon and a white ribbon looped together on his lapel. He chose ribbons because they have been used to raise awareness of issues, and when people asked him about them, he told them he was mourning his wife. "It gave me an opportunity to say that," he explained, and it struck me that, throughout most of history, people had no need of such an opportunity.

As Galleli said, his ribbons were "a way to let folks know that something different had happened." That sounds modest enough, but mourners will tell you there are days when it is crucially important. Mourning clothes provided a marker and thus a kind of insulation for those who wore them – rare luxuries now that we have nothing that alerts the community to the presence of a mourner. I had given Hannah an old locket to hold a lock of Scott's hair, and when people complimented her on her jewelry, she would disconcert them by saying, "It has Scott's hair in it." When I asked her why she sounded almost aggressive, she harked back to the old function of mourning dress: "People think I look okay, I'm going to class and so on. I want them to know that it's not over."

SORROW SHARED

A joy shared is a double joy;
a sorrow shared is half a sorrow.
    – proverb

For several months in the winter of 1999 and again in the
winter of 2000, I sat in on a support group for young
widows and widowers every Monday afternoon. On Tuesday
mornings, as I drove to work, I would find myself thinking
about John and Susie and Donna – their likes, their dislikes,
their blind spots, their habits, endearing and otherwise.

Occasionally I would stop short and remind myself of a
few essential facts: John is dead, and so are Susie and Donna. I
never met them. And all I know about them is what I hear
from their spouses once a week in the faltering light of a winter
afternoon. When I told the psychiatrist who oversaw the group
how vital those dead people seemed to me, he nodded. "The
bereaved bring them to life again in this room, so that they can
let them go in their own time, when they're ready."

Sitting in a room with people who are young and widowed
but otherwise quite different from one another may not seem
the likeliest mourning activity. That these people were originally strangers who were brought together in a doctor's office
is a modern development, but mourners have probably always

sought out the company of mourners. In traditional societies, they met informally. War or plague or the non-existence of antibiotics ensured that the bereaved had abundant companionship. The village sewing circles of the past had their share of widows, and it's easy to imagine them rehearsing their husbands' last illnesses and deaths, the changing relationships with in-laws, the concerns about children and money – the same topics I listened to in a doctor's office in 1999.

Loring Danforth's book *The Death Rituals of Rural Greece* describes the shape of bereavement in Potamia, a village in Thessaly in northern Greece, in 1979. The Greeks follow the custom of double burial, in which the whole corpse is interred at first; one to three years later, when the flesh has disintegrated, the skeleton is dug up and reburied. Alexander Tsiaras's extraordinary photographs show women crouching in the open graves after three years, holding up a skull, kissing it, passing it to each relative in turn, and weeping. Between the first and second burials, while the whole corpse is in the earth, the mourning women go to the village cemetery every evening, sit on the tombs of their loved ones, weed and tidy, pass the time of day with their neighbors, remember those under the ground, bemoan their fate. A bereavement support group, Greek village style.

⌘

One of the few traditional rituals that gathered mourners from different families and that continue today is the saying of Kaddish. Beginning in the 12th century in Jewish communities in France and Germany, the custom arose that sons mourning a parent recited a short prayer of praise to God, in Aramaic. Originally it was meant to lessen the parent's time in the fires of Gehenna, the purgatory-like place where souls were believed to spend up to twelve months after death. Over centuries and countries, the custom flowered. Today Kaddish, still in Aramaic, is said during the daily synagogue services. Many Jews say Kaddish every day for eleven months after the death of a close relative, with variations depending upon the branch of Judaism and local customs. Some go only to the morning service, others attend afternoon and evening services as well. What was originally and correctly translated as the "orphan's Kaddish" is now known as the "mourner's Kaddish."

It is a puzzling obligation to many Jews, because the hymn of praise makes no mention of death or loss. They often report that, especially in the first days after a death, exalting God is a grating, resentful exercise. Once you realize that Kaddish was first said on behalf of the dead, to atone for their sins, the praise makes more sense. But even for those who understand the custom only imperfectly, its communal aspect gives it great force. The service in which Kaddish is said can happen only in the presence of a minyan, the quorum of ten Jews that makes a service valid. You cannot fulfill your Kaddish obligation in solitude; it must be done in a group. As Marian Henriquez Neudel, a Chicago lawyer who said Kaddish for her father, describes the experience, "It draws us into a community (typically a rather small one) at a time when grief might otherwise isolate us. It imposes a routine on us when we might be tempted to let chaos take over. It gives us something to do early in the morning when depression wakes us up earlier than usual."

In many North American congregations, Neudel's "rather small" community – the minyan or more – is by no means a certainty at early-morning service on weekdays. That makes the presence of each and every Kaddish-sayer precious. In almost everyone's memories of saying Kaddish, there are more than a few mornings when someone in the group gets on the phone and beats the bushes for five more people, for two, for one, until the minyan is achieved and the service can go forward. To walk into shul and find yourself "the tenth" is uniquely gratifying. The cliché "I'm here for you" is literally true when it comes to saying Kaddish, but the mourner is also there for his dead, for himself, and for God, if his belief includes God.

Kaddish is a club whose membership shifts. Some finish their eleven months soon after others begin, while others' time overlaps more or less completely. Newcomers become veterans and welcome the newly bereaved into the group as they prepare to leave. Years later, people will say, "Oh yes, we said Kaddish together one spring" or "He began saying Kaddish for his son just as I was finishing for my father." It becomes a kind of metaphor for the fortunes of life – similar and dissimilar – as well as the way people converge and move apart, as fate dictates.

The saying of Kaddish was not intended to provide mourners with group support, and it does not serve that function universally. For women, relative newcomers to the custom, the experience can be harshly unwelcoming. Marian Neudel threatened jokingly to write a "Mourner's Guide to Chicago Synagogues," rating them on non-sexism (equal signs), friendliness (smiley faces), and quality and quantity of the after-service breakfast (forks), as well as liturgical quality (Torah scrolls) and speed (clockfaces). More seriously, she was keenly aware of the synagogues that permitted men and women to sit together but did not count women in the minyan. The one she settled on not only accepted women as part of the minyan, it allowed a woman to lead the service.

She was more fortunate than the New York writer Evelyn Broner. In *Mornings and Mourning*, a journal of 1987, the year she said Kaddish for her father in New York, Broner records an anthology of snubs, delaying tactics, and insults designed to exclude her. The secretary of one shul tells her, "We do not allow our women to mourn." (Broner pictures "women with brimming eyes and fixed smiles.") The secretary advises Broner to hire a professional mourner, predicting rightly that she will find it hard to rouse an amen when she rises to say the mourner's prayer. Broner persists in her search, settling on an almost equally unfriendly Orthodox shul in which to say

Kaddish. When she complains to a friend, he says unsympathetically, "Your mistake is you went into a fish store and asked for chicken." In other words, a woman cannot expect to be accepted in an all-male club.

The dilemma for Broner, as for other women, is that the egalitarian shuls that welcome women often don't offer a daily service. If a female mourner wants to fulfill the traditional daily requirement, she must broach the less predictably genial territory of an Orthodox or Conservative synagogue. Broner did that for her father, although she now thinks her impulse was misguided. After listening to her daughter's frustration for a year, Broner's mother wanted a more accommodating atmosphere for the Kaddish said when she died. She ordered her daughter, "Go where they honor you, and that way they'll honor me." She added, "Promise, no curtains, no balcony, no last row." Broner obeyed, finding an egalitarian congregation without daily services but where an inclusive Kaddish could be said on Fridays and Saturdays.

Other mourners shy away from the communal aspect. One such was Leon Wieseltier, the author of *Kaddish*. Wieseltier, the literary editor of the *New Republic* and temperamentally inclined to "bookishness," wanted to spend the year after his father's death studying the evolution of Kaddish while he prayed three times a day. He began by regarding the group as a necessary hindrance to his scholarly, spiritual aim. Early in the year he writes, "The shul is losing its strangeness for me. This worries me. In a strange place, solitariness is possible. Sociability poses a threat to spirituality. Now I'm coming to know my fellow petitioners. They are no longer strangers, they are becoming friends. How do you pray with friends? How do you pray with anybody? Prayer is a throb of individuation, at least for me. And yet the congregation is one of the conditions of my kaddish."

As the year moves on, Wieseltier notes with something like chagrin that he is being drawn, inexorably, into a community. On a day when he leads the worship at his shul in the

Georgetown district of Washington, D.C., at all three services, a few members congratulate him. He demurs, "Not a big deal. But how on earth did this fine little congregation become dependent on me?" More and more, he refers to a remark made by a "friend" after the service; or he finds himself beguiled by the mien of another mourner, admiring his comportment, wondering about his story.

The shared purpose and daily demands of Kaddish mean that any place that can summon a minyan is a haven (for a man, at least). At one point, Wieseltier decides that going to the Georgetown synagogue for lunchtime service is too difficult in the middle of his workday. He goes instead to the nearby offices of the ultra-Orthodox political lobby in Washington, where he has heard there are services. "Can I help you?" the receptionist asks when he enters the busy office. He answers, "I'm a mourner." "Have a seat," she returns. Here, in a conference room gorged with volumes of U.S. law on one side and Jewish law on the other, is a place for the mourner.

But it is in his regular congregation that Wieseltier feels most unexpectedly at home. Midway through the year he concedes, "After the prayers, this morning and every morning, a few minutes of friendly banter. I have been thoroughly absorbed into the fellowship of these excellent people. I am no longer a stranger in my community. (There is even one of them whom I can't stand.)"

When his allotted time is over, the reluctantly clubbable Wieseltier has acquired more than religious discipline and a formidable understanding of the history of Kaddish. According to Jewish law, he has mourned publicly for his father. "I am no longer a mourner," he writes. "That is to say, my mourning is all mine now. For a year, private was public. In accordance with the requirements of my tradition, and sometimes thoughtfully, I exposed the condition of my heart. But that rite has now expired. The public no longer has any claim on the private . . .

I am alone again with the purities and the impurities, his and mine."

Not only was his mourning necessarily public, it brought with it a responsibility that outlasts the eleven months. Just before the unveiling of his father's gravestone, Wieseltier reads in a 13th-century text that a mourner must leave home, even during the first housebound days after a death, to comfort another mourner. First thinking it cruel that someone fresh from his own family funeral must hustle to another, he accepts the point: the obligation to console trumps the obligation to mourn. And the duty to console is lifelong. His sorrow has made him a "specialist in grief," and that expertise must not go to waste. "The disconsolate are the masters of consolation," Wieseltier concludes. "They offer sympathy without illusion."

Like Wieseltier, the Toronto architect Gordon Pape went to synagogue to pray and discovered a community. When his sister died, his parents said Kaddish for a month, "more out of obligation than spiritual feelings," and stopped. Gordon continued for the full eleven months, saying of the thirty or so people at his regular synagogue, "These people stand up and recite Kaddish and you know they've gone through what you have. You have this club, and this thing in common, not that anyone wants to have it in common."

The club demands a strenuous commitment. The morning service at Gordon's Conservative synagogue begins at 7:30 and lasts about forty minutes; the combined afternoon and evening service, at 7 P.M., takes half an hour. When his father died a few years after his sister, Gordon returned to the mourner's Kaddish. He relished the mutual dependence, remarking on the "sigh of relief" that greets the mourner at an underpopulated service. And he enjoyed "the collective combination of individuals" that rises to recite the prayer: "I've never heard two people recite Kaddish the same. Everyone's personality comes out. Some are very loud, others inaudible, others singsong. Some are very authoritative, others very mournful."

Gordon Pape's experience of Kaddish fits well into Terry Martin and Kenneth Doka's description of instrumental, or masculine, mourning – a mostly unspoken, shoulder-to-shoulder solidarity with his fellow mourners, as they performed the same action. He did not always know the names of those who overlapped the longest with him, and only rarely did he have time for the daily after-service breakfast. When he did go to breakfast, he didn't inquire about the particulars of another's loss, beyond the relationship, and he disliked being asked much about his own loss. But if he heard that someone had had a similar experience and if he thought he could help them, he'd go over quietly and suggest having a chat.

Ending Kaddish is never easy, Gordon says, as it involves letting go of the soul, which has been wandering in Gehenna in a kind of transitional state. "There's an intensity that builds at the end, and the last few times are so poignant," he recalls. "You feel regret that you hadn't done enough for the soul." When the eleven-month period ends, the rabbi often gives a talk at the morning service about the dead person, and the family frequently sponsors the breakfast. Gordon didn't want that, but he did want to mark the end. He brought a bottle of Scotch to the afternoon service. "It's my last day," he told the group, "and I'd like to invite all of you for l'chaim." He gave a little speech about his father, toasting him and the group and hoping to meet in happier times. Now, when he runs into people with whom he said Kaddish, even if he can't summon up their name, there is a profound feeling of fellowship.

⌘

Many Jews like to say that Kaddish is "the world's oldest bereavement support group." Both the ancient religious duty and the modern phenomenon bring together people who may be strangers to one another, with a range in the "age" of their bereavement – they meet at different points along the mourner's path. Veterans of support groups list among its benefits the feeling of universality ("I'm not the only one who has lost someone. Everyone here is a mourner"), the sense of solidarity, and the chance to be altruistic. So do Kaddish veterans.

In fact, the modern support group derives more directly from two streams, the self-help movement and group therapy. Self-help is as old as people banding together for a common objective, although the contemporary incarnation is usually dated from the founding of Alcoholics Anonymous in the 1930s. AA was based on the premise that self-disclosure is essential for change, a belief that continues to fuel self-help groups. Group therapy, which began in the 1940s, is a mysterious, seemingly haphazard alchemy that achieves something more than might be expected from its components – typically, seven to twelve more or less functional people, whose interactions are supervised by a trained therapist.

The bereaved spouses' group I observed was more like a self-help group than group therapy, in that its twelve or so members wanted psychological support in their bereavement rather than more fundamental therapy. The atmosphere was more sympathetic and less analytical than that in thoroughgoing group therapy, which relies on the here-and-now dynamics of its membership to create tension and, ideally, enlightenment.

But it was like group therapy in that it was conducted under the auspices of a psychiatrist and a psychiatric nurse. This particular group was the work of Ed Pakes, a Toronto psychiatrist who has specialized in different kinds of bereavement throughout his career. When he began treating young (which he defines as under forty-five) bereaved spouses in individual therapy, he felt, in his words, he was "getting nowhere." At some point he realized that, because we live in a world where young adult deaths are rare, few of his patients knew another person in their situation. In therapeutic language, they had no "mirrors." In commonsense terms, their loneliness was intensified. So Pakes formed two groups that meet weekly, one in a downtown hospital, the other in his office north of the city. They are open-ended groups in that there is no set length of membership; people may stay for as few as eight meetings or for more than a year.

Pakes led the group I attended with Sandra Freedhoff, a psychiatric nurse, but their guidance often seemed nominal. One of them might begin by asking if the members had begun thinking about the coming holidays, or, midway through a meeting, might ask a silent member how the week had gone for him; very occasionally, they will steer the group away from a tangent. But the members had so much to tell one another that I often wondered if the group would be much different if the professionals were not there. No doubt their relative transparency owed something to their expertise, and more was going on in the way of direction than I realized, but it was clear that the members' most intense desire was to communicate with one another. After all, as Wieseltier noted, the disconsolate are the masters of consolation. The doctor and the nurse wisely deferred to them.

A friend who is a therapist experienced in leading groups once said to me, "Group therapy of whatever kind is the purest form of democracy." I thought of that often while I observed this group. The members ranged from prosperous people with full-time housekeepers to a woman who appeared wearing the uniform of a cleaning service, with her name embroidered on her pocket. In between there were farmers, businesspeople, teachers, students, housewives. There were Christians, Jews, people of no religion; people whose families had been in Canada for generations and new immigrants with sonorous accents. All defined themselves as bereaved spouses, whether married or not, heterosexual or homosexual. They advised one another, agreed or disagreed, teared up sympathetically when someone wept, passed Kleenex to each other as complete equals. They had something in common that dwarfed puny things like class and money. In a word, they commiserated.

At one session, a lawyer in her early thirties began talking about her six-year-old son, who had become violent and uncontrollable after his father's completely unexpected death from an aneurysm. She began sobbing and could not stop. Thérèse, the cleaner, turned to Pakes. In her thick Québécois accent, she pointed out the number of people in the group who had children of roughly similar ages and some difficulty getting them cared for during these late-afternoon Monday sessions. Why didn't the doctor organize a bereavement group for their children, in this building and at the same time? To his credit, he did just that, renting space in the office building and engaging a child therapist. (Each week, when the smiling child therapist collected the variously unruly, sullen, and well-behaved children from the waiting room and led them down the hall, I was reminded of the Children's Crusade.) What struck me was that the least educated person in the group was touched by the plight of the most educated person in the group and came up with an excellent suggestion.

Researchers and practitioners consistently report that altruism is one of the chief motors that make a successful support group work, as well as one of the most valued benefits remarked on by members. Why helping others would make troubled people, in this case bereaved people, feel better is not immediately clear, but it is an ancient strategy. In primitive societies, a distressed person was often ordered to make a celebratory meal or do some other good deed. Perhaps bereaved people prize the opportunity to help others because they feel powerless and inadequate, perhaps because they want to expiate some sense of neglect or guilt (which might only be the guilt of having survived), perhaps because suffering makes us more sensitive to the suffering of others, perhaps because a sense of effective connection with others is crucially important to our well-being. No doubt there are other reasons as well.

Because the members of a support group are, as one researcher put it, both "consumers and deliverers of services" – they help one another and are the beneficiaries of help – their connective web is very tightly woven. That web, called group cohesiveness by therapists, is another critical part of the support group experience. A member of a group used a different metaphor to describe her relationship to the others. She imagined herself as "a lonely ship in the dark. Even though no physical mooring could be made, it was nonetheless enormously comforting to see the lights of other ships sailing the same water."

The presence of other ships sailing the same water is reassuring in a number of ways. First, the very fact that they have gathered is important. A widower in Pakes's group mentioned that a few friends had offered to put him in touch with widowers of roughly his age, but he couldn't be sure they would welcome his call: "When you go to a group, you know you're with people who *want* that contact."

The group allows its members to try on, either actually or in their imagination, solutions they hear about – or bereavements they witness. I imagined that Ellen, a teacher whose husband had died of melanoma, offered hope to several people still in the newer, rawer stages of grief. After leaving the group prematurely, Ellen had returned about two years after her husband's death because she wanted to think, in concert with the group, about the unhappiness of her younger son, and a new relationship in which she was involved. Her troubles were by no means over, and her story of her husband's death, at home, was one of the most wrenching I heard, but she was an immensely calm, appealing presence I could easily picture as a model.

In Ed Pakes's words, the group provides a "mourning map" that allows members to anticipate some of the rough spots ahead as well as the smoother ones. Simply listening to the range of opinions in the room about, for example, what to do with the dead partner's clothing can be liberating. On the other hand, unanimity can be normalizing. Feeling guilty about her impatience with her in-laws, a widow learned that "I will inevitably blame my in-laws and they will blame me. The group gave me the understanding that that's natural, and that's been a big help."

Pakes imposes only two rules: no cellphones, and no judging anyone's way of mourning. Mostly the group members spoke to one another warmly and sympathetically, but on occasion I witnessed breathtaking frankness. Henry, a widower who I imagined was a small-time gangster, because of his flamboyant style of dress – he turned out to be an extremely organized actuary – rather unexpectedly became the moral center of the group. He once rounded on Yvonne, a woman whose husband had committed suicide. She had told her school-age children that their father died of a heart attack. After brooding on this information for some weeks and consulting his own children, Henry said to Yvonne: "You're sitting on a time bomb. Children understand everything, at some level. Your children know what their father did, and you'd better tell them the truth. Right now."

Although any subject is permitted in a support group, I never did hear some things discussed. Henry and Yvonne were the only ones who ever described being angry at their spouse for dying. No one expressed relief at a death. There was almost no discussion of sex after widowhood, and Henry predicted privately that such a discussion would probably split along gender lines. (Men's bereavement groups report that they do discuss sex.)

The group's most captivating practice, to my mind, was their storytelling. Before I began observing Pakes's group, I had attended a course he gave about bereavement at the Toronto Psychoanalytic Society, designed for therapists as well as the general public. One night, Pakes invited two widows from his bereavement group to visit the class and tell their stories. The first was a nurse who specialized in cystic fibrosis. She had married a man with cystic fibrosis, and they had a daughter. About eighteen months before her visit to the class, when their child was three and her husband apparently doing well, he died unexpectedly. Her story included some reflections on the irony of her professional life, and the complications of returning to nursing cystic fibrosis patients after her husband's death.

The other woman had been widowed less than a year, and she wept more often during her story. She had said goodbye to her husband as he set off with their dog on their usual Sunday-morning walk on the shore of a river. Ordinarily she would have gone along, but they were having guests for dinner and she stayed home to cook. A bank of the river gave way, the dog fell in, and her husband drowned trying to save the dog. (The dog survived.) She ended with a coda, which took place about six months after the death, when she made a rather perilous journey by water to say goodbye to an old friend dying of cancer.

The widows left during the coffee break. When we reconvened, a therapist taking the course commented, "My clients can't tell stories. They start in the middle and work sideways, spending too much time on irrelevant details, and they don't quite get to the point. But these two" – pointing dramatically at their empty chairs – "they're from Hollywood!" They were not, of course, from Hollywood. They were normal women who had suffered grievous losses. To say that they were magnificent storytellers sounds like a cold, purely aesthetic judgment that ignores the suffering involved. In fact, they were magnificent largely because of their pain – pain that neither woman denied.

Listening to these women, then to dozens of similarly gripping stories once I began attending the group, I recalled the theory that the first narratives in human history dealt with the deaths of kings and heroes. Hearing about the deaths of these ordinary people, I could believe the theory. The story of any death is awesome. Told in detail by the dead person's partner, with all the attendant emotional ramifications, it put most other narratives I could imagine in the shade.

Aside from their subject, the people in Pakes's group had another advantage as storytellers: repetition. When a newcomer joined the group, she introduced herself with her story, and each member of the group told his story. As the months went by, they shaped and reshaped their material to its best advantage. It is no coincidence that one of Pakes's favorite tasks for mourners is to acquire a sense of mastery, something particularly prized after the mourner has such a drastic experience of powerlessness. Pakes had prompted the second widow who came to our class to tell the story of her journey by water, which he admired because it showed her conquering the fear that arose when her husband drowned. Both content and form, as she took control of the narrative with difficulty, were about mastery.

Paradoxically, the telling and retelling of a terrible event seem to have a certain anesthetizing effect, while they also make the death incontrovertibly real. (Two other tasks of mourning: to accept that the death has truly happened, and to begin to carry on in spite of it.) Certainly there seems to be a compulsion to tell the ur-story, as I began to think of the story of the death, which is then embroidered and amplified, depending on the circumstances. I often noticed this when I set out to interview a mourner about something very specific – the role played by keepsakes, for example, or long-term commemorations. Almost without exception, the mourner would have to "begin at the beginning," and tell the whole story, often starting with the diagnosis.

In the group, this was encouraged. It was fascinating to hear the stories evolve or simply exhibit themselves differently, depending upon the teller's mood or where she was on the mourner's map. One man, for example, had a complicated story of his wife's refusal to have surgery for a non-life-threatening condition and her eventual needless death from painkillers. On an angry, uncommunicative day, he could tell a nonplussed newcomer: "My wife died of sheer stupidity." That was all. Period. On a softer day, he might tell the whole tortuous tale. No doubt both extremes, and those in between, were therapeutic.

At times I felt guilty that I was so gripped (dare I say entertained?) by these sad stories and these brave people. Then I would remind myself that the widows and widowers were also enjoying one another's company. There was a special richness, not surprising in a group where everyone had sustained a loss and gathered together, committed to a notable level of openness. Sometimes it seemed that the whole human comedy was being played out in Ed Pakes's office on Monday afternoons. I heard stories in that crowded room I will never forget: a suicide complicated by family feuds, a lesbian who had to stifle her grief outside her closest circle, a wedding in a cancer ward where the desperately ill bride toasted her groom with pineapple juice. The combination of sorrow, intimacy, and hope made a potent, intensely human brew.

If, as many studies have demonstrated, human companionship improves the ability to deal with life's stresses, perhaps the opposite is also true, that one of the harshest traumas might make people ready for a particular level of intimacy. As the psychologist Louis Lagrand says, "Support groups are especially life affirming. They initially provide the confidentiality that allows us to deal with feelings that society tells us should be held in abeyance. Around the meeting table, hope is mirrored in the eyes of all who have gone before and survived their tragedies."

Although Hannah trusted that she would not continue to feel as wretched as she did in the first year after Scott died, she did feel wretched. As a little girl, she had refused to listen to a story until the reader promised that it ended happily, and now she began collecting happy endings, stories of people who had lived through a similar bereavement. My friend Jane, whose young husband had been killed in a car accident twenty-five years earlier, wrote to her, and Hannah liked thinking about Jane and her subsequently contented life. Another of the condolence letters told about the writer's sister, who eventually thrived after the death of her fiancé. Hannah read and reread that letter; it was an infusion of hope.

Because she took such obvious encouragement from others' stories and because she is incorrigibly sociable, Hannah would probably have been an ideal candidate for a support group. But finding a young bereaved partners' group – and that is what she wanted – is a serendipitous matter. When I learned of their existence, in the second winter of her bereavement, Ed Pakes told me about one in the Vancouver area, but it didn't work with Hannah's hectic, changeable timetable. Believing as he does in the value of "mirrors," Pakes tried to connect her by phone with a medical student he knew in a parallel situation, in Halifax, but their conflicting schedules made that impossible. As it turned out, Hannah did a lot of her mourning in carefully chosen company, with friends who listened sympathetically but had little in the way of reciprocal experience.

Unlike the "talking cure" of one-to-one therapy, a support group is closer to a "talking-and-listening cure." For the majority of adult support groups, that exchange is the raison d'être. Groups for children operate differently, because of children's energy level, their distractibility, and their bent for expressing things through play. A children's group will often include activities: banging Play-Doh to "get the bad feelings out," moving to music, bringing in a picture or possession of the dead person. As an aid to talking, in a group for children aged seven to twelve who have lost a parent or a sibling, the Bereaved Families of Ontario includes a teenager. Acting as a bridge between the children and the adult counselor, the teenager, who is also bereaved, "models" for the children when he talks about his feelings. Out of these activities, as well as conversation, the children say some impressively sage things to one another.

The most evocative exercise I saw involved the children ascribing feelings to particular colors, and using them to draw a picture. Asked to talk about the feelings represented by the colors in his picture, a boy named Kevin, perhaps nine, said the blue was "angry," the green "weird," the yellow "irresponsible," and the orange "guilt." Kevin's younger sister had fallen to her death from a faulty seat on a Ferris wheel. Kevin, who was also on the Ferris wheel with his mother, had chosen that particular ride.

When the counselor asked him to explain more about the "irresponsible" yellow and orange "guilt," he said, "I feel guilty because I chose to sit at the back," that is, in a seat that turned out to be safe. The counselor asked the group, "Can anyone help Kevin with that feeling?" "Wrong place. Wrong time," a boy about Kevin's age responded. "You can't blame yourself – either way, someone would have got killed." It was a wise, sad moment between two school-age boys. Once more, the disconsolate were the masters of consolation.

⌘

One bright September morning in Tokyo, I met five women whose children had been killed in automobile accidents. The most recent death was two years in the past, the earliest nine years before. The mothers were mostly in their thirties or forties, with one woman in her sixties. One wore a T-shirt, another a Lacoste shirt and chino pants, unusually casual attire for downtown Tokyo. The others were dressed more conventionally, in simple, dark clothes. Two held handkerchiefs; they had just come from a trial, and they explained that they were more than usually emotional after such an ordeal. Reckless driving is often treated quite leniently in Japan, and the parents' group to which these women belong attends at least a few trials of offenders each month. Forbidden to speak, they sit with the victims' families, a silent but weighty witness to the grief caused by careless driving.

Their group began eleven years ago, when the daughter of Masako and Wataro Ide was killed. At the funeral, a friend said in her eulogy that the child's death must not be wasted. Masako Ide, round-faced, short-haired, and the group's natural leader, still weeps as she talks about that time. So stunned by sorrow that she could no longer do her job, she kept returning to the eulogy and its hope that their child had not died in vain. Masako and Wataro started advertising for other parents whose children had been killed in car accidents.

Activism is difficult in Japan, as is discussing emotional pain, and the Ides must have known that. Still, they believed that thousands of children were being killed each year by hazardous driving, and that their cause would rally supporters. They were wrong. Their first two advertisements got no response whatsoever. Finally, eight people answered their third advertisement. With no professional expertise or help, and no funds, the parents of nine children started an organization designed to raise public awareness about dangerous driving and to toughen the laws against it, while supporting themselves and other bereaved parents.

Today the situation has improved, but not remarkably. The group has amassed a network of experts, legal, organizational, and therapeutic, who address their meetings. The Tokyo Medical and Dental College now has a center for bereaved families, and it's easier to interest doctors and mental health professionals in their plight. The parents' monthly newsletter alerts members to the dates of upcoming trials and information about recent verdicts. The group's annual national meeting attracts about two hundred people, but that is a small number for a country of 130 million. In a society where acceptance and self-restraint are the norm, the Ides' dream makes for uphill work.

Perhaps as devastating as the general nonchalance about hazardous drivers is the prevailing Japanese belief that grief should be as invisible as possible. Even in private life, self-control is so prized that mourners often report feelings of isolation. Weeping, Tomoko Fujimoto, a girlish-looking woman with rimless glasses, remembers, "I was expected to endure the loss of my child in silence, but I couldn't sleep, I couldn't eat. People said to me, 'Please, get back to normal.' No one understood what I was feeling, so my sorrow was never terminated. I felt that I had done something wrong, committed a crime, because I couldn't stop feeling sad. I tried to act normal, on the surface, with other people. But I was not honest. I had to wear a mask." Everyone in the group nods emphatically at her conclusion. Only in the group, they agree, could they talk about their feelings. They compare it to a family or a village, two elements in Japanese life that were formerly much more cohesive. They also liken it to a *kakekomi*, a Buddhist temple where one goes for refuge.

On the morning we spend together, the women behave like the Western self-help groups I have observed. They cry, they laugh, they tease one another, they tell stories the other women have heard many times before, they get angry – at the legal system, at the Buddhist belief that the death of a child may mean her parents or her ancestors did wrong, at friends who didn't want to hear about their sorrow. As in Western groups, people join who are new to bereavement, and they watch the more experienced members carefully. They are encouraged, Masako Ide notes, thinking, "I'm in great trouble now, but maybe I'll get better too."

One intense woman, Keiko Mitoma, who cries easily, keeps pulling her jacket down over her knees, as if it were a blanket. Motoko Misaki, the oldest, who was sixty-one when her only child was killed, says she is resigned to living twenty more years before she can join her daughter. She feels sorry for the younger mothers, who will have to live much longer. The

Japanese do not touch one another as a rule, whereas in a Western group, the mourners might extend a consoling arm or patting hand to the tearful more often; this was the only cultural difference I noted.

This morning, they become most animated when they discuss Buddhist mourning rituals. For many people, the funeral, followed by commemorative ceremonies on the third and seventh anniversaries of a death, combines arcane rituals with vapid social occasions, and several of these women wanted nothing to do with them. A reception marking the death of an aged parent may reasonably have some party-like elements, but for the death of a child, it is unthinkable. The one most in favor of the conventional rituals is Keiko, whose son was very young when he died. Like many such parents, she resents the idea that his short life could be forgotten. She insisted on all the ceremonies "because it was a proof that my son lived on the earth. It was a demonstration of that. I was saying, 'Please, remember him!'"

If their conversation seems familiar, their regular monthly meeting would strike a Westerner as unusual. For one thing, the length: these meetings, designed for "mental care," as they put it, and attended by twenty to thirty people, begin at 1 P.M. and go on until 9:30 P.M. While a Western self-help group would typically talk in a single group, this group splits into different activities, as they choose. Some knit, taught by Motoko, who finds "you can forget sorrow" while you knit. Others chat; others drink tea; still others meet with a visiting expert, such as a professor of law. There is a rice-bowl supper to which members contribute their specialties. Motoko, who comes from an area famous for its good tea, always prepares the tea. At 7:30, a professional comes and addresses the group, perhaps a politician, perhaps a counselor who specializes in the marital difficulties of bereaved parents.

Yes, the women tell me, the death of a child takes its toll on a marriage. Because the husband has to return to work, while the wife is too shocked to eat or sleep, Tomoko Fujimoto says, it's easy to think, "'He's okay, but I'm not okay.' The wife cannot even deal with herself, so she can't afford to think of her husband." Divorce is often the result. Fewer men than women go to the monthly meetings, but they take an active part in the group's practical and political affairs and faithfully attend the group's December party and annual trip. (The trip is an interesting difference between bereavement groups in Japan and North America. The well-known Japanese penchant for group travel extends to this association, while even very close Western groups for bereaved parents, such as the Compassionate Friends, report a disinclination to socialize outside the meetings, much less travel with one another.) A few of the women note that it's even more difficult for men to voice their grief than it is for their wives, but their husbands become extremely emotional on occasion. The December party, particularly, is a poignant event. It always includes the singing of children's songs, and it is quite usual for fathers as well as mothers to weep while they listen.

⌘

As Tom Miavitz lay dying at forty-eight, his plants also began dying. His mother had taught him about plants when he was a boy; later he studied horticulture in university. He passed on his interest to his only child, Elan, who was studying botany when he became ill with cancer. He had raised his daughter alone, and the two were unusually close. Her father loved two things, Elan Miavitz says, "his garden and me."

For months after his death, despairing and purposeless, she felt that her life was shattered. Solace came in stages. First, still dazed with grief, she remembered the plants in her father's Gainesville, Florida, home. His garden was in ruins, his rex begonias, kalanchoes, and plumeria drooping, his palms burned by the cold. "Plant by plant I repotted, pruned, and fertilized his entire collection," she wrote. "Each day I gave his plants all my attention. Dead and diseased leaves were clipped away. Spent blooms pinched. Lanky perennials hard pruned to encourage branches and flowers. Looking after his garden made him seem not so far away. Caring for his plants felt like continuing to care for him . . . I had found a way to connect with him, wherever he had gone."

Tom Miavitz's garden was a godsend, because the cemetery where he was buried forbade any planting on graves – a deprivation for anyone, in his daughter's view, but particularly cruel for a gardener. Still in a great deal of pain, she began volunteering at Gainesville's Botanical Gardens. Struck by the way the garden mirrors our life – "We grow, go to seed and die, according to the seasons, and something of us continues" – she felt the first peace she had known since her father's death. "The earth continually touched me," she recalls, "as I touched it." Pruning she found particularly soothing, she told me – identifying and cutting off the dead parts and watching the raw stumps heal "really softened me." By this point, she had felt society's spoken and unspoken wish that she "move on," which gave her another reason to value the garden: "The garden never judged me. It did not lecture me to 'get over' my sorrow. It did not hurry my grief. The garden itself cannot be hurried along."

Elan is not the first person to find a measure of serenity in the garden. The Harvard biologist Edward O. Wilson coined the term "biophilia" to describe the innate affinity humans have for living things. It springs, he says, from our evolutionary past, when "the smell of water, the hum of a bee, the directional bend of a plant stalk mattered." A growing body of evidence shows that being in contact with what the gardener Henry Mitchell calls "the great cycle of wheeling life" speeds physical and emotional healing.

At about the same time she began gardening, Elan joined a support group. Here there was none of the stigma attached to loss that she felt in the outside world, no need to hide her hurt, no one who underestimated the impact of her father's death. It occurred to her to combine the companionship she felt in the group with the profound meaning she found in gardening.

At twenty-five, Elan had no experience in running a support group and she knew very little about the burgeoning field of horticultural therapy. Her own twist – the combination of support group and joint gardening project – was relatively unusual. She used the term "grief gardening" to describe what she wanted to do and, with the certainty of someone who has had a transforming experience, she forged ahead. With contributions of land and plants from the garden shop where she worked and the cooperation of the local hospice movement, in 1997 she founded a gardening group of six recently bereaved women. Their ages ranged from thirty-five to fifty. Their losses, including a sister, a husband, a friend, were as various as their gardening experience.

For the first meeting, Elan urged the women to bring pictures of their dead, "so that we can meet everyone involved." As well as the usual biographies of living and dead, she wanted to know about their interest, if any, in plants. She set herself a daunting set of objectives: to mourn the dead, both in conversation and by gardening; to honor any particular horticultural interest they had; to bond the group with a joint project, which would bring pleasure to them and to others; and to teach some gardening skills. Fired by beginner's optimism, she managed to do it all.

The group met for three hours every other week for twelve weeks. They began with an hour and a half of talk, modeled on the support group Elan had attended, followed by gardening. The gardening included individual work, depending on their interests: one woman, who had never grown vegetables, planted her own pepper and tomato garden, as her husband had, to continue his avocation. At the end of each session, Elan gave each member a plant to take home and ordered, "Nurture it!" One member designed her own memorial garden, using all six of the plants.

But they spent most of their gardening time together on their group project, a perennial lily bed, planted with crinum lilies, daylilies, and dahlias. The flowers were chosen for their associations with resurrection as well as to illustrate the cyclically recurring nature of perennials. Since the ninety minutes of talk took place on a porch that overlooked the lily bed, it became their reference point, whose progress the women marked as they talked about their own advances and relapses.

Just as a garden cannot be speeded up, Elan says, grief cannot be overcome in a day. Along with learning about organic fertilizing, dividing lilies, and designing a perennial bed, the women were attempting lessons in tranquillity, patience, hope, even joy. When the twelve weeks were over, the group made a plaque dedicating the bed "in honor of our loved ones." Today the garden still flourishes, as do the friendships made in the group.

⌘

Like the Japanese parents' group, Elan Miavitz added an element to the support group. More and more mourners are subtracting an element – their physical presence – as they join forces on the Internet. As I saw with Hannah's attempts to find a support group, sitting in a real room with other mourners is a luxury available to relatively few people. The Internet's indisputable advantage is its convenience. You need to be awake and available to join a chat group that meets in real time, but other than that, the Net is there twenty-four hours a day, seven days a week, whether you live in a desert, Toronto, or Auckland, New Zealand.

Hundreds of different clusters, tailored to highly specific kinds of bereavement, create virtual communities of mourners. The Compassionate Friends, for example, runs nine separate chat groups that meet for an hour once a week in the evening, including ones for men mourning the death of a child; for single parents who have lost a child; for parents with no surviving child; for parents, grandparents, and siblings in families where a child has been murdered. Grief Net offers correspondence groups for more than thirty different types and stages of loss: for people wishing to discuss the spiritual aspects of bereavement, for people who have lost a loved one through substance abuse, for widows and widowers who have moved past the first stages of grief. There is a "kids-to-kids" group, where "adults may lurk, but only kids may send messages"; there is even a group for those who work with the bereaved. The Website for Tom Golden, the Jungian author of *Swallowed by a Snake*, supplies a small supermarket of possibilities for the mourner: columns by Golden and others, excerpts from his book (as well as information on ordering it), a virtual scrapbook where more than six hundred people have posted their stories, a discussions page with "threads" or links to letters on similar themes. Other sites provide mourners places to honor their dead with obituaries, eulogies, and photograph albums; these are accompanied by appreciative letters from strangers who have perused their homemade memorials.

The facilitators and monitors are volunteers and mental health professionals, with a range of training. Their interventions can be sensible and well timed, such as a checklist of common reactions to large-scale disasters that a facilitator posted after the attacks on the World Trade Center and the Pentagon. But, as with Ed Pakes's support group, the real connections happen between the mourners.

Because I had spent so much time sitting in Pakes's office with bereaved spouses, the obvious limitations of Internet mourning struck me first: the lack of visual and auditory information, the cumbersome nature of the written interchange. Chat groups use punctuation marks and shorthand – :(for "frown"; {{{{ for "hugs"; LOL for "laughing out loud" – to speed communication, but there's not much scope for nuance or ambivalence. At the same time, the anonymity and lack of pressure permitted by the Internet is a great advantage for many people. Men and adolescents report that they find it much easier to discuss their feelings in that forum than face to face. Alcoholics acknowledged 30 percent higher levels of consumption to a computer than to a therapist, and another study found that subjects reported more sexual problems to a computer than to a psychiatrist. Diffident mourners and those with feelings they consider shameful might well prefer to confide in strangers, under cover of anonymity, in their own time.

Hannah is a talker, not a writer, and I'm not sure how often she would have been moved to communicate on the Net. But, had she known about these groups, I can imagine her reading the stories, the plaints, and the small successes of people in her situation, especially in the lonely evenings in the first winter and spring of her bereavement. Certainly the same topics and emotions surface on the Internet and in traditional support groups. Mourners from both groups reported in one study similar gains in terms of hope, a sense of group cohesion and universality, and a feeling that the enterprise was helpful. Significantly, the only category where the virtual group reported lower ratings than the face-to-face group was altruism.

After September 11, 2001, one of the things people grasped quickly was that mourning can often be more bearable in the presence of other people. A spontaneous, communal shrine came into being at the base of George Washington's statue in New York's Union Square. Composed of photographs, cards, flags, paintings, bumper stickers, posters, and sculptures deposited or sent by people all over the world, it was made by and for a bereaved city. Until officials took down this "modern war memorial," as the *New York Times* art critic called it, people by the hundreds came at all hours to contemplate it.

They stood there, often for quite a time, in the company of strangers, looking for comfort or meaning in something constructed incrementally, by strangers. A young man who returned each night explained its appeal: "You get a little bit of hope in togetherness."

Mourners of single, unheralded deaths feel the same, although their search for a community is more difficult. The modern mourner is often doubly bereft, of a circle that understands and supports the loss as well as of the dead person. The proverb "Misery loves company" has a hard, unsympathetic edge. But misery loves company for excellent reasons.

TEN

KEEPSAKES

When this you see, remember me.
　　　– proverb

Shall I say how it is in your clothes?
A month after your death I wear your blue jacket.
The dog at the center of my life recognizes
you've come to visit; he's ecstatic.
In the left pocket, a hole.
In the right, a traffic ticket
delivered up last August on Bay State Road.
In my heart, a scatter like milkweed,
a flinging from the pods of the soul.
My skin presses your old outline.
It is hot and dry inside.
　　　– Maxine Kumin, "How It Is,"
　　　　for Anne Sexton

Hannah's bedroom, when we returned to her Vancouver apartment after the funeral week, was a lamentable sight. Brides' magazines and medical textbooks were strewn on the floor, with some silk pajamas she had brought Scott from Vietnam. A rose saved from the night they had become engaged was drooping behind a picture of the two of them on the wall. Photos from the engagement night were scattered on her desk – Hannah flaunting her ring, Scott looking triumphant. She had returned from Asia the Sunday before his accident and had not expected to see him until the following weekend. But in the baggage retrieval area at the Vancouver airport, she heard, "Hi, Beautiful, do you need a cart?" Typical of Scott, he had driven up from Seattle and surprised her. When he took off early Monday morning for the three-hour drive back, he left the shirt he had worn on Sunday in her closet. It was the last time she would see him conscious.

The brides' magazines were no doubt the first things to go, although no one remembers whisking them away. The Vietnamese pajamas were put in a big box of personal effects that she rummaged through regularly. The pictures on the wall, of Scott alone or Hannah and Scott, multiplied, until Hannah referred to her room as the "shrine." Scott's blue shirt she left in the closet as it was, creased, holding the shape of his body, smelling like him.

As well as his hair in her locket, Hannah wore something of Scott's every day that winter and spring, from among the sweaters, T-shirts, and undershorts she had taken in the dispersal of his clothes. She was not ready to let him go, partly because his death had been so sudden and partly because, like every death, it was so final.

Even when a death is long in the past, survivors cherish some vestige or token of the dead person. Sometimes they call it a memento, a Latin word that means a reminder; sometimes a souvenir, the French word for memory. Or a keepsake, a sturdy English compound that suggests that the picture, the lock of hair, or the letter is valued more for its commemorative power than for its intrinsic worth.

Keepsakes can be ordinary and unemphatic. The dead person's clothes must surely be among the most universal mementoes, and they were frequently distributed in wills. Yet in the past their sentimental force was rarely remarked upon.

Perhaps that is because in times when people had few clothes, their pragmatic value was paramount. An 18th-century man must have been conscious that the linen shirt against his skin had once touched the skin of his dead father or brother, but it is not a thought that often finds expression in letters or diaries.

Now that middle-class people have many clothes, their emotional resonance can be intense. Widowers seem either to dispose of their wives' clothes immediately or to live for a long time with closets full of fragrant dresses – both tributes to the power of clothes. Many gay men who die of AIDS have written extremely specific wills, directing particular sweaters or scarves to carefully chosen friends. Matthew Galleli, the widower who wore black and white ribbons on his lapel to mark his loss, began wearing his wife's T-shirts and straw hat about a year after she died. "Memory" is the tailors' term for the wrinkles at the elbow of a jacket, and memory is what the inheritors of clothes wear. To sleep in your mother's night-gown or to warm yourself in your wife's sweater is to inhabit something very intimate, something that expresses their taste, that knew their story, that touched their body.

My friend Sandra Gwyn loved clothes, especially straw hats, shoes, and rather funky jewelry. Soon after she died, her widower gave some pieces of jewelry and other possessions to close friends, but most of her clothes remained in their house. About six months after her death, a dozen women friends were invited for an evening "at Sandra's." Richard Gwyn left the house, as arranged, and Sandra's sister-in-law Danielle Fraser presided. First we saluted Sandra with champagne ("A great clotheshorse!" was one toast), then we drew numbers. The clothes had been laid out on the lower level of the house and one by one, according to our numbers, we trooped down to make our choices.

At the start of the evening, we were rather tentative. Were we being macabre, or greedy, or both? Some of us weren't even sure that Sandra would approve. Those feelings lessened, as champagne and our memories of Sandra flowed. Each time we returned to the living room, modeling our new acquisitions – and we each had a half-dozen visits to the lower level – we were greeted with happy cries. We remembered when Sandra wore that to such-and-such a party; we'd never seen this one but it was very Sandra; how had we missed that handsome jacket? Sandra was small, but one of the symbolic pleasures of the evening was that her things somehow fit women of widely varying sizes. (And at least one tall man, who frequently wears the sweater his wife brought home for him.) The generosity of her clothes seemed to echo her loyal friendship for very different people. As well as clothes, Sandra loved giving parties, and this memorial potlatch felt as if she had arranged one last party for us.

Because clothes are so personal ("My skin presses your old outline," as Maxine Kumin's poem says), people had varied reactions to the evening. Some wouldn't come at all, and others came to remember Sandra but didn't take part in the clothes draw. Some came intending not to take a number, and then did. And when we went down to that room, with Sandra's shoes neatly arranged along the floor and her clothes on the bed and in the closet, perhaps we all drew our own line between "all right" and "too close." I shared Sandra's shoe size, and the sight of her newish, fur-trimmed Indian moccasins made me sad. They were too intimate, too reminiscent of her illness. But I happily wear her green suede pumps, and I like to think I am walking in Sandra's shoes.

Some mementoes are surprisingly bulky. Few mourners have the resources of Queen Victoria, who ordered the Blue Room in Windsor Castle, where Prince Albert died, to be kept as a perpetual memorial to his life. But parents who have lost a child face a related dilemma. Should the child's bedroom be kept as a kind of museum, or should it be redecorated and used for another purpose? Parents in this situation say it is one

of their most heartrending decisions and fraught with potential conflict.

The solutions that seem most satisfactory strike a balance
between commemorating the child and recognizing the
ongoing life of the family. In one case, a Toronto family kept
the wallpaper, decorations, and some of the furniture from
their toddler's bedroom, while using it as the computer room
for their surviving sons. They added a large aquarium, in the
mother's words, "so there would be something living in
the room." It remains "Adam's room."

A Vancouver family kept their teenage son's room intact for
some years, and their daughter and their son's friends used it as
a teenagers' gathering place. When they decided the time had
come to redecorate, they invited friends and family to a
farewell ceremony for Jess's room. They were given pencils and
asked to draw pictures and write letters to Jess on the walls of
his room. When everyone had had his or her say on Jess's walls,
they shared a meal and began repainting.

Keepsakes can be very graphic. A widow in the Andaman
Islands in the Bay of Bengal, photographed early in the 20th
century, wore her husband's skull on a cord around her neck,
a bulbous, bobbing pendant. In the North Massim in New
Guinea, in the same period, the widow wore a mourning collar
contrived from the band her husband had worn around his
hips. Suspended from the band were mementoes of his life: his
lime gourd, which held the hallucinogenic lime and betel nut
he chewed; the handle of his coconut spoon; three small
packets filled with his hair.

Outlandish? Probably, to modern Western eyes. But these
mementoes are not remarkably different from the necklace
worn by Anne Pierce Guillemard. When her six-year-old son,
Frederic, died in 1847, she took her little boy's hair to London's
fashionable Regent Street. There an "artist in hair" named A.
Forrer made her a braided and tasseled rope necklace with a

gold clasp. Hair jewelry was expensive, and Anne Guillemard may well have paid in the neighborhood of $8, at a time when a normal monthly wage was $25 (in modern American money). According to the note that the Guillemard family keeps with the necklace in its original box, the mother wore her boy's hair "a great deal."

The European tradition that includes Anne Guillemard's necklace and Hannah's locket began in the Middle Ages with something more impersonal and religious, the memento mori. Literally a reminder that death comes to all, a memento mori could be as blunt as a real skull. It could also be an exquisitely wrought if grisly bauble: a tiny ivory and gold skull that opened to show a timepiece, a miniature silver coffin, or an articulated skeleton labeled, "As I am, so must you be." Designed to be kept on a writing table or prie-dieu and meditated upon, they marked human mortality, not individual loss.

By the 16th century, as the medieval world and its stoic attitude to death receded, people began commemorating their own deaths by bequeathing rings to family and friends. The oldest rings, bearing the familiar skulls and coffins, stem from memento mori but with a crucial difference: they invite us to consider not only our common fate but also one very particular fate. The inscription that Anne Lady Newdigate of Arbury chose for her mourning ring in 1637 — "Death is the beginninge of life" — was a traditional one. But the addition of her own crest and initials sounded a new note. It said, Yes, we will all die into a new life, but this rings marks a unique death. Shakespeare's 1616 will ordered rings for his wife and daughter engraved with a more secular, modern sentiment (and a popular one for mourning rings): "Love my memory."

As time went on, mourning rings became more personal and began to be given on behalf of other people. When Anna-Maria Verney died at the age of four in the 1680s, her father, Ralph, sent a ring to his brother, explaining, "Filled with my little girl's haire; she was fond of you and you loved her there-fore I now send you this to keepe for her sake." That an uncle who loved his little niece would "keepe for her sake" a ring is very different from contemplating a generic ivory skull. That the ring was filled with Anna-Maria's hair introduces another element, both intimate and, to some, disturbing.

Hair is a special material. Coming from the body and closely associated with the personality, it is more portable and flexible a souvenir than skulls and ribs. It also resists decay, remaining, in John Donne's words, "a bracelet of bright hair about the bone." And it can be worked, transformed into everything from tightly spiraled watch chains to the multicolored bouquets in which Victorian women gathered together specimens from living and dead relatives. Significant artists and artisans worked in the medium, and they produced the occasional tour de force brooch or locket involving weeping willows, a tomb, and a mourner, all executed in hair. One such small masterwork, dated 1788 and in the National Museums of Scotland in Edinburgh, has inscribed on the tomb, "Tis the survivor dies." That lament takes us very far from the medieval impassivity about death, and even from Shakespeare's wish to be remembered.

It was the Victorians who transformed hair work into an industry that could not keep up with the demand and an elab-orate ladies' handicraft that rivaled tatting and beadwork in popularity. The craft was believed by some to have originated in Norway, by others in Germany, but it was generally agreed that the French had perfected it. Almost everyone could afford it, whether it was a childish curl clumsily entrusted to a black glass locket or Anne Guillemard's smart Regent Street neck-lace. By mid-century the fad had spread throughout much of Europe, the British colonies, and the Americas.

Hair appealed to the Victorians' unabashed interest in the physical body (when it came to death) and their emotional-ism. Another name they used for hair jewelry was "jewelry of sentiment." With a lock of hair from a child or a friend, the English poet Leigh Hunt wrote in 1855, a mourner could look up to heaven and almost exult, "I have a piece of thee here, not unworthy of thy being now."

In their enthusiasm for a "piece of thee," the Victorians learned to manipulate hair into anchors, urns, padlocks, forget-me-nots, yews, ostrich plumes, snakes swallowing their tails (symbolizing eternity), and ears of wheat (symbolizing a mature death). They tortured it into dozens of variations on the chain, including the "striped snake," which combined light and dark hair, and the "Scotch plaid braid," which required white, black, and red hair. They prepared it by boiling it in water with soda, worked it with the help of braiding tables, bobbins, lead weights, and forms. The December 1850 edition of *Godey's Lady's Book* gave instructions for building a home braiding table, accompanied with patterns for hair work. Once the piece was finished, it was fixed by boiling it for five minutes, then roasted until dry in as hot an oven as possible, short of burning the hair.

Elaborate or simple, hair jewelry had Queen Victoria's approval. When she visited her gillie John Brown's mother on the morning of Mrs. Brown's husband's funeral in 1875, she did not appear empty-handed. After watching "the sad procession wending its way sadly down" to the churchyard, the queen wrote, "I went back to the house, and tried to soothe and comfort dear old Mrs. Brown, and gave her a mourning brooch with a little bit of her husband's hair which had been cut off yesterday, and I shall give a locket to each of the sons." The speed with which hair cut from the dead man's head could be integrated into a brooch was probably typical. Presumably the sons would affix their lockets to a watch chain.

After that the two widows sat down and, "according to the universal Highland custom," took some whiskey and water and cheese. Both in black, Victoria and Mrs. Brown communed over the traditional mourning food in front of the kitchen fire. Then the queen left, "begging the dear old lady to bear up."

Hair jewelry helped mourners to bear up to the very end of the century, although its greatest popularity stretched from the 1850s to the 1870s. About mid-century, a new kind of brooch was invented, called the swivel or revolving brooch. It had two glass boxes that swivelled as the wearer wished, displaying perhaps hair on one side and a portrait of the dead person on the other. The portrait might be a costly painted miniature, but more likely it was a photograph, another mid-century invention. At first the two kinds of mementoes complemented each other, one an actual part of the dead person, the other a realistic representation of the person. But, like many things Victorian, the craze for hair jewelry exhausted itself. In addition, something undeniably better was available. Mourners still might keep a lock of hair, but hair twisted and gummed into a setting sun or a scythe could not summon up that person nearly as well as the most rudimentary photograph.

⌘

Only photography would make it possible for almost everyone to have a likeness of their loved ones, but the wish was nothing new. Centuries before the Brownie camera, the prosperous commissioned portraits and statues in life, and death masks, tomb effigies, and memorial statues and paintings after death. In the Renaissance, as the portrait was gaining a new importance, a subgenre became fashionable: the likeness of the dying or newly dead.

In France, Germany, Switzerland, the Low Countries, and Scandinavia, people were pictured writing their wills on their deathbed or in severe close-up, dead and alone, or dead and accompanied by mourners. English examples are rarer – there are only about a half-dozen known survivors – and they derive from the Netherlandish school. Within this category, there were national favorites. Netherlandish artists made a specialty of children and artists. The German tradition of painting dead nobility continued until late in the 18th century. Deathbed portraits of French nuns were often hung in their convents, like personalized versions of the medieval memento mori.

A subject that strikes moderns as ghoulish was a natural outgrowth of the medieval and Renaissance preoccupation with the "good death." Historians have also connected these arresting pictures to the new Protestant emphasis on individual responsibility. Since the Protestants had abolished purgatory, which meant that prayers after death were not going to affect the person's chances of salvation, his fate was sealed at the moment of death. As a result, the ultimate moment of life became even more significant; some even thought a person's dying looks might provide a clue as to the state of his soul. No doubt Protestantism played a role, but deathbed portraits were also popular in Catholic countries. They probably owe more to the Renaissance humanism that inspired portraits, biographies, and an interest in the individual personality in general.

But surely the deathbed has an interest that is not limited to the Renaissance. Only a very death-phobic society would deny that the time shortly before and after death is impressively important. Death is one of the two great passages that every person experiences. As people of the 19th century, another culture not averse to memorializing the deathbed, understood, it is often revealing of character, full of feeling, visually striking.

For Sir Kenelm Digby, the death of his wife, Venetia, in 1633 was catastrophic but fascinating. Theirs had been one of the great love stories of 17th-century England. Aristocratic teenagers who fell in love, they had been separated by Digby's mother, who wished her son to marry a great fortune. A future founder of the Royal Society and the author of treatises on religion, medicine, natural philosophy, and cookery, Digby was so charming that "had he been dropped out of the clouds in any part of the world, he would have made himself respected," as John Aubrey described him in *Brief Lives*. Venetia Stanley, a "most beautiful desirable creature" in Aubrey's eyes and a muse for Ben Jonson and other poets, was a much-sought-after belle at the court of James I. After numerous adventures on both sides, the lovers reunited and made a clandestine marriage.

Once Digby became surveyor general of the navy, secrecy was no longer necessary. They were married for nine years and had four sons. In fairly typical style for a 17th-century aristocrat, Digby's eye wandered occasionally during his marriage, resulting in a duel in one case. But, in a way that was probably not typical, he remained passionately devoted to Venetia. She was, he said, "all the true joy I had" and "the only hinge my content has moved upon."

On April 30, 1633, Venetia went to bed in apparent good health. The next morning her maid found her dead, in the same peaceful position in which she had gone to sleep. She was thirty-two, her husband two and a half years younger. Digby's first reaction on hearing the news was "amazement": "In an instant my fancy ran over more space [than] is between heaven and earth . . . I presently grew as senseless almost as the body that I had in my arms." Shock and days of weeping followed, but he also took action. He ordered that casts be made of Venetia's face and hands and that her hair should be cut off for keepsakes. And he commissioned his friend the Flemish painter Anthony Van Dyck to paint her just as she looked when she was discovered.

Probably all Digby realized was that he wanted to keep some semblance of what had been taken from him so abruptly. Exactly what made him think of a deathbed portrait is unknown. They were unusual but not unheard of in England. Just two years earlier, the poet and divine John Donne had caused a sensation by wrapping himself in a shroud, closing his eyes, and having his portrait painted. Digby definitely knew of Donne's example. Although Van Dyck seems never to have painted a deathbed portrait before this, he came from the Low Countries, where such pictures were popular.

A decisive factor may have been Charles I's order for an autopsy, since Venetia's death was so mysterious. Not only had Digby not had time to assimilate the fact that she had gone, her still-beautiful image in death was going to be disfigured, and soon. He owned portraits painted when she was alive, but something in him needed to freeze her image in death, if only to make himself believe it. (The autopsy established nothing, except the puzzling fact that her brain was much shrunken. Rumors circulated that her scientific husband's custom-made potion of viper wine, which he prescribed to sustain Venetia's health and beauty, had poisoned her, but she had been taking it with no ill effects for nine years. The likelihood is that she died from a cerebral hemorrhage.)

Van Dyck arrived to draw her the day after she died. Digby wrote, "Nobody would have thought other than that she had been fast asleep: and with the same sweetness of looks she continued til the surgeons and women ordered her body for her cold and long bed." Other than adding her pearls and a rose, and rubbing her pale cheeks to give her some "seeming colour," the painter and widower did not alter her appearance.

Van Dyck had painted Venetia the year before, in a large, formal portrait of the couple with two of their children. In blue satin and lace, her hair carefully arranged in curlicues across her forehead, she drapes her arm around a wary-looking little son. *Venetia Stanley, Lady Digby on Her Deathbed*, by contrast, is a startlingly intimate and naturalistic closeup. She is seen from above, as the maid would have discovered her. Lying in a white nest of nightclothes and linen, Venetia is a well-nourished 17th-century beauty with a double chin and curly, unkempt hair. She is framed, almost claustrophobically, by a midnight blue velvet coverlet and bed curtains. One hand props her head, and her left eye is ever so slightly, worryingly open. Less realistically, she wears the pearl necklace and large pearl drop earrings, and the rose drops its petals where the white sheet meets the dark coverlet. These were symbolic elements: the pearls suggesting tears as well as purity, the rose perhaps an allusion to the Blessed Virgin, the dropped petals indicating death.

Van Dyck delivered the painting seven weeks after Venetia's death, and Digby welcomed it as the painter's masterpiece and his own "constant companion." At about twenty-eight by thirty-two inches, it was a good size but portable. The widower carried it from his table by day to his bedside by night: "And by the faint light of candle, methinks I see her dead indeed." Digby's friends objected to the portrait as a particularly morbid part of what they saw as his excessive mourning, but he loved it so much that he ordered a miniature of it. Two and a half inches square, it has the same barely open left eye and is carefully marked with Venetia's exact age: thirty-two years, four months, twelve days.

Van Dyck's painting, now in the Dulwich Picture Gallery outside London, is the most famous of Digby's memorials to Venetia, but not the only one. He gathered forty-five of his letters written in mourning, with five "meditations" or essays, into a volume called *In Praise of Venetia*. He commissioned a grandiose classical monument of black marble and bronze to mark her grave, with Venetia as a Roman matron accompanied by mourners. He ordered at least two other statues of her, probably designed for domestic monuments. A year after Venetia's emotional night funeral at Christchurch, Newmarket Street, Digby organized an anniversary sermon in the same church that included a eulogy of his wife. He collected a volume of memorial verse to Venetia composed by Ben Jonson and members of his school, "the tribe of Ben," as well as by lesser poetic lights, including himself.

Part of Digby's mourning was specific to his own confident, rather histrionic character. Part of it related to the fashionable cult of melancholy that had entered England via

Italy at the end of the 16th century. But, although more self-conscious and extravagant than the average, in most ways Digby was a textbook mourner.

Because he documented his feelings so thoroughly in his letters, it's possible to follow him as he works his way through the complex and contradictory terrain of grief. A 21st-century therapist would find Digby's reactions absolutely familiar. He complains of loss of appetite, and the portraits painted of him in mourning do show a frailer, gaunter man. Scarcely getting "an hour's slumber in a whole night" and obsessed with thoughts of his loss, he is unable to concentrate in conversation. Neither can he read: "If I force myself to read a few lines, I understand them not, although the matter be never so plain." Indifferent to most things, he has visions of and conversations with Venetia so vivid he can hardly believe they are imaginary. His grief and his tears come in bursts, and for a long time Wednesday morning, when Venetia died, is a particularly difficult time. Berating himself for his infidelities and other sins against his wife, Digby converts her into an angel, listing her virtues again and again, minutely describing her bodily perfections. Even the weight she gained in her latter years meets with his uxorious approval: "She had a replete body, full of fatness and succulency."

He grasps the therapeutic power of the telling and retelling of his sad story and writes that although his thoughts hurt him, "when I set them down in writing some part of their acrimony is stolen from them by committing them to paper." After the first weeks of shock and raw pain, Digby moved to a familiarity with his grief. Five months after Venetia's death, he writes of his bereavement, "As long as I wrestled with it, it used violence to throw me; but now I lie quietly upon the ground and am contented with my fall, it lieth gently upon me."

In *Bereavement: Studies of Grief in Adult Life*, Colin Parkes discusses the early, searching stage of mourning: the agitated, pining, seeking behavior of lower and higher animals who have lost their mates, their young, or their parents. In humans, this involves brooding on the dead person, imagining conversations and sightings, going to the places and things that seem to summon them up. Another task is the "painful repetitive recollection of the loss experience," which makes it real and irrevocable. This is more necessary and perhaps more painful if the death, like Venetia's, has been completely unanticipated.

Digby did the work of grieving, in Colin Parkes's terms, materially helped by Van Dyck's portrait. As a life-size, realistic image of Venetia apparently sleeping peacefully, it was a crucial part of his searching, pining stage, "the only constant companion I now have." When he praised it, paradoxically, by saying that when he beheld it by candlelight, "methinks I see her dead indeed," he seemed to understand the necessity of making himself believe that that calm, lovely image was actually that of a dead woman. That is what Parkes calls the "painful repetitive recollection of the loss experience." The suddenness of Venetia's death and her sleeping appearance made the portrait doubly valuable: it was a keepsake of his beautiful wife that also helped Digby, as he said, "to look . . . death in the face."

⌘

Looking death in the face was not something our ancestors shrank from. They could hardly have avoided it. Everyone was at risk, but particularly children. From about 1650 to 1750, parents had to expect that one out of four children under the age of ten would die. This worsened in some places in the 19th century, when the survival rate dropped to 50 percent. And when death occurred, it was at close quarters. People were sick and died in their own homes; they were laid out at home, and in pioneer settlements or rural places, they might be buried in the back yard.

With death a constant, familiar presence, people decorated their parlors, bedrooms, and schoolrooms with mourning pictures and grouped around the piano to sing sentimental songs such as "Cradle's Empty, Baby's Gone." They slept under memory quilts, as they called them, pieced together from the clothes of a dead family member, perhaps embroidered with consoling verses. Sometimes they used mourning clothes or even pieces of the shroud in quilts dedicated to a loved one. In one of these, made around 1900, an unknown widow took apart her black silk mourning coat and used it to make a crazy quilt about her husband. Around a central coffin she embroidered biographical symbols of their life together: flags, ships, hearts, fans. Bits of appliquéd fabric look as if they came from her wedding dress.

One of the most famous American mourning quilts was made by Elizabeth Roseberry Mitchell in Kentucky in about 1839. Two of her sons had died in Ohio, where the family had lived before they moved to Kentucky. When she returned, grief-stricken, from a visit to their graves in Ohio, she designed a quilt as a substitute burial ground. The background is a fairly cheerful pattern of stars alternating with calico blocks, but all eyes travel up the embroidered path from the bottom border that leads to the Mitchell burial plot pictured at the center of the quilt. Behind a carefully stitched fence entwined with symbolically drooping flowers, Elizabeth Mitchell appliquéd two hexagonal coffins labeled with her sons' names. Even more startling, around the border of the quilt she appliquéd a coffin for each living family member. The plan was that a labeled coffin would be added to the border with each birth and transferred to the burial plot at the person's death. (In fact, only two coffins joined the original two in the plot, and nineteen remain in the border.)

The idea of greeting the birth of a child by adding a coffin to a quilt is a telling example of how much the world has changed in the last 150 years – and it is important to note that Elizabeth Mitchell's quilt was not considered in any way unhealthy. Quite the contrary, she expressly began it as a way to ease her distress, to make a "place" where she could visit her dead sons. The quilt, a memento mori only a little less unblinking than a medieval skull, was intended to console. Whether it did is not known, but its wear indicates that Mitchells slept under its bleak design for many years.

Mourning needlework was not limited to adult women. The sampler, which displayed alphabets, numbers, a verse, and a simple picture in embroidery, was an important part of every girl's education, and little girls regularly embellished them with gravestones and meditations on death. The mourning sampler, which became a popular variation, focused on the names and death dates of family members and a verse that expressed sorrow, resignation, or both. Because a sampler was a rather ad hoc affair, a girl might be able to cross-stitch additional deaths in after it was hung on the wall. That happened in the case of Sarah Gould of Long Island, who commemorated the deaths of her sister Jennet and her brother Egbert in a sampler she completed in 1815. Sadly, another brother and sister, James and Levina, died in 1820 and 1825. Sarah managed to squeeze their names in and even to add two cramped little *s*es in her verse, so that it read, "My Brother[s] and my Sister[s] dear."

The mourning picture was another way the dead could be commemorated in needlework. Unlike the educational sampler, a mourning picture was all art, a complex painting in silk embroidery using a wide variety of stitches. Mourning pictures were the creations of a leisured class, often made by girls at finishing schools. Abby Bishop was thirteen and a pupil at Miss Balch's Academy in Providence, Rhode Island, when her mother died in 1796. Miss Balch's pupils were famous for their polychrome silk embroidery pictures. On a pumpkin-colored background, Abby embroidered the twin-towered Providence Congregational Church, surrounded first by an arch and then by an undulating border of blossoms. Underneath she stitched, "My Mother departed this life March 24th 1796," and a home-made verse: "Then art thou gone my tender Parent dear / An drop my friends the Sympathizing tear / Gone! gone! And left your Children, Ere' they knew / One half the favors they received from you."

A thirteen-year-old who responds to the loss of her mother by executing a painstaking piece of embroidery is not our idea of a bereaved teenager. Nor would we expect a fifteen-year-old girl to commemorate her dead sister by an elaborate ink painting and inscription on her workbag, the cotton bag that held her needlework supplies and current project. That is what Rebecca Tenney did in Bluehill, Maine, in 1819, to honor her sister Abigail, who had died of measles three years before at the age of four. The picture is the usual one of a woman weeping at a tomb, shaded by weeping willows.

Mementoes like this became so predictable that Mark Twain took deft aim at them in *The Adventures of Huckleberry Finn*. Puzzling over the sensitive Emmeline Grangerford's mourning pictures, Huck sees a black-veiled woman underneath the obligatory weeping willow "leaning pensive on a tombstone" and clutching a white handkerchief. The picture was called *Shall I Never See Thee More Alas*. Another of Emmeline's tributes, this one to a dead bird, was captioned *I Shall Never Hear Thy Sweet Chirrup More Alas*. Yet another, showing a young woman, in Huck's description, "mashing a locket with a chain to it against her mouth," was titled *And Art Thou Gone Yes Thou Art Gone Alas*.

Alas, it is easy to laugh at Emmeline's mechanical creations, and there is no denying that Victorian rooms were full of such morose keepsakes. Abby's picture, Rebecca's workbag, and Sarah's sampler might seem unhealthy occupations for young girls. But we live in a world where few children lose a sibling or a parent. Those plain-speaking pieces of handicraft, hung in the parlor or bedroom, integrated the dead into the daily life of the family. The 19th century thought that was natural, as do many therapists today.

The quilts and samplers and memorial pictures of the past are more structured, with less scope for personal expression, than the drawings and designs contemporary bereaved children make in support groups. But they all represent a union of hand and eye and mind that allows the mourner to ruminate on the dead while they work. As well, the needlework must have given their makers the satisfying sense that order can come out of disorder, that beauty can emerge from suffering, that humans are not simply the tools of malevolent fate.

⌘

Needlework keepsakes had the advantage that half the population could make them, and they were cheap. People still longed for realistic likenesses of their dead, but professional artists were expensive. If someone in the family could draw, they were enlisted to sketch the mortally ill or newly dead. Lyman Beecher's one-month-old daughter, Harriet, died from whooping cough in 1809 in Long Island. Years later, he wrote to another daughter, "After the child was laid out, she looked so very beautiful that your mother took her pencil and sketched her likeness as she lay. That likeness, a faint and faded little thing, drawn on ivory, is still preserved as a precious relic." (Two years later, another girl was born and given the same name as the child who died, a common 19th-century practice. She grew up to become Harriet Beecher Stowe.)

Families without artistic talent might spend a large sum for a painting. William Gookin, a New Hampshire artist who made something of a specialty of postmortem paintings, was engaged by the family of a Dr. Cowan who died in 1848. Gookin charged $40 for the painting, $15 for the frame, $3 for hiring a horse, and $7 for "time in going." When a family realized a case was hopeless, they might call in the painter before death. Gookin was called to the Cushing house when their daughter Hannah was ill and shown the sick child, her best dress, and the family dog. He returned to his studio and painted Hannah in her finery, standing against the trees with the dog at her feet.

Painting a dead person as if he were living was the 19th-century preference, especially in the case of children. A child could sicken and die within a few days, and parents would have no image with which to remember his childish vitality or characteristic gestures. Posthumous painters went to considerable trouble, measuring the corpse (sometimes with calipers), studying earlier portraits if they existed, posing siblings with similar coloring. Grieving parents were understandably difficult to please, and at least one well-known portrait painter, William Sidney Mount, advised charging double the usual price for "the anxiety of mind" involved in a posthumous portrait.

In the late 1850s, Marcus Ward of Newark, New Jersey, commissioned two family portraits from the painter Lilly Martin Spencer. One shows four children grouped around an armchair, concentrating on a parrot. The other picture, an equally realistic, life-size portrait of a fifth child, Nicholas Longworth Ward, shows a toddler trembling between babyhood and boyhood. Dressed in the short-skirted dress worn by little boys in the 1850s, he tilts his head to one side and trustingly offers an orange to someone just outside the frame. The 19th-century viewer would have assumed that the children in the first picture were alive and known immediately that Nicholas was dead. The clue was the broken-stemmed rose in the goblet at Nicholas's left. Roses held downwards or with broken stems signified death, just as the rose petals on Venetia Stanley's counterpane communicated that this was no ordinary sleep.

Sometimes a family could not bear even a symbol breaking the illusion of life, and there was none. At other times the painter or the family invented an idiosyncratic symbol. Nicholas's orange, parted into seven sections and offered so beguilingly, has puzzled scholars. Perhaps Nicholas simply liked oranges, or he had just reached the stage when a child learns to share things with other people. But fruit was often associated with fertility, and the orange may well symbolize the seven members of the Ward family, including Nicholas. (Seven pieces of fruit lie on a plate in the portrait of the living children.)

Part of the point of a posthumous portrait was to affirm the dead person's continuance in the life of the family, and some paintings portrayed the living and dead members together, in an idealized portrait. The Wards chose not to do that, but the two paintings, clearly companions, announce, "This is our family." That it is the dead child who may be proffering a symbol of the complete family would have struck the 19th-century viewer as poignant but not ironic.

Posthumous paintings remained an upper-class preserve, and their popularity began to fade by about 1860. In 1839 something more limited but more reliable appeared: the daguerreotype. Almost immediately, it occurred to people that this new invention could capture the dead as well as the quick. (At the dawn of photography, it was much easier with the dead, because subjects had to hold their pose for such a long time.) The first posthumous daguerreotypes appeared in the 1840s, and posthumous photographs continued to be made routinely at least through the first decades of the 20th century in Europe and the Americas. Their popularity extended from working men to Queen Victoria, who slept with a large photograph of Prince Albert taken shortly after his death.

In 1846, the Boston firm of Southworth and Hawes advertised, "We make miniatures of children and adults instantly, and of Deceased persons either at our rooms or at private residences ... We take great pains to have Miniatures of Deceased Persons agreeable and satisfactory, and they are often so natural as to seem, even to Artists, in a quiet sleep." Albert Southworth gave businesslike advice to his colleagues about such matters as positioning the body, the possibility of liquids escaping from the mouth, and the use of a mirror to produce an "easy graceful, natural" image. Photographic supply houses designed dignified cases for postmortem pictures as well as framing mats in black with subdued floral embellishments. Their efforts paid off, as the advertisement for a daguerreotype business in 1854 indicates: "The only establishment in a city of 20,000 inhabitants and where pictures of deceased persons alone will pay expenses."

One of the motives behind posthumous paintings and early postmortem photographs was the lack of a likeness made when the person was living. But even after the 1890s, when the Kodak camera had put snapshots within the reach of most North American families, people continued to photograph their loved ones after death. They might have six photographs of Uncle William, but his death was too significant to go unrecorded. A typical postmortem photograph from the turn of the century might include twenty or more family members grouped around an open coffin on the lawn, just before the arrival of the hearse.

Not only was it important to have a picture of the dead person, it might be important to be in the picture oneself. When James Garfield, the future American president, learned that his infant had died, he hurried home from his Civil War regiment to be photographed with the child in his arms. A West Virginia funeral director tells a 20th-century story of two sisters whose brother had died. They had never been photographed with him, so they took his embalmed body home one last time. There they had a family portrait taken, with their brother propped up between them.

Social and photographic historians are naturally attracted to postmortems, as these images are called, and there are large collections of them in the Burns Archive of Death and Dying in New York City, the Strong Museum in Rochester, and other institutions. The thought of poring over images of dead people now tends to make people shudder, but no more than

Victorians would have flinched at the idea of pictures of people having sex. As Freud pointed out in *Totem and Taboo*, a culture is defined by what it represses, and ours has decided that an interest in death is a peculiarly creepy form of pornography.

Nonetheless, for sheer human interest, it would be hard to surpass a few hours or days spent looking at postmortem photographs. There is considerable beauty in these pictures, especially in the early daguerreotypes. They tended to be intense, carefully composed portraits in closeup, enclosed in a case and designed for intimate viewing. Often the subject is apparently sleeping, and the only indications to the contrary are the telltale roses placed in a hand. Occasionally medicine bottles stand on a table, a symbolic reference to useless remedies that is also seen in posthumous paintings.

Sometimes the inscription is as striking as the image: on the back of a picture of a young girl taken nine days after death is written, "Mother could not bear to part with only daughter." Sometimes a combination of care and carelessness suggests a family's distress, as in a picture from the 1850s of a dead girl in a neat plaid dress seated on a loveseat, but with blood visible on her face and neck. And there are images that could inspire a novel. One of those, taken in Atlanta in 1863, shows black twin boys about ten years old. Their father was a slave owner, their mother a slave. One beautifully dressed boy is dead, lying on a bench; the other, identically dressed, contemplates his mirror image.

There are grotesque images, although not as many as might be imagined. Occasionally a corpse is emaciated by cholera or dysentery, but death came more often with savage swiftness in the 19th century. People were carried away so quickly by infections that there was not time for cheeks to lose their roundness.

The postmortem photograph evolved along with photography as a whole and society's attitude to death. By the 1870s, the dignity of the first generation of postmortems was giving way to something less studied, more a record of the event of death. The invention of paper prints, such as the *carte de visite*, meant that a postmortem could be displayed in an album rather than in its own case, looked at in company rather than individually. Perhaps the sometimes daunting focus on the face in the early postmortems seemed inappropriate for the family album. In addition, the new emphasis on what funeral directors had begun to call the "beautiful memory picture" meant that the fashionably padded and trimmed coffin (now renamed the casket in America for its resemblance to a jewel box) became the dominant feature in a postmortem.

Even in England, where coffins remained coffins, the beautification of the death scene and its preservation in a photograph became increasingly important. When Lord Frederick Cavendish was assassinated in Dublin in 1882, the nurses surrounded his hospital bed with flowers, and photographs were taken. Finding the pictures "too beautiful – such a deep comfort," his widow framed them in velvet and sent them to friends and relatives.

In urban, mainstream America, the demand for postmortems lessened considerably after about 1920, when many of our contemporary attitudes to death were formed. But although postmortem photographs have not been openly acceptable in middle-class America for a long time, the impulse to make a record of the dead persists. The photographic historian Jay Ruby was told by a Pennsylvania funeral director in the 1970s that he often found used flashbulbs in the wastepaper basket after the family had been alone with a body. A friend of mine considered photographing her mother, who died very emaciated from cancer in 1996, and only decided not to "because she would have hated people seeing her like that." Another friend's mother did photograph her husband after death but has never shown the Polaroids to anyone.

Hannah's outsize album of Scott's photographs in life – six years' worth of dances, camping trips, family occasions, hikes – was a vitally important component of her mourning. She regularly showed it to visitors and toted it with her on plane trips across the country in the first year after his death. When we drove to see her grandparents in the summer, she stowed it in the car and told me she didn't like to introduce the subject of the album: that was my job. Dutifully, I mentioned it that evening, and Hannah sat between her grandparents and took them through her years with Scott. She carried it to San Francisco for the first anniversary of Scott's death, which she spent with his parents. For Marilyn particularly, paging through those pictures, most of which she had never seen, was harrowing and heartening in about equal measures.

I assumed that Hannah would not have wanted pictures of Scott in the hospital, attached to respirators and other machines, and then free of them in death. But I was wrong. It was not a strong wish, and she did not spend time regretting that she did not have any such pictures. But the days around Scott's death had been so meaningful that having some photographic record seemed natural to her. Few things seem to divide people as sharply as postmortem pictures, and Scott and Hannah's friends were no exception: to some the idea sounded reasonable, while others were horrified.

There is one situation where postmortem photographs have become acceptable again in mainstream North America, and that is in the case of stillbirths and infant deaths. Beginning in the late 1970s and early 1980s, obstetrical nurses and social workers turned their attention to the plight of parents who entered the hospital expecting to take home a baby and left with nothing. "You have to hold someone before you can give them up," as one social worker explained to me. The holding involves encouraging parents to spend time seeing, touching, and embracing their baby, to name their baby, and to take home as many mementoes as possible: locks of hair, foot and hand prints, crib card, ID bracelet, and photographs.

At virtually all North American hospitals, photographs taken by staff are a standard, central part of the services offered to grieving parents. The baby may be photographed alone or held by parents, grandparents, siblings, staff. Many hospital volunteer organizations make tiny smocked gowns and knitted hats for the photography sessions, and these clothes, often the only ones ever worn by their child, are also taken home by the parents. Most parents are grateful for the photographs, but if they decline, the pictures are labeled and kept on file. In many cases, parents return months or years later, sometimes after the birth of another child, wanting the photographs of the baby who died.

In 1985, the Centering Corporation in Omaha, Nebraska, produced "A Most Important Picture," a brief guide for nurses, doctors, and social workers about photographing stillborn babies and infants who die. There is practical advice on types of cameras and backgrounds (a loosely wrapped baby on a colored sheet or paper produces a good result). There are interesting suggestions – "Showing the baby's shoulders also adds to the picture" – and a picture of a baby, fists clenched above a receiving blanket, to prove it. The authors recommend that the family also take their own pictures, which promotes talk. As usual with postmortem photographs, even the disturbing pictures in the manual are impressive. An anencephalic newborn lies unclothed but with a cap over his head. Twins, born after twelve weeks' gestation, share a receiving blanket. A little boy listens intently to his grandmother as she holds his dead sibling.

Laurel, a healthy nine-pound girl, died during her birth in Toronto in 1995. Her parents, Ann Martin and Tom Clement, were completely unprepared for her death, which happened suddenly when Ann's uterus ruptured and the baby asphyxiated. Laurel died in the evening, and Ann spent the first night "howling. It was an animal response. I liken it to a husky on an ice floe or a wolf, where you howl out your devastation."

The nurse assigned to them told Ann and Tom they could see their baby whenever they wished, but they refused. The next day, after some sleep, Ann changed her mind. "I stepped out of shock and into mourning. I realized that there was only so much time, and if I said no, it would be gone forever. To hold your baby is tangible proof that you've had a baby, and that was really important . . . I will never forget seeing Tom walking the baby around our hospital room and realizing that he had really learned how to hold a baby. With Mallory, our first child, he had been unsure. Here he was cradling Laurel, knowing just what to do."

At this point, Laurel had been dead about sixteen hours. Tom remembers, "She was so cold, that was so hard. I kept feeling her cold bottom and thinking that I should change her diaper."

For Ann, Laurel remains a perpetual newborn. Tom is conscious of the milestones she will never cross, painfully aware of "where she would be now." When the two-and-a-half-year-olds entered Mallory's daycare in 1997, he thought, "Laurel would have been there." In 2002, he says of her, "She remains with us every day."

Although Laurel never lived outside the womb, her parents have a drawerful of keepsakes in the room she would have shared with her sister, and others that Ann keeps in her lingerie drawer "because I see them every day." In the first drawer they keep the clothes the hospital dressed Laurel in for her photographs, booties and a gown, with a receiving blanket. Ann says, "That's all you have and they've been against her skin and you can caress them. That's all you have to caress." She points out the smocking on the gown: "We appreciate that it was done with care. There were days when I would just come in here and bury my face in the blanket." Also in the drawer is the tape of Laurel's funeral service, which Tom and Ann listen to on the anniversary of her death, the plastic-covered death notice from the newspaper, the sympathy notes they received, even a list of the people who brought them meals in the first weeks.

In her lingerie drawer, Ann keeps a lock of dark hair, tiny handprints, an early ultrasound picture, and the diary she kept in the months after Laurel died. Meticulous records of her blood sugar that Ann, a diabetic, kept throughout her pregnancy are also here, proof that she was ensuring a healthy future for her baby.

Pride of place goes to six Polaroid pictures of a round, perfectly formed, brown-haired baby. Ann notes how pummeled she looked, after the nurses and doctors worked fruitlessly to revive her. "She was such a feisty little thing. I would have expected her to fight the good fight." After carrying Laurel for nine months, Ann had a strong sense of what her daughter was like, and seeing her confirmed it. Now the pictures keep that impression alive. "She had this shock of dark hair and this look of absolute determination. She was a little bruiser in the womb." In one picture she is being held by a nurse, and Ann says, "I love that someone is holding her."

The diary she kept after Laurel's death shows how important the pictures were in Ann's mourning. Very much as Sir Kenelm Digby used his portrait of Venetia to stimulate his feelings, to remember her dear image, to convince himself that she really was gone and to imagine that she was not, Ann used her Polaroids. On a particularly bad day, she visited Laurel's grave and had an impulse to resurrect her, to hold her and protect her: "Her picture is in my mind all day." Once, when she wailed in despair over the pictures, Tom gently took them away from her. Later she offered to show a friend her pictures. "I could tell in an instant that the idea made her uncomfortable and I felt bad, but it's her choice – not everyone wants to see pictures of dead babies. It's just that I want Laurel to be alive so much that it gives me comfort to pretend she is by seeing her."

Maybe "pictures of dead babies" or dead wives, or other unconventional mementoes, strike onlookers as dubious or creepy because the onlookers have no need for such comforts at the moment. When a friend told me that her sister was keeping her late husband's greeting on their telephone message, months after his death, I winced. The friend pointed out that a recording of Sam's voice was not much different from a picture of his face; we just aren't yet familiar with telephone greetings as keepsakes. And, most important, Cathy, Sam's widow, loved hearing his voice. My reaction to that and the story of Ann Martin's reluctant friend stirred memories of Digby's friends. Chiding him for poring over Venetia's portrait, they told him he was doting on a shadow. Digby's defense of his desperate but ultimately wholesome remedies was a good one, appropriate for Ann's use of her Polaroids and Cathy's voice recording: "Mine is not a light and disjointed madness, but a serious and coherent one." Not madness at all, in other words.

ELEVEN

AS GENTLY AS POSSIBLE

Now, I think maybe you never get over anything, you just find a way of carrying it as
gently as possible.
    – Bronwen Wallace, "Heart of My Heart"

As the first anniversary of her son's death approached,
Karen Tallman wanted a gathering at the place where he
died. Close friends – a Haida man, a Greek couple, and a
Jewish woman – tried with some heat to dissuade her. The
prescribed year of mourning, they argued from their separate
traditions, was about to end. They needed to mark the closing
of that period, and a ceremony at the place where Jess died
would be going backward, not forward.

The setting for the discussion was one of the Friday-night
suppers that Karen and her husband, Brian DeBeck, had held
since Jess's death. Some of the guests were horrified to hear
their friends accusing Karen and Brian of clinging to their grief,
of dragging out their mourning. But Karen, with typical objec-
tivity, emphasizes how much she valued the argument because
it made her grasp the firmness of her position. She didn't need
other people to accompany her to the ritual she was imagining,
but "I was very clear that I was nowhere near a turning point. I
was not finished with grieving."

Jess DeBeck was in his last year of high school in 1996 when the van in which he was sleeping caught fire on a quiet Vancouver street overlooking the water. His family mourned him deeply and imaginatively. They are still mourning.

Brian is a labor organizer, Karen a psychologist. Jess's sister, Cora, was fifteen when he died. They are an unusual family in the public, social way they conduct their private life. Their bereavement was gregarious and eclectic because they are gregarious and eclectic. Responsive to the suggestions and customs of their friends, they were conscious from the first that they wanted to include and accommodate other people who grieved for Jess and for them. Perhaps the most remarkable thing about Karen and Brian was their understanding that the heightened mode of ritual – borrowed, adapted, or improvised – is a way to keep people connected during a tragedy.

Much of the first year after Jess's death was organized with that goal in mind. In the DeBecks' living room, a shrine went up to Jess, with his ashes, pictures, candles, and flowers. For forty-nine days, the prescribed first stage of Tibetan mourning, at 8 A.M. and 8 P.M., a bell would be rung, a candle lit, and from five to fifteen people gathered for a reading from E.J. Gold's *The American Book of the Dead*, a rendition of the Tibetan Book of the Dead. It gave a rhythm to the day and made it possible for people still reeling from the shock of Jess's death to be together for perhaps twenty minutes of reading, prayers, and comments. Unexpectedly, some of the regulars found themselves mourning their own family and friends, something that happened consistently at rituals for Jess, and that Karen and Brian welcomed.

Devoted to her work as a psychologist at Vancouver General Hospital and a fairly driven personality, Karen was dubious when a colleague, a psychiatrist, advised her not to work full-time for six, eight, perhaps twelve months. At first it took courage not to return to the hospital but, as it turned out, she worked only a day and a half a week for a full year after Jess's death. Once Karen realized, with surprise, that she was going to be able to stay home, she began to think of herself as one of "the old Greek women who live in black and tend the churches in the villages, sweep and light candles and putter. Because really for that first year, I didn't want to do anything much but light candles, make things pretty, arrange flowers."

Brian, for his part, has a strong attachment to stone. With his brother, he spent the first month after Jess's death building a stone wall around their house. A graphic symbol of protection and enclosure, it was a reminder that nothing had managed to keep Jess safe, and nothing could have. But as the family lived more and more within its house during the first year of mourning, as Karen found what consolation she could in making it beautiful, as it became even more of a center for their friends, the wall seemed increasingly appropriate.

The stone wall led to the building of a large memorial cairn at the DeBecks' cabin at Storm Bay on the Sunshine Coast of southern British Columbia. In the first summer after Jess's death, they rafted a sizable load of stone over to their land, and about twenty friends and family formed a chain that moved it from the raft to the place appointed on the beach for the cairn. The strenuous work of passing the stones one to another and building the five-foot-high cairn took about four hours. By the end, Karen understood something about the relationship between stone and grief, how many hands could make it bearable but never rob it of its weight, its hardness, its obduracy.

The Storm Bay cairn, which endures, is an example of a successful ritual where everyone takes a part and where the process and the result are both peculiarly correct. The cairn's cumulative element and the metaphorical rightness of stone led to an extraordinary first-anniversary ritual. Karen had prevailed, and they held it on the hilly street where the van had caught fire. A trailerful of rock had been unloaded about a block up from the site, and in the evening about a hundred people picked up a rock in one hand and a candle in the other.

By the time Brian and Karen arrived, they were streaming slowly down the steep hill in silence, lit by their candles. One by one, each added a rock to the growing pile.

Karen has a vague memory that she read something, and that a few people spoke, but the important thing was the people silently constructing, one by one, the four-foot-high cairn. Unlike the Storm Bay cairn, they knew this one was temporary, but what was important was the process. If it stayed for one minute, that was enough. As it happened, it lasted for six weeks. By the time the city took it down, it was piled with flowers and someone had positioned a picture of Jess on it.

⌘

Karen and Brian's Haida, Greek Orthodox, and Jewish friends had not been misrepresenting their cultures. The Greek Orthodox Church's memorial service on the first anniversary of a death is an important milestone. Jewish mourning officially ends eleven months after the death, when the daily saying of Kaddish is concluded and many families unveil the headstone at the grave. The Haida also erect a headstone at the end of a year and hold a potlatch to signal the conclusion of mourning.

Of course, that mourning officially ends does not mean the dead are forgotten. The Jews say commemorative prayers at four points during the year, as well as remembering the anniversary of the death, called *yahrzeit*. (Or, as a five-year-old friend reminded her father, "Isn't it almost time for Zayde's yard sale?") In Greece on the third anniversary, the body is exhumed for the second burial, and that date is often marked by Greek Orthodox people in North America with a memorial service. Because Jesus lay in his tomb on a Saturday, Greek Orthodox remember the dead on four Saturdays in the year, called Psychosavato, the Saturday of Souls.

But most people, at least in North America, rarely mention the anniversary of a death after a few years, outside their most intimate circle. When I lived in Holland in the late 1970s, I was leafing one day through a friend's family calendar, which in the practical Dutch way was hung in the bathroom. On a certain date was the notation *"Moeder's sterfdag"* – Mother's death-day. An American as yet untouched by the death of anyone close to me, I was surprised. My friend's mother had been dead more than fifteen years, but the anniversary was still a day to be reckoned with, marked down along with birthdays, wedding anniversaries, and other happier family occasions. By that point, the annual return of the day probably prodded my friend to spend some minutes remembering her mother. In earlier years, there may have been an anniversary mass.

The Japanese are particularly tenacious about commemorating their dead, holding memorial services on the first anniversary of the death, then after 3, 7, 13, 25, 33, 50, and sometimes 100 years. Naturally, relatively few people remember someone fifty years after his death, much less a hundred years. In Japan, as elsewhere in Asia, memory and grief become transmuted over the years into a more generalized respect for one's ancestors.

Some Japanese, such as Motoori Norinaga, design their own death-day observance. Norinaga, the 18th-century scholar whose lifework was returning the Japanese to their own traditions, devised a gathering in his study, decorated with his self-portrait, seasonal flowers, and a lighted lamp, but no incense. His desk was to be set up. The memorial tablet on display, unlike the usual Buddhist tablet the Japanese keep on the family altar, had no Chinese words, only Norinaga's posthumous name in Japanese. After a meal that included fish and sake, Norinaga's friends and disciples were to spend the evening composing poems.

It was a highly personal memorial, echoing Norinaga's taste in food and pastimes and his deeply felt patriotism. Few people anywhere have the will or the means to endow such a yearly observance, but in Japan it is not necessary to be wealthy, accomplished, or even beloved to have an annual remembrance after death. The midsummer holiday called Obon, by and large a jolly occasion, turns the country into a confraternity of mourners who tend, nourish, and celebrate the family's dead.

In mid-July or mid-August, depending on the region, the dead are believed to return to their old houses. To welcome them, what seems like the majority of Japanese clog the nation's highways to return to their family village and cemetery. There they clean the family graves, light a fire at home so that the smoke can guide the dead back, and make offerings of food and drink to the dead at an altar set up in the home. A priest may attend, reading prayers to aid the dead on their long journey to full enlightenment. Dances, called *bon odori*, are held to entertain the dead. In some localities, eggplants and carrots are carved into models of horses, so the deceased can ride back to the other world when Obon is finished.

An American married to a Japanese woman described Obon for the *Japan Times* in 1987 as a relaxed family reunion occupied with gossiping, eating, and cleaning the family graves together. But it is also a time when the dead exert a vigorous, generally benevolent influence. As they left the graveyard, the head of the family said of his mother, dead for a quarter-century, "See how my mother keeps us together."

In spite of the general good spirits, at least the first few Obons after a death can be piercingly sorrowful. At the end of the holiday, the dead return to the other world, their way lit again by fires. In Nagasaki, they depart symbolically in large model boats that have been specially constructed, first for a happy, noisy parade through the streets and then for their voyage out to sea. At Obon in 1984, a group of college students pulled a boat of some twenty feet, decorated with a photograph of a young girl and messages of love to her. During the parade, they threw firecrackers and made merry along with everyone else, but minutes after they had pushed their boat out from the harbor, they were in tears, "clutching each other in the grief of the recently bereaved," struck again by the finality of the separation. When a loved one who was celebrating Obon a year ago is now being celebrated, there is nothing abstract about it, no comfortable sense of ancestors long settled in another world.

Other places observe a collective commemoration of the dead, and the best-known Western example has a strong family resemblance to Obon. On Mexico's Day of the Dead, the dead also return to their earthly home for twenty-four hours. As with the smoke at Obon, some Mexicans light incense to direct the spirits back to their house; others make trails of marigold petals. (Marigolds are the flower associated with the dead from Aztec times.)

An altar or *ofrenda*, meaning offering, is built at home with pictures of the dead, candles, and special food and drink for them. Graves are cleaned and decorated with special flowers. Although the Day of the Dead springs from the confluence of Aztec beliefs about the importance of death with the Catholic feast of All Souls' Day on November 2, it is, like Obon, a holiday where the main celebrants are family members. In Mexico as in Japan, the clergy have minor or no roles to play.

At first the Day of the Dead sounds exotic and touristic, more about spectacle than about feeling. Mexicans will advise you to go to Xochimilco for the candlelight parade; go to Mixquic on Lake Chalco, where the *trajineras*, shallow lake boats, are decorated with *ofrendas*. All over Mexico, beginning in the last weeks of October, rows of sugar skulls, each decorated with a name, grin ghoulishly in markets and candy shops. People present them to their namesakes, and children particularly look forward to receiving these macabre sweets. Round loaves of special Day of the Dead bread are topped with crossed bones, modeled in dough. Cheeky toys made of wood, pottery, and paper depict skeletons driving cars, filling teeth, teaching classes, playing instruments. People write irreverent descriptions of their living friends' deaths, called *calaveras*, or skulls, and give them to the subjects. It all seems to underline the contradictory stereotypes about Mexicans and death: they embrace it, they jeer at it, they are gloomily obsessed with it, they make friends with it.

Always celebrated with special fervor by Indians, the Day of the Dead is making something of a comeback with educated, urban Mexicans and artists. They like what they see as its insouciance, its outrageousness, its creative opportunities. Mexico City newspapers at the beginning of November are filled with satiric *calaveras* addressed to politicians. Every museum and community center has its own altar. When I asked a Mexican diplomat whose wife, an artist, builds a Day of the Dead altar in their house each year whether Mexicans actually mourn or even remember their dead on November 2, he said, "Only generically."

I got very different answers to that question when I spent the Day of the Dead in Valle de Bravo. A twisting Indian town about two hours from Mexico City, Valle de Bravo is a popular weekend retreat for people from the capital. But during the week the city dwellers are nowhere to be seen, and the town is much as it has been for hundreds of years.

On the Day of the Dead in 1999, Tere Mercado Goncalez served me a lunch of tortilla soup and chicken stew in the Valle de Bravo house where she works as a maid. She is a compact, beautiful woman in her early forties, with a square, copper-colored face and gleaming black hair. Once she had finished the dishes, she was on her way to the cemetery, to clean her mother's and mother-in-law's graves and decorate them with *nube*, cloud-flowers, a white, gypsophila-like bloom. Many people spent the whole day in the cemetery, but Tere could spare only three hours. When the graves had been tidied, she and her two daughters would eat a meal of *mole* tamales on her mother's grave.

At home, she had already set up the family altar. The basic offerings to the dead are fruit, flowers, candles, bread, and some sugar skulls. If the family's circumstances permit, *moles* or other favorite foods of the dead are added. November 1 is dedicated to dead children, the *angelitos* or little angels. At noon on October 31, the candles are lit in memory of the family's dead children. Twenty-four hours later, those candles have burned out and new ones are set out and lit for the adults. Families who can afford it add cigarettes and tequila to the altar. The customary belief is that the dead consume the essence of the offerings, leaving the rest for the family to eat, smoke, drink. When I asked Tere if she believed that, she smiled. "No. It's a tradition."

Then, unprompted, she recounted a Day of the Dead legend told all over Mexico with minor variations, as a true story that happened in that particular village. It concerns a man who was so miserly that he gave his wife no money for their *ofrenda*. She could only put the commonest herb on their altar for their dead. That night, as the man was returning from the bar, he saw the dead walking from their old houses back to the cemetery. At the end of the group were his own relatives, ragged and hungry because they had not been fed. Contrite, he rushed home and gave his wife money for a proper offering, but it was too late.

For Tere, it's a bittersweet time, shot through with obligation and melancholy. She feels a satisfaction when she has done her duty to her mother, but, she says, "you can't take the sadness out of it." Her mother died when she was eight, thirty-five years ago, and the days in the year when Tere remembers her most vividly are Mother's Day and the Day of the Dead. In particular, she remembers her mother setting up the Day of the Dead altar in their house, as she expects her daughters to remember her on November 2, after she is dead. She is confident they will carry on with the tradition, since everyone in her village, with the exception of the converts to Protestantism, observes the holiday just as they did in her childhood. Why don't the Protestants celebrate the Day of the Dead? Because they think it is superstitious, she says, and they don't see its point. Its point, for Tere, seems devoid of superstition, simply a day or so reserved to remember her mother at home and in the graveyard.

Valle de Bravo has two cemeteries, and early in the afternoon the approach to the smaller one, next to the Church of Santa Maria, is lined with women selling the three classic Day of the Dead flowers: long-stemmed marigolds; crinkled, velvety flowers that resemble brains; and cloud-flowers. Beer, candles, and thin wooden crosses painted black are also for sale.

The scene at the cemetery itself is quiet and purposeful. A mass in the packed little chapel is concluding; one is celebrated here at noon on November 1 and 2. Yesterday's flowers for the *angelitos*, deposited on the many quite recent children's graves, are already tired-looking. Every family is intent now on its adult graves, mounding the earth into a new, pronounced hump if there is no stone to distinguish it (and often there is not), putting out heaps of marigolds in empty, economy-size chile jalapeño cans.

Luisa Riley and her husband, Ariel Garcia, are tending the grave of her father, who died four years ago. She offers me a beer in the hot sun and volunteers, "It's a sad day." Her school-age son is pounding holes in the chile jalapeño cans that will cover the candles they will light when they leave. Another woman, in the flounced and many-layered dress of bright blue, red, and pink worn by the Mazahua Indians, is painstakingly painting a name on a black wooden cross. Nearby, a child's tomb has a brilliant turquoise-painted crucifix with a heart affixed at the crossing.

One intoxicated Indian who can't read approaches some Mexicans and asks them to find the grave of his father, whom he names. When they locate it, he approaches, weeping; stands there smoking a cigarette; weeps some more and leaves. Although Tere told me that the men in her family use the holiday as an excuse to get drunk and don't do the grave-tending, this man is an exception in the cemetery. As many men as women are weeding, neatening, setting out flowers. What is most striking is that among the hundreds of graves I cannot find a single one left untended and undecorated.

Valle de Bravo's older cemetery, near the entrance to the town, does have a few neglected graves, but they are among the oldest, the tall, dark stones dating from the 18th century. It also has 18th-century graves that are groomed and beflowered as if their inhabitants were within living memory. The stability of Valle de Bravo's population has something to do with it, but the importance of the Day of the Dead means that even the most remote ancestors will have their resting place spruced up on November 2 more often than not. (Just as the Japanese pity those souls condemned to hover near the scene of death because they have no family to care for them, Mexicans sometimes erect a small altar with flowers outside the cemetery to all the dead whose families have died out or moved too far away to tend their graves.)

At dusk, the long alley that leads to this cemetery is also thronged with flower sellers, only now the long-stemmed marigolds, which are expensive, are offered at cut rates. Most graves by this time sport big cans bursting with baby's breath, marigolds, birds of paradise, and an airy yellow flower that self-seeds on the graves. Everywhere there is the acrid scent of marigolds and the softer, insinuating perfume of calla lilies. In the coming dark, sheltered under the pierced chile tins, the candles glow.

At this point, the family groups have mostly done their work and stand pensively at their graves. As in the Santa Maria cemetery, there are a surprising number of children who have died in the past thirty or so years, and many late-20th-century graves of Indian women in their thirties. The Indians favor big, bright crosses covered in plastic roses or marigolds. In the softness of the candlelight, they take on a mellow but still extravagant look.

Two women are saying the rosary by a family grave. Children play hide-and-seek among the tombs, but decorously. I don't see any passionate outpourings of grief, although, as at Obon, the first Days of the Dead must be sharply painful for those left behind. It is a sober scene of familial piety, meant to honor the well-remembered and the never-known, far from the grinning skeletons for sale in the market or the satirical *calaveras* of Mexico City.

⌘

Feeding the dead, from the Day of the Dead to Obon and beyond, is so widespread it must speak to several impulses: denial, guilt, fear, the wish to nurture and cherish. In the late 1930s, Kibisaburo Sasaki traveled from Tokyo to Düsseldorf, where he studied metallurgy for three years. For the rest of his long life in Japan, he ate the same Western breakfast every day without fail: strong coffee, a slice of white bread and a slice of rye bread, marmalade, blue cheese. He passed on his taste for coffee to his wife, and when she died, he offered her spirit a small cup every day at the family altar. When he died in his nineties in Tokyo in 1997, his granddaughter-in-law packed coffee, bread, marmalade, and blue cheese and placed it in his coffin. But that was not the end of Sasaki's excellent coffee. On special occasions, his daughter Reiko Ryuzoji brews some and brings a small cup of it to the family altar along with a little container of rice. On ordinary days, she offers rice, tea, and the family news. Educated, well traveled, and resident for several years in California, Reiko chats with her dead father about, for example, a grandchild who faces an important job interview that day.

In the Japanese tradition, which stresses the obligation to care for the dead, food offerings are crucial. Every day before the living members of an observant family eat, they must bring

rice and tea to the ancestors at the family altar. Memorial services almost always include an offering of a food prized by the
dead person. When Emperor Hirohito and Empress Nagako
attended the memorial service on the first anniversary of their
daughter's death, they brought to their son-in-law's house *soba*,
or buckwheat noodles. They had been one of the princess's
favorite dishes.

Special gifts of food brought to a family, such as foreign
food or chocolates, are frequently offered to the dead at the
altar before the family partakes of them. Because the spirits
are believed to be continually involved in the eating habits of
the family, this can cause problems as families incorporate more
Western foods into their diet. Sugimoto Etsu, a little girl in the
late-19th-century Meiji era, came home one day to find her
grandmother and the maid covering the Buddhist altar with
white paper. The girl's father had become convinced that the
addition of meat to the family's diet would be a good thing.
Horrified, the grandmother was trying to seal off the vegetarian ancestors from the pollution that would ensue. It was an
ominous day, because "this was the first family meal that could
not be shared with the ancestors."

Karen Tallman and Brian DeBeck heard about offering
food to the dead from a Haida woman in the Queen Charlotte
Islands. In the Haida's ceremonial food burnings, dishes the
dead person particularly enjoyed are cooked (no menstruating
women are allowed to take part in the preparation) and blessed
by a shaman. Then the food as well as the surface on which it
is arranged are burned.

In the second summer after Jess's death, Karen and Brian had
a food burning at Storm Bay for eight dead people. Each household involved prepared food for their dead. Karen and Brian
brought sushi, and Brian made Jess's favorite fish and chips. A
friend whose daughter had died brought her cherished, very
expensive Belgian chocolates. They built a cedar table, set it

with eight plates, and ceremoniously placed the food on it; after some blessings, they burned table and food.

For Karen and Brian, it was a wholly satisfactory ritual, a dramatized expression of their continuing wish to feed and cherish Jess and of their inability to do it in the normal way. Not all the participants saw it in that light. One friend offering food to his parents had been in China when his mother died, and this was his first ritual in connection with her death. He wept a little during the burning, but later told Karen that it felt unutterably phony and he hated it. If they did it again, he didn't want to be involved.

Karen is keenly aware of ritual's potential to feel contrived, which is when people go into what she calls "foot-shuffling mode." And new or borrowed rituals are particularly liable to feel embarrassing. Karen distinguishes between rituals that are about letting go and those that are about staying in touch, and maintains that the former are more acceptable in the West. "There are a lot of people who will take part in the goodbye rituals," she says, "spreading the ashes and things like that. But when they have a sense that the ritual involves hanging on to, connecting with, keeping your relationship with the person who's gone, they don't want to do that."

Offering food is a way of keeping in touch with the dead, which is perhaps why Karen and Brian's friend found it both moving (he cried) and repulsive. Karen is unambivalently intent on staying in touch with Jess. She understands the mourning model of gradual detachment and reinvestment as well as anyone, and accepts that for people without religion, it's probably inevitable. But, she says, "it doesn't work with a kid, at least early on."

Rather than letting go, she has focused on connecting with Jess's spirit, surprising herself with her willingness to dabble in spiritualism and other adventures she would formerly have scorned. She finds herself on a tricky, sometimes lonely path at odds with her training, her professional behavior, her secular childhood, even her temperament. Unlike Brian, whom she describes as a "natural" and who communicates with Jess as a matter of course, Karen suffers from what the Buddhists call "doubting mind." She struggles constantly with what has become almost a secret life, she laughs at its flakier aspects, but she never denies that it has become a necessity.

⌘

The scar remains, but we are more than a scar.
 – Therese Rando, *How to Go On Living*
 When Someone You Love Dies

At the newspaper where I once worked, we had a callous half-joke we trotted out when someone discovered the death, a few or several days before, of a person who merited an obituary. "Don't worry," the journalist, chagrined that he had missed a story, would be told, "he's still dead."

Because the dead are still dead, and will always be dead, our relationship with that fact and with them goes on forever. Sometimes the relationship seems to persist almost unchanged over many years. When Queen Victoria lay on her deathbed in 1901, she rallied ever so slightly when a clergyman recited the conclusion of her favorite hymn, John Henry Newman's "Lead Kindly Light": "And in the morn those angel faces smile / Which we have loved long since and lost awhile." It had been thirty-nine years since she had lost Prince Albert, and she had been looking forward – sometimes fretfully, sometimes serenely – to the "morn" of their reunion ever since. She was buried, as she had instructed, in white, wearing both her wedding veil and her mourning cap. Unknown to her children, she had ordered that mementoes, including Albert's dressing gown, one of his cloaks, and a plaster cast of his hand, were to be placed at the bottom of the coffin, over a layer of charcoal. A quilted cushion concealed them and the queen's body was placed on that.

Something else about the queen's meticulous planning was unknown to her children. As she had directed, a photograph of her beloved gillie, John Brown, had been placed in her hand, which was then covered with flowers.

Queen Victoria remains a byword for extravagant, excessive mourning. But it is a reputation she does not entirely deserve. According to the yardsticks of contemporary psychiatrists and psychologists, she mourned "successfully." And, as the furnishing for her coffin indicated, she had found a significant place in her affections for John Brown while maintaining her attachment to Albert.

In spite of the hot water and fresh clothes she ordered to be laid out daily in Albert's dressing room, the queen never doubted that her husband was really dead. The custom may have begun when she found it too harrowing to rescind the usual arrangement, and it hardened into habit. The making of the Blue Room, where Albert died, into a shrine was an accepted 19th-century practice in households with a room to spare. As her biographer Elizabeth Longford says, "Royal death-chambers were rarely disturbed – except by revolution." In fact, Queen Victoria disapproved of the dusty, lugubrious German *Sterbezimmer*, or death chamber, and prided herself on the repainting and installation of new china and pictures in the Blue Room.

Clearly, the Queen suffered a traumatic depression when Albert died, which included the classic symptoms of weight loss, headaches, and overwhelming lassitude. But from her first days of near-suicidal grief, she climbed very slowly, but steadily, upwards. About eighteen months after Albert died, Queen Victoria was involved in a carriage accident and realized in the first few minutes that she wanted very much to live. It was a decisive moment. In the same year, she was seen laughing in public.

Although she refused to open Parliament for more than four years after Albert's death, she resumed her desk work with document boxes and conferences with the prime minister within weeks. Before Albert's death, she had not chosen a dress without his approval, much less settled questions of state. By 1864, she was congratulating herself on her involvement in the Schleswig-Holstein war with the astonishing statement to her eldest daughter: "I am glad darling Papa is spared this worry & annoyance, for he could have done even less than I can."

The widow who had moaned by her husband's bed in 1863, "Albert, Albert, where art thou?" was consulting her spiritual adviser Dean Gerald Wellesley in 1866 about her worry that she was missing Albert less painfully. (By now, her affectionate friendship with John Brown was a source of comfort.) On her forty-seventh birthday in 1866, four and a half years after Albert died, Queen Victoria returned to an old birthday custom and counted her blessings. They were: "Affectionate children and friends; the ability to make others happy and to be of use." She does not mention her own happiness as such but, before the 1860s ended, the Widow of Windsor was enthusiastically taking foreign holidays to places she had never been with Albert and building her own house in Scotland.

It is true that Queen Victoria abhorred the idea of remarriage for her widowed ladies-in-waiting as well as for herself; she established what Elizabeth Longford calls a "Sacred College of Vestal Widows." She was a self-dramatizing personality capable of using her bereavement to mask her old aversion to public appearances and to entertaining foreign royalty. Working hard at her job behind closed doors, she never grasped that a monarch is a necessarily public figure. That was her chief mistake, and the source of her image as a self-indulgent, lifelong mourner. The English people held it against her until the mid-1870s.

But the severest period of her mourning was over within three years of Albert's death – not excessive, by modern standards, for a long primary relationship. The queen resumed her old zestful, anxious, high-strung, and occasionally hot-tempered attitude to life, but stiffened now with a self-reliance she would never have achieved had Albert lived. Because her grandchildren tended to occupy its thrones, her interest in Europe was intense and proprietary. As "head of all the family," she did everything from sitting by the bedsides of daughters and granddaughters in childbirth to mediating international squabbles. She worked hard, danced, sang, and enjoyed the theater well into her seventies.

Similarly, Sir Kenelm Digby's florid grief for his wife merged gradually into a new life of scholarship. In 1634, the second year of his widowhood, after moving restlessly from house to house, he retreated to Gresham College in London, where he spent his days in chemistry experiments. According to John Aubrey, "He wore there a long mourning cloake, a high crowned hatt, his beard unshorne, lookit like a Hermite, as signes of sorrowe for his beloved wife." While at Gresham College, Digby modified his "assumptive world," as a modern therapist would say, by returning to the Catholicism of his childhood. This career-ending decision was made so that he could pray for Venetia's soul. After various sojourns in Paris, Rome, England, and prison, depending on the prevailing political winds, he returned to England at the restoration of Charles II. Unmarried, he lived modestly in a small house in Covent Garden with a laboratory and a library.

But mourning leaves few people unchanged. When Digby died in 1665, his epitaph proclaimed without much exaggeration, "This age's wonder for his noble parts, skilled in six tongues and learned in all the arts." One of the Royal Society's earliest members, he was the author of its first publication, *The Vegetation of Plants*. Most of his learning, which resulted in books on several subjects, had been marshaled in the years after

Venetia's death. He credited his bereavement with inspiring his studies: they calmed the restlessness of his grief and provided his only solace.

Digby's work on the immortality of the soul, published in 1644 in *Two Treatises*, was even more directly inspired by the loss of Venetia. Like his earlier experiments with the regeneration of crayfish, his pursuit of a rational foundation for immortality sprang from his passionate wish to be reunited with Venetia. "Without such lively stirrers up," he acknowledged, "it is not unlikely but that I might have content my selfe with walking dully and implicitly in the way that my birth and education had sett me in." As Therese Rando makes clear, returning to the person you were before the death is not an option. As Sir Kenelm Digby makes clear, being shaken out of "walking dully and implicitly" is not a bad thing.

⌘

At the lunch after Scott's funeral, Jamie Roche talked about what he called the "takeaways" of his brother's brief life – takeaways being a management term for the lasting benefits of an experience. When my sister Carole walks Seattle's downtown streets, she looks up at the decorated tops of the buildings, something Scott taught her to do. That is one of her takeaways.

For me, Scott could shine the freshest, clearest light on something quite ordinary. He had grown up without pets and had given Hannah a cat, Matilda, for Valentine's Day. Occasionally he would say to her, genuinely wide-eyed at the wonder of it, "Can you believe we're living *with an animal* right in this house?" Every so often, when the everyday suddenly acquires a gloss, I'm reminded of Scott's innocent eye.

Another takeaway is inscribed on the bench at English Bay in Vancouver that the Roches donated in memory of their son. Hannah chose the location, and together we wrote the text on the plaque, trying to capture in the allotted words something of

Scott's welcoming spirit and his focus on the important things in life. Below "Scott Roche, 1973–1998," it reads: "He loved friendship and the out of doors. May you who pass by here enjoy them also."

Thinking of takeaways from Scott's life is easy. Are there any from his death? Has grieving for Scott, even from my relatively distant position on the mourner's bench, left any marks?

One of my takeaways is either laughably trivial or more meaningful than I understand: I have not worn a watch since Scott died. My watch had broken beyond repair in Vietnam and after borrowing my niece's briefly in Seattle, I gave it up. When I returned to Toronto, going into a store for anything less basic than food was impossible. With Scott dead, shopping seemed almost obscenely inappropriate. Weeks, months, and years went by. I returned to shopping, but I still go watchless.

Sometimes I look at my naked wrist and think, That is the visible sign of my mourning for Scott. Or perhaps it's just become a habit, like the previous twenty-five years when I wore a watch daily. There are ways to look at it symbolically, which I didn't in 1998. The time had gone tragically out of joint, so why wear a timepiece? Scott's death put so much of our lives in perspective that reminding myself of my cluttered, overscheduled days seemed peculiarly pointless. Some day I'll probably buy a watch. But meanwhile my watchlessness divides my life into before-Scott-died and after-Scott-died.

There are other divides. Anyone's bereavement is a serious business to me now, no matter that the dead person was very old or the connection distant. I am ashamed how meagerly I acknowledged some people's losses, before Scott. I always write condolence letters, because I saw how much hers meant to Hannah, and their staying power lasts as long as the mourner wishes. Funerals that I would have considered optional in the past summon me now.

Scott's death opened my tear ducts. Before, I rarely wept. Now I do much more easily, usually when it's something to do with young people or rites of passage. And since I heard the funeral director Todd Van Beck say, "Unless there's walking, it's not a ritual," I weep reliably at processions of any kind. Something about people moving gravely, in concert, now seems unbearably poignant.

The humanity and ingenuity of mourning customs move me, particularly when expressed in a ritual. A container in which mourners of different styles can meet and find a comfortable place, a performance where the script is largely written and the steps mapped out, a ritual is precious after the disequilibrium of death. The mourner whose culture provides viable ones is fortunate, but increasingly rare. Mourners like Karen Tallman and Brian DeBeck who devise their own are even rarer.

Hannah too wishes she lived in a society with more rituals. Although she apparently had little difficulty designing her mourning, she would have preferred to have "things you do automatically, rather than think them up." Anniversaries she finds particularly awkward: "You don't know what to do with yourself." On September 5, 1998, which would have been Scott and Hannah's wedding day, she and I went with my sister and her daughters to their weekend house on Decatur Island off the coast of Seattle. It was a place Scott and Hannah loved. We toasted Scott, and Scott and Hannah, at dinner; Hannah went for a walk alone on the beach. It felt sad and rather aimless, no doubt appropriate reactions.

For the first anniversary of Scott's death, Hannah joined the Roches in San Francisco for a family dinner, a memorial mass, and a hike in the nearby hills. On the second anniversary, she spent the evening reminiscing about Scott with a friend, and on the third she went to see a movie made from one of Scott's favorite books, Cormac McCarthy's *All the Pretty Horses*. Other than the first year, it has never seemed quite right, or quite enough.

When I tell Hannah she has a gift for mourning well, she shrugs it off. I explain Freud's theory that the mourner who has slowly and painfully divested herself of her attachment to the *living* beloved is liberated, and that is what she seems to have achieved. She agrees that there are no shortcuts to mourning, but she points to her advantages: youth, lots of friends ("And you have to seek out the ones who are good at grief, because they aren't all"), and the engrossing demands of medical school.

But I maintain that, by some stroke of luck, Hannah was a talented mourner. Somehow she understood that attention had to be paid to Scott, to her, and to the destruction of their present and future together. She had to plot it herself, at times almost systematically. As well as her private, wordless grief, she marked her way on the mourner's path with objects and actions: her orange silk vest, her locket, the Scott album, the Scott coffee, the anniversaries. Out of her own stubbornness, she allowed no one to direct her or embarrass her, to speed her up or slow her down. And she has won the freedom Freud forecasts, but without sacrificing her connection with Scott.

Hannah, now a doctor, has decided to become a radiation oncologist. Perhaps she would have chosen a specialty that cares for large numbers of mortally ill people even if Scott had lived. We will never know. But death has fewer terrors for her than for many people her age. And when she has to break bad news to a family or be involved in a debate about life support, she remembers those days in Harborview Medical Center in 1998.

Every January 10, on the anniversary of Scott's death, Sybil, Hannah, and I send a perennial plant to his parents with the message, "Scott lives forever in our hearts." So he does, but the heart is capacious.

About three and a half years after Scott's death, Hannah became engaged again. Her fiancé, Bruce Townson, is an old boyfriend – they had been counselors at a summer camp – who reconnected with a condolence card. Whenever I visited Vancouver and read through Hannah's box of cards and letters, Bruce's made me grin. Probably he had not bought many condolence cards in his young life. In among the tasteful white-on-white doves and flowers, his was a brightly colored "thinking of you" card, featuring a moose wearing overalls and smoking a corncob pipe. (In his defense, he reminds me that he was working as an engineer in a small Alberta town, where the card supply was limited.) Every January, on Scott's death-day, he sent Hannah flowers, not so much a courtship tactic as a gesture of admiration. In addition to the other reasons to love Hannah, Bruce was moved by the way she mourned Scott. Othello says, to explain the growth of love between Desdemona and himself: "She loved me for the dangers I had passed, / And I loved her that she did pity them." Something similar happened between Hannah and Bruce.

The Roches greeted the engagement with the generosity we have come to expect from them. Soon after Scott's death, they had decided that, since they could not watch Scott's life go forward, rejoicing in Hannah's milestones would be the next best thing. After Hannah had told the Roches, and Marilyn and I talked on the phone, I sent Marilyn a letter. I told her that when Scott died, Hannah's medical school classmates had made her a gigantic sympathy card covered with their individual messages. One, written by a man wise beyond his twenty-four years, said, "Never forget him. Never try to replace him. Learn to love him in a new way." Hannah has done that, I wrote Marilyn. And Bruce would not want it otherwise. Mourning, after all, is one of the prices we pay for attachment. Perhaps Bruce also suspects that someone so adept at the mourner's dance is likely to be good at something even more complicated – the dance of life.

NOTES

Prologue

5   "I will not tear": Alexiou, *Ritual Lament*, pp. 32–33.

Chapter One: The Bustle in a House

8   John Galt: Galt, *Annals*, pp. 89–90. The novel was first published in 1821.

9   anthropologists: See, for example, Hertz, *Death and the Right Hand*, pp. 33–34; O'Suilleabhain, *Irish Wake Amusements*, pp. 166–72; Rush, *Death and Burial*, pp. 108, 168–69; Schauss, *Lifetime of a Jew*, pp. 287–93; Turner, *Houses for the Dead*, pp. vii–x, 120–23; van Gennep, *Rites of Passage*, pp. 151–52.

10 Newfoundland fishing villages: Memorial University of Newfoundland Folklore & Language Archive (MUNFLA), accession 73-64, collected by Elizabeth Moore, p. 4; accession 71-42 (1971), collected by Tom Moore, p. 35; accession 72-115 (1972), collected by Helen Tuff, p. 40.

10 Anne Brener: conversation with the author, spring 1999.

13 ancient protocol: Lamm, *Jewish Way*, pp. 244–45.

13 Arnold van Gennep: van Gennep, *Rites of Passage*, pp. 10–13, 146–65.

13 Artas: Granqvist, *Muslim Death and Burial*, p. 64.

14 Roman republic . . . Europe: Rush, *Death and Burial*, p. 152; McManners, *Death and the Enlightenment*, p. 272.

15 attitude to the body: Anne Brener speculates that Jewish mourning practices were tailored around what is for them the most grievous bereavement: the loss of a parent. Perhaps, she says, their aversion to watching with their dead springs from the feeling that it would be too great an intimacy, bordering even on disrespect, to keep a wake over a dead parent. That, however, does not explain how many other cultures overcame the aversion.

19 Joany Power: MUNFLA, accession 74-115 (1974), collected by Hubert McGrath, p. 5.

21 social heart: Butler, "Sacred and Profane Space," pp. 27–32.

22 "Poor Paddy": de Boileau, *Recollections of Labrador Life*, p. 85.

22 "The nights were long": MUNFLA, accession 73-64 (1972), p. 7.

24 Peter Narvaez: Narvaez, "'Tricks and Fun.'"

24   Highland wake: O'Suilleabhain, *Irish Wake Amusements*, p. 31.

24   Leinster: ibid., p. 72.

25   Patrick's Cove: MUNFLA, accession 74-115 (1974), p. 13.

30   European widows . . . Burgundian court: Lou Taylor, *Mourning Dress*, pp. 52–56.

30   polar Inuit: Paterek, *American Indian Costume*, p. 422.

30   Elizabeth Grant: Grant, *Highland Lady*, pp. 249–52.

Chapter Two: Wailing Time

33   We do not wail much: Lutz, *Crying*, pp. 193–224.

33   Kol women . . . Maoris: van Gennep, *Rites of Passage*, p. 151; Oppenheim, *Maori Death Customs*, pp. 50–51.

33   Relatives might stand . . . *goos*: Alexiou, *Ritual Lament*, p. 11.

34   Plato: *Laws*, vol. 2, p. 535, lines 959–66.

34   Solon . . . Cicero: Rush, *Death and Burial*, p. 176.

34   1992 study: P.C. Smith, Range, and Ulmer, "Belief in Afterlife," p. 217.

35   tombstone epitaphs: Rush, *Death and Burial*, pp. 185–86; translations by Thomas Robinson.

36   his sister Macrina: Gregory, *Life of St. Macrina*, especially pp. 27, 33, 59–60, 69, 71, 73.

39   Christian onlooker: quoted in Alexiou, *Ritual Lament*, p. 30.

40   Hilma Granqvist: Granqvist, *Muslim Death and Burial*, pp. 54, 147–51, 159.

42   Boccaccio: Boccaccio, *Decameron*, pp. 54–55.

42   "Sing me": Alexiou, *Ritual Lament*, p. 40.

42   forbidden paid keeners: O'Suilleabhain, *Irish Wake Amusements*, pp. 138–41.

43   poetic tug-of-war: ibid., pp. 141–42.

43   Margaret Alexiou: Alexiou, *Ritual Lament*, pp. 40–41.

48   first centuries after Christ: Schauss, *Lifetime of a Jew*, pp. 245, 252.

48   the Rama: quoted in Schindler, "Mourning and Bereavement," p. 122.

49   Jewish scholars: Feldman, "Death as Estrangement," pp. 84–94.

50   Margaret Holub: Holub, "Cosmology of Mourning," pp. 345–46.

Chapter Three: The Celebration

54   Robert Garland: Garland, *Greek Way*, pp. 20–37.

54   Roman republic: Patterson, "Patronage," p. 15.

55   Victor Turner: quoted in Woodward, *Theatre of Death*, p. 2.

55   transitional realm: Houlbrooke, *Death, Religion and the Family*, pp. 34–35.

56   one-third of a person's fortune: Gittings, "Urban Funerals," p. 171.

57   Cromwell's rule: ibid., p. 174.

57   Elie Brackenhoffer: Castan, Lebrun, and Chartier, "Two Reformations," p. 107.

57   Queen Victoria: Victoria, *Letters and Journals*, pp. 240–41.

58 Dutch New York: Earle, "Death Ritual," pp. 36–37.
58 practice of praying: Houlbrooke, *Death, Religion and the Family*, p. 39.
61 Thomas Attig: lecture at a meeting of Bereaved Families of Ontario, Oakville, Ont., April 27, 1999.
62 Steven Holl: Olson, "What Is Sacred Space?" p. 41.
64 Todd Van Beck: lecture at a conference of Bereaved Families of Ontario, Toronto, April 24, 1998.
64 ambivalent . . . object: Woodward, *Theatre of Death*, p. 11.
65 "with grett lyght": Duffy, *Stripping of the Altars*, pp. 361–62.
69 ancient . . . and modern Greeks: Garland, *Greek Way*, p. 25.
69 minor tractate . . . marriage contract: quoted in Meltzer, *Death: An Anthology*, pp. 257–58.
69 Cheremis villages: quoted in ibid., p. 260.
69 Portsmouth . . . Scandinavian countries: Lou Taylor, *Mourning Dress*, pp. 183–86.
72 Dorothy Woodsworth: quoted in Gittings, *Death, Burial and the Individual*, pp. 62–63.
72 costly coffins: Mitford, *American Way of Death*, pp. 198–200.
73 Basques: William A. Douglas, *Death in Murelaga*, p. 47.
75 Todd Van Beck: lecture at a conference of Bereaved Families of Ontario, Toronto, April 24, 1998.

Chapter Four: Final Destination
80 Sophocles: Sophocles, *Antigone*, p. 165, lines 206–07.
84 Bissoondath: conversation with the author, April 2000. Bissoondath also told this story in "Set Free by Lighting a Holy Fire," *Toronto Star*, May 23, 1999, p. B3.
89 "Henceforth": Ariès, *Hour of Our Death*, p. 30.
90 winged death's-head . . . another life: Sloane, *Last Great Necessity*, pp. 21–22.
92 Basil Hall: quoted in French, "Cemetery as Cultural Institution," p. 76.
92 foul air: Etlin, *Architecture of Death*, p. 24.
92 Montpellier: ibid., p. 16.
92 Saulieu: ibid., p. 31.
93 Holy Innocents: ibid., p. 33.
93 Richard Etlin: ibid., p. ix.
93 Père Lachaise: Sloane, *Last Great Necessity*, pp. 49–51.
94 primary tourist attraction: Linden-Ward, "Strange but Genteel Pleasure Grounds," p. 305.
94 Fanny Kemble: quoted in French, "Cemetery as Cultural Institution," p. 70.
94 Guides . . . stereoscopic cards: Linden-Ward, "Strange but Genteel Pleasure Grounds," pp. 302–04.
94 Franklin Pierce: ibid., p. 302.

94 descendants of Mount Auburn: ibid., pp. 307–17; Sloane, *Last Great Necessity*, p. 56; French, "Cemetery as Cultural Institution," p. 85.

95 Rochester in the 1830s: Thomas and Rosenberg-Naparsteck, "Sleepers' City," pp. 3–22.

95 "labor at Mount Hope": Reisem, *Mount Hope*, p. 8.

96 Pharcellus Church: quoted in Thomas and Rosenberg-Naparsteck, "Sleepers' City," p. 8.

96 Henry Arthur Bright: Linden-Ward, "Strange but Genteel Pleasure Grounds," p. 305.

97 day trip: *Rochester Gem and Ladies Amulet*, August 7, 1841, pp. 125–36.

97 Marcia Webster: *Rochester Gem and Ladies Amulet*, September 5, 1840, p. 142.

98 fifty choice trees: Reisem, *Mount Hope*, p. 10.

100 letter thanked Anthony: Rochester *Democrat and Chronicle*, July 15, 1998.

100 Civil War . . . original people's parks: Linden-Ward, "Strange but Genteel Pleasure Grounds," p. 323.

101 In 1909: Jackson and Vergara, *Silent Cities*, p. 108.

101 park cemetery: Sloane, *Last Great Necessity*, pp. 97–127.

102 Hubert Eaton: Rubin, Carlton, and Rubin, *L.A. in Installments*; Sloane, *Last Great Necessity*, pp. 157–90; Kath, *Forest Lawn Memorial-Parks*.

107 About ten thousand families: Information on Forest Lawn in 2002 comes from Paula Woodley in its communications office.

109 twenty-seven hundred visitors: information supplied by Joan Hunt of the Friends of Mount Hope.

111 Fingland family: Laura Meade, "Parents' Pride Is in Son's Grave," Rochester *Democrat and Chronicle*, April 22, 1984, pp. 1B, 5B; Ernest Fingland Jr., conversation with the author, spring 2000.

Chapter Five: After Great Pain

115 two Oregon psychologists: Bolton and Camp, "Funeral Rituals," p. 349.

116 "O, thou coffee pestle": Granqvist, *Muslim Death and Burial*, p. 106.

119 "Who's the Host?": Lipnick, "Who's the Host?"

120 "unbearable": Joyce Slochower, conversation with the author, February 2000.

120 "something that's meaningful": ibid.

121 "powerfully diminished capacity": Slochower, "Mourning," pp. 355–56.

121 "brilliant structure": Slochower, "Therapeutic Function," p. 143.

121 "perhaps unique": ibid., p. 150.

122 "body odor": Joyce Slochower, conversation with the author, February 2000.

123 "emotionally present": Slochower, "Therapeutic Function," p. 149.

123 "may actually begin": ibid., p. 151.

124 "traumatically unprotected": Slochower, "Mourning," p. 364, note 3.

124 "prepsychoanalytic adaptation": Slochower, "Therapeutic Function," p. 151; Slochower, "Mourning," p. 365.

Chapter Six: How to Mourn

133 Clifford Geertz: Geertz, *Religion of Java*, pp. 68–70.

133 Romans officially urged: Shelton, *As the Romans Did*, p. 97.

133 Tullia . . . Sulpicius's carefully wrought composition: ibid., pp. 20, 94–96.

135 Chuang Tzu: quoted in Meltzer, *Death: An Anthology*, p. 282.

135 Buddha: ibid., p. 283.

136 John Ruskin: quoted in Kingsland, *Book of Good Manners*, p. 333.

136 Anne Bradstreet: Bradstreet, *Works*, pp. 235–39.

138 consolation literature: In "The Domestication of Death," a chapter in her book *The Feminization of American Culture*, Ann Douglas discusses the work of Anne Bradstreet, Lydia Sigourney, and Theodore Cuyler, among many others.

138 Queen Victoria: Darby and Smith, *Prince Consort*, p. 4.

138 *Letters*: Sigourney, *Letters to Mothers*, pp. 260–97.

139 Strangers wrote her: Haight, *Mrs. Sigourney*, pp. 103–04.

139 follow a pattern: Sigourney, *Poems Religious and Elegiac*.

140 in "the hope" . . . Dean Arthur Stanley: Cuyler, *Recollections*, pp. 96–97.

141 American historian: Ann Douglas, *Feminization of American Culture*, p. 205.

141 "largest household": Cuyler, *Empty Crib*, p. 10.

142 "sustaining grace": ibid., p. 44.

142 "fine vein" . . . "horses never": ibid., pp. 16–17.

142 "felt a secret" . . . meeting Jesus: ibid., pp. 26–27, 28, 31.

142 Theo: ibid., pp. 51–52.

143 "It would be" . . . "only imagine": ibid., p. 58.

143 "Had you": ibid., p. 99.

143 "but they do not": ibid., p. 64.

143 "Jesus loves me": ibid., pp. 53–54.

143 "My only answer": Cuyler, *God's Light*, p. 49.

144 "bright sunny boy" . . . "No bereavements": Cuyler, *Empty Crib*, pp. 100–01.

144 "As I look": ibid., p. 104.

146 "all society" . . . "The more the heart": Sherwood, *Manners and Social Usages*, p. 201.

146 "To advise a mourner": ibid., p. 210.

146 "If one chooses": ibid., p. 198.

146 "to a certain extent" . . . "The heart knoweth": Harland, *Complete Etiquette*, pp. 214–15.

147 "the whole evening": Fenwick, *Vogue's Book*, p. 155.

148 "selfishly mourning": Post, *Etiquette* (1965), p. 335.

148 "may start to have": ibid., p. 337.

148 "the lonely widow" . . . "outwardly mourning person": Vanderbilt, *Etiquette* (1972), pp. 130–31.

150 something peculiarly American: Starker, *Oracle at the Supermarket*. See especially pp. 2, 13–14, 37–38, 59, 63, 109.

151 "which temporarily makes": ibid., p. 170.

152 Steven Starker reports: ibid., pp. 153–55.

154 "the club": Mehren, *After the Darkest Hour*, p. 145.

154 The guidelines: ibid., pp. 157–58.

154 Mehren endorses: ibid., pp. 174–76.

154 "Grief is": ibid., p. 163.

154 Studies support: See Sanders, "Risk Factors," pp. 255–67; Parkes and Weiss, *Recovery from Bereavement*; Rando, *Treatment of Complicated Mourning*.

155 Sigmund Freud: Freud, "Mourning and Melancholia," p. 154.

155 Francine du Plessix Gray: Gray, "At Large," p. 8.

156 Colin Murray Parkes: Parkes, *Bereavement*, p. 7.

156 "like nest-building behavior": Silverman and Klass, "What's the Problem?" p. 11.

156 "a rough guide": Parkes, "Historical Overview," p. 30.

158 Therese Rando: speech to a conference of Bereaved Families of Ontario, Toronto, April 24, 1998.

159 "You know": Brener, *Mourning and Mitzvah*, p. 94; Brener, speech at Kolel Centre for Liberal Jewish Learning, Toronto, March 21, 1998.

159 Dennis Klass: Klass, "Bowlby's Model of Grief," p. 31.

159 move "adaptively": Rando, *How to Go On*, p. 285.

163 "form of denial": O'Connor, *Letting Go with Love*, p. 50.

163 "This is the choice": ibid., p. xv.

163 "*You will survive*": ibid., p. xiv.

164 "a state": ibid., p. 44.

Chapter Seven: The Gender of Mourning

165 Akan funeral: Aborampah, "Women's Roles."

166 Shuddhitattva: Narasimhan, *Sati*, p. 11.

167 female keening: Kay Carmichael, *Ceremony of Innocence*, p. 108.

168 E.M. Forster: Forster, *Marianne Thornton*, pp. 67–73.

170 Colin Parkes: quoted in Jalland, *Death in the Victorian Family*, p. 251.

170 chances of remarrying: ibid., p. 253.

170 Pat Jalland: ibid., pp. 253–55.

171 William Harcourt: ibid., pp. 257–60.

171 "Victorian widows": ibid., p. 259.

173 widow sacrifice . . . honorary gateways: Thompson, *Suttee*, pp. 24–25.

174 Alexander: ibid., p. 28.

174 narrowing of possibilities . . . Angirasa: Narasimhan, *Sati*, pp. 17–19.

174 motives advanced: Thompson, *Suttee*, pp. 47–50.

175 Richard Hartley Kennedy: Courtright, "Iconographies of Sati," pp. 42–47.

175 "Congratulatory address": Narasimhan, *Sati*, p. 70.

176 "chastity belt": ibid., p. 33.

176 eloquent handprint: Thompson, *Suttee*, p. 30.

176 proceeded to the pyre: Narasimhan, *Sati*, pp. 89, 95; Courtright, "Iconographies of Sati," p. 45.

177 "morally . . . drugged": quoted in Thompson, *Suttee*, p. 133.

177 7,941 women: Narasimhan, *Sati*, p. 70.

177 at least forty satis: Oldenburg, "Roop Kanwar," p. 101.

177 Roop Kanwar: ibid., pp. 101–30.

177 numbered in the thousands: Hawley, *Sati*, p. 7.

179 In 1990: Narasimhan, *Sati*, pp. 1–2.

180 Aristotle: quoted in Lutz, *Crying*, p. 176.

181 Carol Staudacher: Staudacher, *Men and Grief*, especially pp. 1, 3, 5, 6, 8–9, 35.

182 Terry Martin and Kenneth Doka: Martin and Doka, *Men Don't Cry*.

182 gold standard: Moss, Rubinstein, and Moss, "Middle-aged Son's Reactions," p. 260.

182 counselors and educators: Stillion and McDowell, "Women's Issues."

183 Robert Frost: Frost, *Collected Poems*, pp. 55–58.

184 Wilbur: Martin and Doka, *Men Don't Cry*, p. 37.

185 Dave Eggers: Eggers, *Heartbreaking Work*, p. 88.

185 Fred Alger: quoted in Burton, "What They Were Thinking."

186 Freud reacted . . . "attitude towards life": quoted in Bronfen, *Over Her Dead Body*, pp. 15–16.

186 "Since I am": quoted in Silverman and Klass, "What's the Problem?" p. 6.

187 "And actually": ibid.

189 "simply less intense": Martin and Doka, *Men Don't Cry*, p. 41.

190 "feeling rules": Hochschild, "Emotion Work," pp. 551–73.

190 floridly emotional: Carmichael, *Ceremony of Innocence*, p. 50.

190 team of psychologists: Rosenblatt, Walsh, and Jackson, *Grief and Mourning*.

192 Barbara Dorian: Margaret Wente, "The Era of Sadness," *Globe and Mail*, February 22, 1997.

192 study of boys: Rose and Asher, "Seeking and Giving."

193 the Bara: Huntington and Metcalf, *Celebrations of Death*, pp. 102–07.

Chapter Eight: Sad Clothes

194 Geoffrey Gorer: Gorer, *Death, Grief and Mourning*, pp. xvi, xviii.

194 "Ma's sad cap": Victoria, *Letters and Journals*, July 1, 1862, p. 165.

195 Maori widows: Mead, *Traditional Maori Clothing*, p. 67.

195 ancient Greece: Bonfante, *Etruscan Dress*, p. 130, note 60.

195 New Caledonia: Biebuyck and Van den Abbeele, *Power of Headdresses*, p. 44.

195 Haya people: Weiss, "Dressing at Death."

196 Cicero: quoted in Sebesta and Bonfante, *World of Roman Costume*, p. 141.

196 Scarlett O'Hara: Mitchell, *Gone with the Wind*, pp. 190–99. The novel was first published in 1936.

197 death of Adonis: Sappho, *Sappho*, p. 35.

197 ancient Romans: Sebesta and Bonfante, *World of Roman Costume*, p. 50.

197   Alfonso . . . of Portugal: Anderson, *Hispanic Costume*, pp. 138–39.

198   Hindu widows . . . Igbo widows: Dar, *Costumes of India and Pakistan*,
      p. 138; de Negri, *Nigerian Body Ornament*, p. 16.

198   North American tribes: Paterek, *American Indian Costume*, especially
      pp. 273, 276.

198   Bereaved men: Newton, *Dress of the Venetians*, pp. 87, 154, 173.

199   Leon Wieseltier: Wieseltier, *Kaddish*, p. 65.

199   Anne Brener: Brener, *Mourning and Mitzvah*, pp. 129, 131.

199   Palestine: Weir, *Palestinian Costume*, pp. 105–07.

199   *Keriah* is reserved: Lamm, *Jewish Way*, pp. 39–44.

201   Anzia Yezierska: Yezierska, *Bread Givers*, pp. 255–56.

202   ancient Greeks . . . Romans: Johnston, *Ancient Greek Dress*, p. 101; Sebesta
      and Bonfante, *World of Roman Costume*, p. 65.

202   Roman widow . . . Roman funerary laws: Sebesta and Bonfante, *World of
      Roman Costume*, p. 50; Shelton, *As the Romans Did*, p. 97.

202   Monastic colors . . . drab: Cunnington and Lucas, *Costume*, p. 146.

203   Henry VIII: ibid.

203   Mary, Queen of Scots: Lou Taylor, *Mourning Dress*, p. 82.

203   White Queen . . . widow's peak: ibid., p. 81.

204   Samuel Pepys: Pepys, *Shorter Pepys*, pp. 747, 780.

204   "Women of inferior Rank": quoted in Lou Taylor, *Mourning Dress*, p. 108.

205   Dying clothes: Ribeiro, *Dress in Eighteenth-Century Europe*, p. 61.

205   special newspaper . . . petitions: Delpierre, *Dress in France*, p. 78.

205   mourning accessories: Strutt, *Fashion in South Africa*, pp. 86–87.

205   Virginia Woolf: Woolf, *Orlando*, pp. 209, 212.

206   middle-class demand . . . department store: Lou Taylor, *Mourning Dress*,
      pp. 189–91; Cunnington and Lucas, *Costume*, p. 248.

206   Australian tailor: Fletcher, *Costume in Australia*, p. 148.

207   Princess Alice: Staniland, *In Royal Fashion*, p. 157.

207   queen of Hawaii: Longford, *Victoria*, p. 364.

207   American cartoon: Coffin, *Death in Early America*, p. 202.

208   "Mun" Verney: Cunnington and Lucas, *Costume*, p. 273.

208   George II: Lou Taylor, *Mourning Dress*, p. 173.

209   M.M. Sherwood: Cunnington and Lucas, *Costume*, p. 275.

209   "Darling Beatrice": quoted in Lou Taylor, *Mourning Dress*, p. 179.

209   Edmund Verney: ibid., p. 177.

209   Ethel Wilson: Ethel Wilson, *Innocent Traveller*, pp. 15–16.

210   Frances Hodgson Burnett: Burnett, *Secret Garden*, pp. 27, 31.

210   After 1918 . . . incompatible with modern life: Lou Taylor, *Mourning Dress*,
      pp. 263–77.

211   M.E.W. Sherwood: Sherwood, *Manners and Social Usages*, pp. 188–206.

211   Ella Wheeler Wilcox: Wilcox et al., *Correct Social Usage*, pp. 146–48.

212   Edith Ordway: Ordway, *Etiquette of To-Day*, pp. 224–30.

212   Emily Holt: Holt, *Encyclopedia of Etiquette*, pp. 327–33.

212 Millicent Fenwick: Fenwick, *Vogue's Book*, pp. 154–59.
213 Elizabeth Post in 1965: Post, *Etiquette* (1965), pp. 335–38.
213 published in 1967: Vanderbilt, *New Complete Book of Etiquette*, pp. 129–31.
213 1972 edition: Vanderbilt, *Etiquette*, p. 191.
214 Queen Victoria: Longford, *Victoria*, pp. 347–48.
214 Colette: Colette, *Seven by Colette*, pp. 120–21.

Chapter Nine: Sorrow Shared
219 "orphan's Kaddish": Wieseltier, *Kaddish*, p. 442.
219 Marian Henriquez Neudel: Neudel, "Saying Kaddish," p. 180.
220 threatened jokingly: ibid.
220 Evelyn Broner: Broner, *Mornings and Mourning*, pp. 6–7, 164, 221, and conversation with the author.
221 Leon Wieseltier: Wieseltier, *Kaddish*, pp. 19, 235, 270, 273, 319, 576, 581.
225 Alcoholics Anonymous: Lund et al., "Resolving Problems," p. 204.
225 The atmosphere: Yalom, *Group Psychotherapy*, p. 484.
226 members ranged: Some names, occupations, and sexes have been changed.
227 Researchers and practitioners: Yalom, *Group Psychotherapy*, pp. 12–13; Klass, "Bereaved Parents," p. 356; Lagrand, "United We Cope," p. 209.
227 ancient strategy: quoted in Yalom, *Group Psychotherapy*, pp. 12–13.
228 "consumers and deliverers": Lagrand, "United We Cope," p. 209.
228 "a lonely ship": Yalom, *Group Psychotherapy*, p. 96.
229 Men's bereavement groups: Staudacher, *Men and Grief*, pp. 172–73.
232 Louis Lagrand: Lagrand, "United We Cope," p. 217.
233 Groups for children: *A Child's Grief*.
238 Elan Miavitz: Miavitz, "Grief Gardening," pp. 17–20, and conversation with the author.
239 Edward O. Wilson . . . Henry Mitchell: York, "Grief Gardening."
243 Men and adolescents . . . Alcoholics: Gary and Remolino, *Coping with Loss*, p. 108; Weinberg et al., "Computer-Mediated Support Groups," p. 46.
243 reported in one study: Weinberg et al., "Therapeutic Factors," pp. 62–65.
244 "You get": Michael Kimmelman, "Offering Beauty, and Then Proof That Life Goes On," *New York Times*, December 30, 2001, Arts and Leisure, p. 35.

Chapter Ten: Keepsakes
247 "Memory": Stallybrass, "Worn Worlds," p. 36.
249 Andaman Islands . . . New Guinea: Lou Taylor, *Mourning Dress*, pp. 51, 225.
249 Anne Pierce Guillemard: ibid., pp. 242–43.
250 Anne Lady Newdigate . . . Shakespeare: Cunnington and Lucas, *Costume*, p. 253.
250 Anna-Maria Verney: Lou Taylor, *Mourning Dress*, p. 232.
251 small masterwork: Hunter, "Mourning Jewellery," p. 11.

252 Leigh Hunt: Bell, *Hairwork Jewelry*, p. 7.

252 In their enthusiasm . . . burning the hair: Campbell, *Art of Hair Work*, pp. 4–12.

252 Queen Victoria's approval . . . "bear up": Victoria, *Letters and Journals*, pp. 240–41.

253 new kind of brooch: Hunter, "Mourning Jewellery," p. 18.

253 France, Germany . . . Renaissance humanism: Gittings, "Venetia's Death," pp. 54–68.

254 Sir Kenelm Digby: Aubrey, *Brief Lives*, pp. 97–99.

255 "all the true joy": All quotations in the section that follows are from Digby, "Digby Letter-Book."

258 Colin Parkes: Parkes, *Bereavement*, pp. 43–59, 77–78.

260 memory quilts: Trechsel, "Mourning Quilts," p. 53.

260 Elizabeth Roseberry Mitchell: ibid., pp. 55–56.

261 Sarah Gould: P.G. Buckley, "Truly We Live," p. 117. Sarah Gould's sampler belongs to the Huntington Historical Society, Huntington, New York.

261 Abby Bishop: Ring, "Balch School," pp. 660–71; Pike and Armstrong, *Time to Mourn*, pp. 129–31.

262 Rebecca Tenney: Pike and Armstrong, *Time to Mourn*, p. 156.

262 Mark Twain: Twain, *Huckleberry Finn*, p. 160.

263 Lyman Beecher: quoted in Buckley, "Truly We Live," p. 110.

263 William Gookin: Coffin, *Death in Early America*, pp. 204, 206.

264 Posthumous painters . . . William Sidney Mount: Lloyd, "Posthumous Mourning Portraiture," p. 73.

264 Marcus Ward: ibid., pp. 74–75.

265 Southworth and Hawes: Ruby, "Post-Mortem Portraiture," pp. 206, 209.

266 James Garfield: Coffin, *Death in Early America*, p. 203.

266 West Virginia funeral director: Crissman, *Death and Dying*, pp. 75–76.

267 Sometimes the inscription: All the posthumous photographs described here are in the Burns Archive of Death and Dying, reproduced in Burns, *Sleeping Beauty*.

267 postmortem photograph evolved: Bowser, "Post-Mortem Photography," pp. 30–51.

268 Lord Frederick Cavendish: Jalland, *Death in the Victorian Family*, p. 182.

268 Jay Ruby: Ruby, "Post-Mortem Portraiture," p. 213.

270 "A Most Important Picture": Johnson et al., "A Most Important Picture."

Chapter Eleven: As Gently as Possible

278 Motoori Norinaga: Robert J. Smith, *Ancestor Worship*, pp. 77–78.

279 relaxed family reunion: Reader, *Religion in Contemporary Japan*, p. 99.

279 group of college students: ibid., p. 101.

286 Emperor Hirohito: Robert J. Smith, *Ancestor Worship*, p. 133.

286 Sugimoto Etsu: ibid., pp. 137–38.

288   on her deathbed . . . covered with flowers: Longford, *Victoria*, p. 561;
       Staniland, *In Royal Fashion*, p. 172; St. Aubyn, *Queen Victoria*, p. 598.

289   Elizabeth Longford: Longford, *Victoria*, p. 311.

290   "I am glad": ibid., p. 320.

290   "Albert, Albert": ibid., pp. 335, 326–27.

290   "Affectionate children": ibid., pp. 363.

290   "Sacred College": ibid., p. 310.

291   she did everything: ibid., p. 373.

291   John Aubrey: Aubrey, *Brief Lives*, p. 99.

291   epitaph: ibid.

291   Royal Society . . . foundation for immortality: Sumner, "Opportunism Versus
       Principle," pp. 8–23.

292   "Without such lively": Digby, "Digby Letter Book," pp. 415–16.

REFERENCES

Abbott, G.F. *Macedonian Folklore*. Chicago: Argonaut, 1969.

Aborampah, O.M. "Women's Roles in the Mourning Rituals of the Akan of Ghana." *Ethnology* 38, no. 3: 257–71.

Alcott, Louisa May. *Eight Cousins; or, The Aunt-hill*. Boston: Little, Brown, 1940.

Alexiou, Margaret. *The Ritual Lament in Greek Tradition*. Cambridge: Cambridge University Press, 1974.

Andersen, Ellen. *Danske Dragter: Moden i 1700-arene*. Copenhagen: Nationalmuseet, 1977.

Anderson, Ruth Matilda. *Hispanic Costume, 1480–1530*. New York: Hispanic Society of America, 1979.

Ariès, Philippe. *The Hour of Our Death*. Trans. Helen Weaver. New York: Oxford University Press, 1991. First published 1981.

———. *Images of Man and Death*. Trans. Janet Lloyd. Cambridge: Harvard University Press, 1985.

———. *Western Attitudes Toward Death: From the Middle Ages to the Present*. Trans. Patricia M. Ranum. Baltimore: Johns Hopkins, 1974.

Ariès, Philippe, and Georges Duby, eds. *A History of Private Life: Passions of the Renaissance*. Trans. Arthur Goldhammer. Cambridge: Harvard University Press, Belknap Press, 1989.

Ashelford, Jane. *The Art of Dress: Clothes and Society, 1500–1914*. London: National Trust, 1996.

Attig, Thomas. *How We Grieve: Relearning the World*. New York: Oxford University Press, 1996.

Aubrey, John. *Brief Lives*. Ed. Oliver Lawson Dick. London: Secker and Warburg, 1949.

Bagneris, Vernel. *Rejoice When You Die: The New Orleans Jazz Festival*. Baton Rouge: Louisiana State University Press, 1998.

Balsdon, J.P.V.D. *Life and Leisure in Ancient Rome*. London: Bodley Head, 1969.

Bassett, Steven, ed. *Death in Towns: Urban Responses to the Dying and the Dead, 100–1600*. Leicester, Eng.: Leicester University Press, 1992.

Beardsley, Richard K., et al. *Village Japan*. Chicago: University of Chicago Press, 1959.

References

Bell, C. Jeanenne. *Collectors' Encyclopedia of Hairwork Jewelry*. Paducah, Ky.: Collector Books, 1998.

Biebuyck, Daniel P., and Nelly Van den Abbeele. *The Power of Headdresses*. Brussels: Leopold III Foundation for Exploration and Nature Conservation, 1984.

Bland, Olivia. *The Royal Way of Death*. London: Constable, 1986.

Bligh, E.W. *Sir Kenelm Digby and His Venetia*. London: Sampson, Low, Marston, 1932.

Bloch, Abraham P. *The Biblical and Historical Background of Jewish Customs and Ceremonies*. New York: Ktav, 1980.

Boase, T.S.R. *Death in the Middle Ages: Mortality, Judgment and Remembrance*. London: Thames and Hudson, 1972.

Boccaccio, Giovanni. *The Decameron*. Trans. G.H. McWilliam. Harmondsworth, Eng.: Penguin, 1975.

Bolton, Christopher, and Delpha J. Camp. "Funeral Rituals and the Facilitation of Grief Work." *Omega* 17, no. 4 (1987): 343–52.

Bonfante, Larissa. *Etruscan Dress*. Baltimore: Johns Hopkins, 1975.

Bowlby, John. *Attachment and Loss*. 3 vols. New York: Basic Books, 1969–80.

Bowser, Kent Norman. "An Examination of Nineteenth Century American Post-Mortem Photography." MA thesis, Ohio State University, 1983.

Bradstreet, Anne. *The Works of Anne Bradstreet*. Ed. Jeannine Hensley. Cambridge: Harvard University Press, 1967.

Brasch, R. *How Did It Begin? Customs and Superstitions and Their Romantic Origins*. New York: David McKay, 1965.

Brener, Anne. *Mourning and Mitzvah*. Woodstock, Vt.: Jewish Lights Publishing, 1993.

Broner, E.M. *Mornings and Mourning: A Kaddish Journal*. San Francisco: HarperCollins, 1994.

Bronfen, Elisabeth. *Over Her Dead Body: Death, Femininity and the Aesthetic*. New York: Routledge, 1992.

Buck, Anne. *Clothes and the Child: A Handbook of Children's Dress in England 1500–1900*. Carlton, Eng.: Ruth Bean, 1996.

Buckley, Anna-Kaye. "The Good Wake: A Newfoundland Case Study." *Culture & Tradition* 7 (1983): 6–16.

Buckley, P.G. "Truly We Live in a Dying World: Mourning on Long Island." In *A Time to Mourn: Expressions of Grief in Nineteenth Century America*, edited by Martha V. Pike and Janice Gray Armstrong. Stony Brook, N.Y.: Museums at Stony Brook, 1980.

Burnett, Frances Hodgson. *The Secret Garden*. London: Octopus, 1978.

Burns, Stanley B. *Sleeping Beauty: Memorial Photography in America*. Altadena, Cal.: Twelvetrees Press, 1990.

Burton, Susan. "What They Were Thinking: Starting Over." *New York Times Magazine*, November 11, 2001, pp. 52, 54.

Butler, Gary R. "Sacred and Profane Space: Ritual Interaction and Process in the Newfoundland House Wake." *Material History Bulletin*, no. 15 (Summer 1982): 27–32.

Byron, George Gordon, Baron. *The Complete Poetic Works*. Oxford: Clarendon, 1980.

Campbell, Mark. *The Art of Hair Work: Hair Braiding and Jewelry of Sentiment with Catalog of Hair Jewelry*. Berkeley, Cal.: Lacis, 1989.

Cardozo, Arlene Rossen. "After the Year, What?" In *Wrestling with the Angel: Jewish Insights on Death and Mourning*, edited by Jack Riemer. New York: Schocken, 1995.

Carmichael, Elizabeth, and Chloe Sayer. *The Skeleton at the Feast: The Day of the Dead in Mexico*. Austin: University of Texas Press, 1995.

Carmichael, Kay. *Ceremony of Innocence: Tears, Power, and Protest*. London: Macmillan, 1991.

Castan, Yves, François Lebrun, and Roger Chartier. "The Two Reformations: Communal Devotion and Personal Piety." In *A History of Private Life: Passions of the Renaissance*, edited by Philippe Ariès and Georges Duby, translated by Arthur Goldhammer. Cambridge: Harvard University Press, Belknap Press, 1989.

A Child's Grief. Bereaved Families of Ontario. Associated Producers, Toronto, 1994. Videocassette.

Coffin, Margaret M. *Death in Early America*. New York: Elsevier/Nelson Books, 1976.

Colette. *Seven by Colette*. Trans. Una Vicenzo Troubridge and Enid McLeod. New York: Farrar, Straus and Cudahy, 1955.

The Compassionate Friends [online]. [Cited March 5, 2002.] <compassionatefriends.org>.

Coryell, Deborah Morris. *Good Grief: Healing Through the Shadow of Loss*. Santa Fe, N.M.: Shiva Foundation, 1998.

Courtright, Paul B. "The Iconographies of Sati." In *Sati: The Blessing and the Curse*, edited by John Stratton Hawley. New York: Oxford University Press, 1994.

Crissman, James K. *Death and Dying in Central Appalachia: Changing Attitudes and Practices*. Urbana: University of Illinois Press, 1994.

Cunnington, Phillis, and Catherine Lucas. *Costume for Births, Marriages and Deaths*. London: Adam & Charles Black, 1972.

Curl, James Stevens. *A Celebration of Death*. London: Constable, 1980.

———. *The Victorian Celebration of Death*. London: David & Charles, 1972.

Cuyler, Theodore Ledyard. *The Empty Crib: A Memorial of Little Georgie*. New York: Baker and Taylor, 1868.

———. *God's Light on Dark Clouds*. New York: Fleming H. Revell, 1913.

———. *Recollections of a Long Life*. New York: Baker and Taylor, 1902.

Danforth, Loring. *The Death Rituals of Rural Greece*. Princeton: Princeton University Press, 1982.

Daniell, Christopher. *Death and Burial in Medieval England 1066–1550*. London: Routledge, 1997.

Dar, S.N. *Costumes of India and Pakistan*. Bombay: D.B. Taraporevala, 1969.

Darby, Elisabeth, and Nicola Smith. *The Cult of the Prince Consort*. New Haven: Yale University Press, 1983.

de Boileau, Lambert. *Recollections of Labrador Life*. Ed. Thomas Bredin. Toronto: Ryerson Press, 1969.

Delpierre, Madeleine. *Dress in France in the Eighteenth Century*. Trans. Caroline Beamish. New Haven: Yale University Press, 1997.

de Negri, Eve. *Nigerian Body Ornament*. Lagos: Nigeria Magazine, 1976.

Dickinson, Emily. *Complete Poems of Emily Dickinson*. Ed. Thomas H. Johnson. Cambridge, Mass.: Belknap, 1983.

Digby, Kenelm. "A New Digby Letter-Book: 'In Praise of Venetia.'" Ed. Vittorio Gabrieli. *National Library of Wales Journal* 9, no. 2 (Winter 1955): 113–48; 9, no. 4 (Summer 1955): 440–62; 10, no. 1 (Autumn 1955): 81–106.

Dinn, Robert. "Death and Rebirth in Late Medieval Bury St. Edmunds." In *Death in Towns: Urban Responses to the Dying and the Dead, 100–1600*, edited by Steven Bassett. Leicester, Eng.: Leicester University Press, 1992.

Dobrinsky, Herbert C. *A Treasury of Sephardic Laws and Customs*. Hoboken, N.J.: Ktav, 1988.

Doka, Kenneth J. *Disenfranchised Grief: Recognizing Hidden Sorrow*. San Francisco: Jossey Bass, 1989.

Doka, Kenneth J., and Joyce D. Davidson, eds. *Living with Grief: Who We Are, How We Grieve*. Philadelphia: Taylor and Francis, Brunner/Mazel, 1998.

Domotor, Tekla. *Hungarian Folk Customs*. Trans. Judith Elliott. Budapest: Corvina, 1972.

Douglas, Ann. *The Feminization of American Culture*. New York: Knopf, 1977.

Douglas, William A. *Death in Murelaga: Funerary Ritual in a Spanish Basque Village*. Seattle: University of Washington Press, 1969.

Duffy, Eamon. *The Stripping of the Altars: Traditional Religion in England, c. 1400–c. 1580*. New Haven: Yale University Press, 1992.

Dunlevy, Mairead. *Dress in Ireland*. London: B.T. Batsford, 1989.

Earle, Alice Morse. "Death Ritual in Colonial New York." In *Passing: The Vision of Death in America*, edited by Charles O. Jackson. Westport, Conn.: Greenwood Press, 1977.

Eggers, Dave. *A Heartbreaking Work of Staggering Genius*. Toronto: Vintage Canada, 2001.

Elkins, Dov Peretz. *Humanizing Jewish Life*. South Brunswick, N.J.: A.S. Barnes, 1976.

Enright, D.J., ed. *The Oxford Book of Death*. Oxford: Oxford University Press, 1987.

Etlin, Richard A. *The Architecture of Death: The Transformation of the Cemetery in Eighteenth-Century Paris*. Cambridge, Mass.: MIT Press, 1984.

Farrell, James J. *Inventing the American Way of Death, 1830–1920*. Philadelphia: Temple University Press, 1980.

Feldman, Emanuel. "Death as Estrangement: The Halakhah of Mourning." In *Jewish Reflections on Death*, edited by Jack Riemer. New York: Schocken, 1975.

References

Fenwick, Millicent. *Vogue's Book of Etiquette*. New York: Simon and Schuster, 1948.

Fletcher, Marion. *Costume in Australia 1788–1901*. Melbourne, Australia: Oxford University Press, 1984.

Floersch, Jerry, and Jeffrey Longhofer. "The Imagined Death: Looking to the Past for Relief from the Present." *Omega* 35, no. 3 (1997): 243–60.

Forster, E.M. *Marianne Thornton*. Ed. Evelyne Hanquart-Turner. London: Andre Deutsch, 2000.

French, Stanley. "The Cemetery as Cultural Institution: The Establishment of Mount Auburn and the 'Rural Cemetery' Movement." In *Death in America*, edited by David Stannard. Philadelphia: University of Pennsylvania Press, 1975.

Freud, Sigmund. "Mourning and Melancholia." In *Collected Papers*, edited by Ernest Jones, translated by Joan Riviere. Vol. 4. London: Hogarth, 1953.

———. *Totem and Taboo: Some Points of Agreement Between the Mental Lives of Savages and Neurotics*. Trans. James Strachey. London: Routledge & Kegan Paul, 1950.

Frost, Robert. *Robert Frost, Collected Poems, Prose & Plays*. Ed. Richard Poirier and Mark Richardson. New York: Library Classics of the United States, 1995.

Galt, John. *Annals of the Parish*. London: J.M. Dent, 1920. First published 1821.

Garland, Robert. *The Greek Way of Death*. Ithaca, N.Y.: Cornell University Press, 1985.

Garrett, Valery M. *Chinese Clothing: An Illustrated Guide*. Hong Kong: Oxford University Press, 1994.

Gary, Juneau Mahan, and Linda Remolino. "Coping with Loss and Grief Through On-Line Support Groups." In *Cybercounseling and Cyberlearning*, edited by John W. Bloom and Garry Walz. Alexandria, Va.: American Counseling Association, 2000.

Geertz, Clifford. *The Interpretation of Cultures: Selected Essays*. New York: Basic Books, 1973.

———. *The Religion of Java*. New York: Free Press, 1960.

Giesey, Ralph E. *The Royal Funeral Ceremony in Renaissance France*. Geneva: Librairie E. Droz, 1960.

Gittings, Clare. *Death, Burial and the Individual in Early Modern England*. London: Croom Helm, 1984.

———. "Expressions of Loss of Early Seventeenth-Century England." In *The Changing Face of Death: Historical Accounts of Death and Disposal*, edited by Peter C. Jupp and Glennys Howarth. Basingstoke, Eng.: Macmillan, 1997.

———. "Urban Funerals in Late Medieval and Reformation England." In *Death in Towns: Urban Responses to the Dying and the Dead, 100–1600*, edited by Stephen Bassett. Leicester, Eng.: Leicester University Press, 1992.

———. "Venetia's Death and Kenelm's Mourning." In *Death, Passion and Politics*, edited by Ann Sumner. London: Dulwich Picture Gallery, 1995.

Glick, Ira O., et al. *The First Year of Bereavement*. New York: Wiley, 1974.

REFERENCES

Goldberg, Helene S. "Funeral and Bereavement Rituals of Kota Indians and Orthodox Jews." *Omega* 12, no. 2 (1981): 117–28.

Golden, Thomas R. *Swallowed by a Snake: The Gift of the Masculine Side of Healing.* Gaithersburg, Md.: Golden Healing, 2000.

———. *Crisis, Grief, and Healing* [online]. 2000. [Cited March 5, 2002.] <webhealing.com>.

Gordon, Anne. *Death Is for the Living.* Edinburgh: Paul Harris, 1984.

Gorer, Geoffrey. *Death, Grief, and Mourning in Contemporary Britain.* New York: Doubleday, 1967.

Granqvist, Hilma. *Muslim Death and Burial: Arab Customs and Traditions Studied in a Village in Jordan.* Helsinki: Societas Scientiarum Fennica, 1965.

Grant, Elizabeth. *Memoirs of a Highland Lady.* London: John Murray, 1911.

Gray, Francine du Plessix. "At Large and at Small: The Work of Mourning." *American Scholar* 69, no. 3 (Summer 2000): 7–13.

Gregory of Nyssa, Saint. *The Life of St. Macrina.* Willits, Cal.: Eastern Orthodox Books, 1975.

GriefNet [online]. Supervised by Cendra Lynn, Ph.D. Rivendell Resources. [Cited March 5, 2002.] <griefnet.org>.

Habenstein, Robert W., and William M. Lamers. *The History of American Funeral Directing.* Milwaukee: Bulfin, 1962.

Haight, Gordon S. *Mrs. Sigourney: The Sweet Singer of Hartford.* New Haven: Yale University Press, 1930.

Harland, Marion. *Marion Harland's Complete Etiquette.* Indianapolis: Bobbs-Merrill, 1914.

Hawley, John Stratton, ed. *Sati: The Blessing and the Curse.* New York: Oxford University Press, 1994.

Heathcote, Edwin. *Monument Builders: Modern Architecture and Death.* Chichester, Eng.: Academy Editions, 1999.

Hendrickson, Hildi, ed. *Clothing and Difference: Embodied Identities in Colonial and Post-Colonial Africa.* Durham, N.C.: Duke University Press, 1996.

Hertz, Robert. *Death and the Right Hand.* Trans. Rodney and Claudia Needham. Glencoe, Ill.: Free Press, 1960.

Hochschild, A.R. "Emotion Work, Feeling Rules and Social Support." *American Journal of Sociology* 85 (November 1979): 551–73.

Hoffman, Frances, and Ryan Taylor. *Much to be Done: Private Life in Ontario from Victorian Diaries.* Toronto: Natural Heritage/Natural History, 1996.

Holt, Emily. *Encyclopedia of Etiquette.* Toronto: Musson, 1921.

Holub, Margaret. "A Cosmology of Mourning." In *Lifecycles: Jewish Women on Life Passages and Personal Milestones*, edited by Debra Orenstein. Vol 1. Woodstock, Vt.: Jewish Lights, 1994.

Homer. *The Iliad.* Trans. Richmond Lattimore. Chicago: University of Chicago Press, 1951.

Houlbrooke, Ralph. *Death, Religion and the Family in England, 1480–1750.* Oxford: Clarendon, 1998.

REFERENCES

————, ed. *Death, Ritual, and Bereavement*. London: Routledge, 1989.

Housman, A.E. *The Collected Poems of A.E. Housman*. London: Jonathan Cape, 1946.

Hunter, Margaret. "Mourning Jewellery: A Collector's Account." *Costume* 27 (1993): 9–25.

Huntington, Richard, and Peter Metcalf. *Celebrations of Death: The Anthropology of Mortuary Ritual*. Cambridge: Cambridge University Press, 1979.

Irish, Donald, Kathleen Lundquist, and Vivian Jenkins Nelsen, eds. *Ethnic Variations in Dying, Death, and Grief*. Washington, D.C.: Taylor and Francis, 1993.

Issenman, Betty Bobayashi. *Sinews of Survival: The Living Legacy of Inuit Clothing*. Vancouver: University of British Columbia Press, 1997.

Jackson, Charles O., ed. *Passing: The Vision of Death in America*. Westport, Conn.: Greenwood Press, 1977.

Jackson, Kenneth T., and Camilo Jose Vergara. *Silent Cities: The Evolution of the American Cemetery*. New York: Princeton Architectural Press, 1989.

Jalland, Patricia. *Death in the Victorian Family*. Oxford: Oxford University Press, 1996.

James, John W., and Russell Friedman. *The Grief Recovery Handbook: The Action Program for Moving Beyond Death, Divorce, and Other Losses*. New York: HarperPerennial, 1998.

Jenkins, Bill. *What to Do When the Police Leave: A Guide to the First Days of Traumatic Loss*. Richmond, Va.: WBJ Press, 1999.

Johnson, Joy, et al. "A Most Important Picture." Omaha, Nebr.: Centering Corporation, 1985. Booklet.

Johnston, Marie, ed. *Ancient Greek Dress*. Chicago: Argonaut, 1964.

Jupp, Peter C., and Glennys Howarth, eds. *The Changing Face of Death: Historical Accounts of Death and Disposal*. Basingstoke, Eng.: Macmillan, 1997.

Kath, Laura, *Forest Lawn Memorial-Parks: A Place for the Living*. Glendale, Cal.: Forest Lawn Memorial-Park Association, 1994.

Kingsland, Mrs. Burton. *The Book of Good Manners*. Garden City, N.J.: Doubleday, Page, 1912.

Klass, Dennis. "Bereaved Parents and the Compassionate Friends: Affiliation and Healing." *Omega* 15, no. 4 (1984–85): 353–73.

————. "John Bowlby's Model of Grief and the Problem of Identification." *Omega* 18, no. 1 (1987–88): 13–32.

Klass, Dennis, Phyllis R. Silverman, and Steven L. Nickman, eds. *Continuing Bonds: New Understandings of Grief*. Washington, D.C.: Taylor and Francis, 1996.

Kübler-Ross, Elisabeth. *On Death and Dying*. New York: Macmillan, 1979.

Kumin, Maxine. *The Retrieval System*. New York: Viking Penguin, 1978.

Kurtz, Donna C., and John Boardman. *Greek Burial Customs*. Ithaca, N.Y.: Cornell University Press, 1971.

Lagrand, Louis E. "United We Cope: Support Groups for the Dying and Bereaved." *Death Studies* 15, no. 2 (March–April 1991): 207–30.

Lamm, Maurice. *The Jewish Way in Death and Mourning.* New York: Jonathan David, 1979.

Lawrence, D.H. *Sons and Lovers.* New York: Viking, 1963.

Leick, Nini, and Marianne Davidsen-Nielsen. *Healing Pain: Attachment, Loss and Grief Therapy.* Trans. David Stoner. London: Routledge, 1996.

Levine, Aaron. *To Comfort the Bereaved.* Northvale, N.J.: Jason Aronson, 1994.

Lewis, C.S. *A Grief Observed.* London: Faber & Faber, 1961.

Linden-Ward, Blanche. "Strange but Genteel Pleasure Grounds: Tourist and Leisure Uses of Nineteenth-Century Rural Cemeteries." In *Cemeteries and Gravemarkers: Voices of American Culture,* edited by Richard E. Meyer. Ann Arbor, Mich.: UMI Research Press, 1989.

Lipnick, Bernard. "Who's the Host? Who's the Guest?" In *Wrestling with the Angel: Jewish Insights on Death and Mourning,* edited by Jack Riemer. New York: Schocken, 1995.

Little, M. Ruth. *Sticks and Stones: Three Centuries of North Carolina Gravemarkers.* Chapel Hill: University of North Carolina Press, 1998.

Lloyd, Phoebe. "Posthumous Mourning Portraiture." In *A Time to Mourn: Expressions of Grief in Nineteenth Century America,* edited by Martha V. Pike and Janice Gray Armstrong. Stony Brook, N.Y.: Museums at Stony Brook, 1980.

Longford, Elizabeth. *Victoria R.I.* London: Weidenfeld & Nicholson, 1964.

Lund, D.A., ed. *Older Bereaved Spouses: Research with Practical Applications.* New York: Taylor and Francis/Hemisphere, 1989.

Lund, D.A., et al. "Resolving Problems Implementing Self-Help Groups." In *Older Bereaved Spouses: Research with Practical Applications,* edited by D.A. Lund. New York: Taylor and Francis/Hemisphere, 1989.

Lutz, Tom. *Crying: The Natural and Cultural History of Tears.* New York: Norton, 1999.

Lynch, Thomas. "Socko Finish." *New York Times Magazine.* July 12, 1998, p. 34.

———. *The Undertaking: Life Studies from the Dismal Trade.* New York: Norton, 1997.

Mandelbaum, David G. "Social Uses of Funeral Rites." In *The Meaning of Death,* edited by Herman Feifel. New York: McGraw-Hill, 1959.

Martin, Andrew, ed. *Scottish Endings: Writings on Death.* Edinburgh: National Museums of Scotland, 1996.

Martin, Terry L., and Kenneth Doka. *Men Don't Cry . . . Women Do: Transcending Gender Stereotypes of Grief.* Philadelphia: Taylor and Francis, Brunner/Mazel, 2000.

McManners, John. *Death and the Enlightenment.* Oxford: Clarendon, 1981.

Mead, S.M. *Traditional Maori Clothing.* Wellington, N.Z.: A.H. and A.W. Reed, 1969.

Mehren, Elizabeth. *After the Darkest Hour the Sun Will Shine Again: A Parent's Guide to Coping with the Loss of a Child.* New York: Simon and Schuster, Fireside, 1997.

Meinwald, Dan. *Memento Mori: Death in Nineteenth Century Photography.* Riverside, Cal.: California Museum of Photography, 1990.

Meltzer, David, ed. *Death: An Anthology of Ancient Texts, Songs, Prayers, and Stories.* San Francisco: North Point Press, 1984.

Memorial University of Newfoundland, St. John's, Newfoundland. Folklore & Language Archive (MUNFLA).

Meyer, Richard E., ed. *Cemeteries and Gravemarkers: Voices of American Culture.* Ann Arbor, Mich.: UMI Research Press, 1989.

Miavitz, Elan Marie. "Grief Gardening: A Horticultural Therapy Program for the Bereaved." *Journal of Therapeutic Horticulture* 9 (1988): 17–20.

Millay, Edna St. Vincent. *Collected Poems.* New York: Harper & Row, 1955.

Mitchell, Margaret. *Gone with the Wind.* New York: Macmillan, 1961. First published 1936.

Mitford, Jessica. *The American Way of Death.* New York: Simon and Schuster, 1963.

Moffat, Mary Jane, ed. *In the Midst of Winter: Selections from the Literature of Mourning.* New York: Vintage, 1992.

Morgenstern, Julian. *Rites of Birth, Marriage, Death and Kindred Occasions Among the Semites.* Cincinnati: Hebrew Union College Press, 1966.

Morley, John. *Death, Heaven and the Victorians.* London: Studio Vista, 1971.

Moss, S.Z., R.L. Rubinstein, and M.S. Moss. "Middle-Aged Son's Reactions to Father's Death." *Omega* 34, no. 4 (1996–97): 259–78.

Myers, Edward. *When Parents Die.* New York: Penguin, 1997.

Narasimhan, Sakuntala. *Sati: A Study of Widow Burning in India.* New Delhi: Penguin, 1990.

Narvaez, Peter. "'Tricks and Fun': Subversive Pleasures at Newfoundland Wakes." *Western Folklore* 53, no. 4 (October 1994): 263–93.

Neudel, Marian Henriquez. "Saying Kaddish: The Making of a 'Regular.'" In *Wrestling with the Angel: Jewish Insights on Death and Mourning,* edited by Jack Riemer. New York: Schocken, 1996.

Newman, John Henry. *Prayers, Poems, Meditations.* New York: Crossroad, 1990.

Newton, Stella Mary. *The Dress of the Venetians, 1495–1525.* Aldershot, Eng.: Scolar Press, 1988.

Ochs, Donovan J. *Consolatory Rhetoric: Grief, Symbol, and Ritual in the Greco-Roman Era.* Columbia: University of South Carolina Press, 1993.

O'Connor, Nancy. *Letting Go with Love: The Grieving Process.* New York: Bantam Books, 1989.

Oldenburg, Veena Talwar. "The Roop Kanwar Case: Feminist Responses." In *Sati: The Blessing and the Curse,* edited by John Stratton Hawley. New York: Oxford University Press, 1994.

Olson, Sheri. "What Is Sacred Space? Steven Holl's Chapel of St. Ignatius Answers with Texture, Light and Color." *Architectural Record* (July 1997): 41–53.

Oppenheim, R.S. *Maori Death Customs.* Wellington, N.Z.: A.H. and A.W. Reed, 1973.

Ordway, Edith. *The Etiquette of To-Day.* New York: Sully & Kleintech, 1913.

Orenstein, Debra, ed. *Lifecycles: Jewish Women on Life Passages and Personal Milestones.* Vol. 1. Woodstock, Vt.: Jewish Lights, 1994.

O'Suilleabhain, Sean. *Irish Wake Amusements.* Dublin: Mercier Press, 1967.

Parkes, Colin Murray. *Bereavement: Studies of Grief in Adult Life*. London: Penguin, 1996.

———. "A Historical Overview of the Scientific Study of Bereavement." In *Handbook of Bereavement Research: Consequences, Coping, and Care*, edited by Margaret S. Stroebe et al. Washington, D.C.: American Psychological Association, 2001.

Parkes, Colin Murray, and R.S. Weiss. *Recovery from Bereavement*. New York: Basic Books, 1983.

Parsons, Elsie Clews. *Kiowa Tales*. New York: American Folk-Lore Society, 1929.

Paterek, Josephine. *Encyclopedia of American Indian Costume*. Santa Barbara, Cal.: ABC-CLIO, 1994.

Patterson, John R. "Patronage, *Collegia* and Burial in Imperial Rome." In *Death in Towns: Urban Responses to the Dying and the Dead, 100–1600*, edited by Steven Bassett. Leicester, Eng.: Leicester University Press, 1992.

Paxton, Frederick S. *Christianizing Death: The Creation of a Ritual Process in Early Medieval Europe*. Ithaca, N.Y.: Cornell University Press, 1990.

Pepys, Samuel. *The Shorter Pepys*. Ed. Robert Latham and William Matthews. London: Bell and Hyman, 1985.

Pike, Martha V., and Janice Gray Armstrong. *A Time to Mourn: Expressions of Grief in Nineteenth Century America*. Stony Brook, N.Y.: Museums at Stony Brook, 1980.

Plato. *The Laws*. Trans. R.G. Bury. 2 vols. Cambridge: Harvard University Press, 1926.

Post, Elizabeth, ed. *Emily Post's Etiquette: The Blue Book of Social Usage*. New York: Funk & Wagnalls, 1965.

———. *Emily Post's Etiquette*. New York: Harper & Row, 1984.

———. *Emily Post's Etiquette*. New York: HarperCollins, 1992.

Puckle, Bertram S. *Funeral Customs: Their Origin and Development*. New York: Frederick A. Stokes, 1926.

Quigley, Christine. *The Corpse: A History*. Jefferson, N.C.: McFarland, 1996.

Radcliffe-Brown, A.R. *The Andaman Islanders*. New York: Free Press, 1964.

Rando, Therese. *How to Go On Living When Someone You Love Dies*. New York: Bantam Books, 1991.

———. *Treatment of Complicated Mourning*. Champaign, Ill.: Research Press, 1993.

Rappoport, Angelo. *The Folklore of the Jews*. Detroit: Singing Tree Press, 1972.

Reader, Ian. *Religion in Contemporary Japan*. Basingstoke, Eng.: Macmillan, 1991.

Reisem, Richard O. *Mount Hope: America's First Municipal Victorian Cemetery*. Rochester, N.Y.: Printing Methods, 1994.

Ribeiro, Aileen. *Dress in Eighteenth-Century Europe, 1715–1789*. London: B.T. Batsford, 1984.

———. *Fashion in the French Revolution*. London: B.T. Batsford, 1988.

Riemer, Jack, ed. *Jewish Reflections on Death*. New York: Schocken, 1976.

———. *Wrestling with the Angel: Jewish Insights on Death and Mourning*. New York: Schocken, 1995

Ring, Betty. "The Balch School in Providence, Rhode Island." *Antiques* (April 1975): 660–71.

Rose, A.J., and S.R. Asher. "Seeking and Giving Social Support Within a Friendship." Paper presented at the biennial meeting of the Society for Research in Child Development, Albuquerque, New Mexico, April 1999.

Rosenblatt, Paul, R. Walsh, and D. Jackson. *Grief and Mourning in Cross-Cultural Perspective*. Washington, D.C.: HRDF Press, 1976.

Rubin, Barbara, Robert Carlton, and Arnold Rubin. *L.A. in Installments: Forest Lawn*. Santa Monica, Cal.: Westside, 1979.

Ruby, Jay. "Post-Mortem Portraiture in America." *History of Photography* 8, no. 3 (July–Sept. 1984): 201–22.

———. *Secure the Shadow: Death and Photography in America*. Cambridge, Mass.: MIT Press, 1995.

Rumford, Beatrix T. "Memorial Watercolors." *Antiques* (October 1973): 688–95.

Rush, Alfred C. *Death and Burial in Christian Antiquity*. Washington, D.C.: Catholic University of America Press, 1941.

Ryan, Joan. "Silent Barter." *Omega* 14, no. 2 (1983–84): 145–54.

Salomone-Marino, Salvatore. *Customs and Habits of the Sicilian Peasants*. Trans. Rosalie Morris. Rutherford, N.J.: Fairleigh Dickinson University Press, 1981.

Sanders, C. "Risk Factors in Bereavement Outcome." In *Handbook of Bereavement: Theory, Research, Intervention*, edited by Margaret Stroebe et al. Cambridge: Cambridge University Press, 1993.

Sappho. *Sappho: Lyrics in the Original Greek*. Trans. Willis Barnstone. New York: New York University Press, 1965.

Schauss, Hayyim. *The Lifetime of a Jew*. Cincinnati: Union of American Hebrew Congregations, 1950.

Schindler, Ruben. "Mourning and Bereavement Among Jewish Religious Families: A Time for Reflection and Recovery." *Omega* 33, no. 2 (1996): 121–29.

Schneider, Marelyn. *History of a Jewish Burial Society*. Lewiston, N.Y.: Edward Mellen, 1991.

Schreier, Barbara A. *Becoming American Women: Clothing and the Jewish Immigrant Experience, 1880–1920*. Chicago: Chicago Historical Society, 1994.

Sebesta, Judith Lynn, and Larissa Bonfante, eds. *The World of Roman Costume*. Madison: University of Wisconsin Press, 1994.

Shelton, Jo-Ann, ed. *As the Romans Did: A Source Book in Roman Social History*. New York: Oxford University Press, 1988.

Sherwood, Mrs. John (M.E.W.). *Manners and Social Usages*. New York: Harper and Brothers, 1897.

Sigourney, Lydia H. *Letters to Mothers*. New York: Harper and Brothers, 1845.

———. *Poems Religious and Elegiac*. London: Robert Tyas, 1841.

Silverman, Phyllis R., and Dennis Klass. "Introduction: What's the Problem?" In *Continuing Bonds: New Understandings of Grief*, edited by Dennis Klass et al. Washington, D.C.: Taylor and Francis, 1996.

Sloane, David Charles. *The Last Great Necessity: Cemeteries in American History*. Baltimore: Johns Hopkins, 1991.

Slochower, Joyce. "Mourning and the Holding Function of *Shiva*." *Contemporary Psychoanalysis* 29, no. 2 (1993): 352–67.

———. "The Therapeutic Function of Shivah." In *Wrestling with the Angel*, edited by Jack Riemer. New York: Schocken, 1995.

Smith, P.C., L.M. Range, and A. Ulmer. "Belief in Afterlife as a Buffer in Suicidal and Other Bereavement." *Omega* 24, no. 3 (1991–92): 217–25.

Smith, Robert J. *Ancestor Worship in Contemporary Japan*. Stanford, Cal.: Stanford University Press, 1974.

Sophocles. *Antigone*. In *The Complete Greek Tragedies*, edited by David Greene and Richmond Lattimore. Trans. Elizabeth Wyckoff. Vol. 2. Chicago: University of Chicago Press, 1959.

Spiegel, Maura, and Richard Tristman, eds. *The Grim Reader: Writings on Death, Dying, and Living On*. New York: Doubleday, 1997.

Stallybrass, Peter. "Worn Worlds: Clothes, Mourning, and the Life of Things." *Yale Review* 81, no. 2 (April 1993), 35–50.

Staniland, Kay. *In Royal Fashion: The Clothes of Princess Charlotte of Wales and Queen Victoria, 1796–1901*. London: Museum of London, 1997.

Stannard, David. *The Puritan Way of Death*. New York: Oxford University Press, 1977.

———, ed. *Death in America*. Philadelphia: University of Pennsylvania Press, 1975.

Starker, Steven. *Oracle at the Supermarket: The American Preoccupation with Self-Help Books*. New Brunswick, N.J.: Transaction, 1989.

St. Aubyn, Giles. *Queen Victoria: A Portrait*. London: Sinclair-Stevenson, 1991.

Staudacher, Carol. *Men and Grief*. Oakland, Cal.: New Harbinger Publications, 1991.

Stillion, J., and G. McDowell. "Women's Issues in Grief." Presented to the annual meeting of the Association for Death Education and Caring, Washington, D.C., June 1997.

Strocchia, Sharon T. *Death and Ritual in Renaissance Florence*. Baltimore: Johns Hopkins University Press, 1992.

Stroebe, Margaret, et al. "Broken Hearts or Broken Bonds?" In *Continuing Bonds: New Understandings of Grief*, edited by Dennis Klass et al. Washington, D.C.: Taylor and Francis, 1996.

Stroebe, Margaret, Wolfgang Stroebe, and Robert Hausson, eds. *Handbook of Bereavement Research: Consequences, Coping, and Care*. Washington, D.C.: American Psychological Association, 2001.

Strutt, Daphne H. *Fashion in South Africa, 1652–1900*. Cape Town: A.A. Balkem, 1975.

Sumner, Ann, ed. *Death, Passion and Politics*. London: Dulwich Picture Gallery, 1995.

Taylor, Jeremy. *Holy Living; and, Holy Dying*. Ed. P.G. Stanwood. Oxford: Clarendon, 1989.

Taylor, Lou. *Mourning Dress: A Costume and Social History*. London: George Allen and Unwin, 1983.

REFERENCES

Tennyson, Alfred Tennyson, Baron. *In Memoriam.* Oxford: Clarendon, 1982.

Thomas, W. Stephen, and Ruth Rosenberg-Naparsteck. "Sleepers' City: The Sesquicentennial History of Mt. Hope Cemetery." *Rochester History* 50 (October 1988): 3–22.

Thompson, Edward. *Suttee.* London: George Allen and Unwin, 1928.

Trechsel, Gail Andrews. "Mourning Quilts: That Distress, by Industry, May Be Removed." *Piecework* (March–April 1994): 52–57.

Turner, Ann Warren. *Houses for the Dead: Burial Customs Through the Ages.* New York: David McKay, 1976.

Twain, Mark. *The Adventures of Huckleberry Finn.* Harmondsworth, Eng.: Penguin, 1975.

Vanderbilt, Amy. *Amy Vanderbilt's Etiquette.* Garden City, N.J.: Doubleday, 1972.

———. *Amy Vanderbilt's New Complete Book of Etiquette.* Garden City, N.J.: Doubleday, 1967.

Van Der Zee, James, Owen Dodson, and Camille Billops. *The Harlem Book of the Dead.* Dobbs Ferry, N.Y.: Morgan and Morgan, 1978.

van Gennep, Arnold. *The Rites of Passage.* Trans. Monika B. Vizedom and Gabrielle Caffee. London: Routledge and Kegan Paul, 1965.

Victoria, Queen of Great Britain. *Queen Victoria in Her Letters and Journals.* Ed. Christopher Hibbert. London: John Murray, 1984.

Wallace, Bronwen. "Heart of My Heart." In *Eighty-eight: Best Canadian Stories,* edited by David Helwig and Maggie Helwig. Ottawa: Oberon Press: 1988.

Walter, J.A. *The Revival of Death.* London: Routledge, 1994.

Watson, James L., and Evelyn S. Rawski. *Death Ritual in Late Imperial and Modern China.* Berkeley: University of California Press, 1988.

Waugh, Evelyn. *The Loved One: An Anglo-American Tragedy.* London: Chapman & Hall, 1969.

Weinberg, Nancy, et al. "Computer-Mediated Support Groups." *Social Work with Groups* 17, no. 4 (1995): 43–54.

———. "Therapeutic Factors: Their Presence in a Computer-Mediated Support Group." *Social Work with Groups* 18, no. 4 (1995): 57–69.

Weir, Shelagh. *Palestinian Costume.* London: British Museum, 1989.

Weiss, Brad. "Dressing at Death: Clothing, Time, and Memory in Buhaya, Tanzania." In *Clothing and Difference: Embodied Identities in Colonial and Post-Colonial Africa,* edited by Hildi Hendrickson. Durham, N.C.: Duke University Press, 1996.

Wieseltier, Leon. *Kaddish.* New York: Knopf, 1998.

Wilcox, Ella Wheeler, et al. *Correct Social Usage.* New York: New York Society of Self-Culture, 1909.

Wilson, Ethel. *The Innocent Traveller.* Toronto: McClelland & Stewart, 1990.

Wilson, Verity. *Chinese Dress.* London: Victoria and Albert Museum, 1986.

Wolfelt, Alan D. *Healing Your Grieving Heart: 100 Practical Ideas for Kids.* Fort Collins, Col.: Companion Press, 2000.

REFERENCES

Woodward, Jennifer. *The Theatre of Death: The Ritual Management of Royal Funerals in Renaissance England, 1570–1625*. Woodbridge, Eng.: Boydell, 1997.

Woolf, Virginia. *Orlando*. London: Hogarth, 1933.

Yalom, Irvin D. *The Theory and Practice of Group Psychotherapy*. New York: Basic Books, 1995.

Yezierska, Anzia. *Bread Givers*. New York: Persea Books, 1975.

York, Karen. "Grief Gardening." Paper presented at the Horticultural Therapy conference in Calgary, Alberta, March 29–31, 2000.

ACKNOWLEDGMENTS

Friends, acquaintances, and family responded to the subject of mourning with a cornucopia of books, clippings, poems, suggestions, information about their own mourning culture, and, most of all, stories. Many of them found their way into these pages. My benefactors include Norman Ashenburg, Rochelle Diamond, Oona Durbach, Rabbi Baruch Frydman-Kohl, Robert Fulford, Sarah Fulford, Phyllis Grosskurth, George Kapelos, Malcolm Lester, Jennifer Levine, Jacqueline Park, Jack Rabinowitz, Morton Ritts, Geraldine Sherman, Carl Solomon, Craig Stephenson, Andrew Watson, Robin Whitaker, Nicholas Wilson, and Karen York.

Maire O'Dea and Shane O'Dea smoothed my way in Newfoundland. Beth Ashenburg introduced me to the cemeteries of Rhode Island. Thanks to Gabriel Guerra Castellanos, Sabrina Villasenor Guerra, and Tom Robinson, I was well prepared for Mexico's Day of the Dead. Once in Mexico, in Valle de Bravo, I was the recipient of Regina Ruffo and Enrique Hülsz's extraordinary hospitality.

Susan Swan, Bernice Eisenstein, and Ramsay Derry provided advice and encouragement when it was most needed. Val Ross located archival material with her usual efficiency and good cheer.

I owe many thanks to my agent, Bella Pomer, for her enthusiasm, expertise, and companionship. To Gary Ross, for the subtitle, and to Ljiljana Vuletic, for research assistance. To

Barbara Czarnecki, whose preternatural grasp of grammar and passion for accuracy seem only to increase with the years. She goes the extra mile as a matter of course. And grateful thanks to Jan Walter, an editor of great sagacity and humanity, who prodded and cajoled me in all the right directions, and then waited calmly for me to see the light.

The Canada Council, the Ontario Arts Council, and the Toronto Arts Council all provided welcome funding for this project. I am also grateful to the Asia-Pacific Foundation, which made possible my trip to Japan.

Special thanks go to Carole Ashenburg, who supplied me with the finest of writers' retreats and Nellie, a dog with a rare gift for contemplation. To Andrew Frank, whose message on Hannah's condolence card is quoted in the last chapter. And, finally, to Mary Hanson, consummate listener, who has already heard most of this book.

⌘

I wish to thank the copyright holders for permission to quote from the following previously published materials.

Emily Dickinson, "The Bustle in a House" and "After great pain, a formal feeling comes." Reprinted by permission of the publishers and the Trustees of Amherst College from *The Poems of Emily Dickinson*, Thomas H. Johnson, ed., Cambridge, Mass.: The Belknap Press of Harvard University Press, Copyright © 1951, 1955, 1979 by the President and Fellows of Harvard College.

Homer, *The Iliad*, trans. Richmond Lattimore. Copyright 1951 by The University of Chicago. All rights reserved. Published 1951. Reprinted by permission of the University of Chicago Press.

ACKNOWLEDGMENTS

A.E. Housman, "To an Athlete Dying Young," from "A Shropshire Lad" – Authorized Edition from *The Collected Poems of A.E. Housman*. Copyright 1924, © 1965 by Henry Holt and Company. Reprinted by permission of Henry Holt & Co., LLC.

Edna St. Vincent Millay, "Dirge Without Music." From *Collected Poems*, HarperCollins. Copyright © 1923, 1951 by Edna St. Vincent Millay and Norma Millay Ellis. All rights reserved. Reprinted by permission of Elizabeth Barnett, literary executor.

Alan D. Wolfelt, *Healing Your Grieving Heart: 100 Practical Ideas for Kids*. Copyright © 2000 by Companion Press. Reprinted by permission of Alan D. Wolfelt.

Elizabeth Mehren, *After the Darkest Hour the Sun Will Shine Again*. Copyright © 1997 by Elizabeth Mehren. Used by permission of Simon & Schuster.

Robert Frost, "Home Burial," from *The Poetry of Robert Frost*, edited by Edward Connery Lathem. © 1969 by Henry Holt and Company. Reprinted by permission of Henry Holt & Co., LLC.

Eric Clapton, "Born in Time," by Bob Dylan, adapted by Eric Clapton. Copyright 1990 by Special Rider Music. All rights reserved. International copyright secured. Reprinted by permission.

Sappho, "On the Death of Adonis." From *Sappho: Lyrics in the Original Greek*, trans. Willis Barnstone, New York University Press, 1965. Reprinted by permission of New York University Press.

Ethel Wilson, *The Innocent Traveller*, © 1990 by University of British Columbia, by arrangement with Macmillan of Canada. Reprinted by permission of Macmillan Canada.

ACKNOWLEDGMENTS

Colette, *My Mother's House and Sido*, translated by Una Vicenzo Troubridge and Enid McLeod. Translation copyright © 1953 by Farrar, Straus & Young. Translation copyright renewed © 1981 by Farrar, Straus & Giroux, Inc. Reprinted by permission of Farrar, Straus and Giroux, LLC.

Nell Altizer, "The Widow Teaches Poetry Writing." Copyright © 1989 by Nell Altizer, *The Man Who Died en Route*, published by the University of Massachusetts Press. Reprinted by permission of the author.

Maxine Kumin, "How It Is." Copyright © 1978, from *Selected Poems 1960–1990*, by Maxine Kumin. Used by permission of W. W. Norton & Company, Inc.

Bronwen Wallace, "Heart of My Heart." *People You'd Trust Your Life To*, McClelland & Stewart, 1990. Reprinted by permission of McClelland & Stewart.

Every reasonable effort has been made to locate and acknowledge the owners of copyright in texts reproduced in this volume. The author and publishers would welcome any information regarding errors or omissions.

INDEX

Muslim practices, 40–42
outlive men, 170
reactions to death, 167–70, 171–72,
    180–81, 189–93
responsibility for mourning
    current Western practices, 166–67
    in various cultures and times,
        41–42, 45–46, 165–67, 193
    why, 5, 166–68, 172
sati, 166, 173–80

Woolf, Virginia, 205
Worden, William, 156
Wordsworth, Dorothy, 72
World Trade Center, New York, 6,
    185, 242, 243–44
Wyman, Jane, 104

Yezierska, Anzia, 201

Zwinglian theology, 56

The text in this book is set in Bembo, a typeface
produced by Stanley Morison of Monotype in 1929. Bembo
is based on a roman typeface cut by Francesco Griffo in
1495; the companion italic is based on a font designed
by Giovanni Tagliente in the 1520s.

Book design by Blaine Herrmann